Character Design for Graphic Novels

A ROTOVISION BOOK

Published and distributed
by RotoVision SA
Route Suisse 9
CH-1295 Mies
Switzerland

RotoVision SA
Sales and Editorial Office
Sheridan House
114 Western Road
Hove BN3 1DD, UK

Tel: +44 (0)1273 72 72 68
Fax: +44 (0)1273 72 72 69
www.rotovision.com

10 9 8 7 6 5 4 3 2 1

ISBN: 978-2-940361-52-6

Art Director: Tony Seddon
Design: Studio Output

Reprographics in Singapore
by ProVision Pte.
Tel: +65 6334 7720
Fax: +65 6334 7721

Printing and binding in Singapore by Star Standard Industries (Pte) Ltd

Character Design for Graphic Novels

Steven Withrow & Alexander Danner

RotoVision

clunkier than either 70's or 90's designs.

CONTENTS:

SECTION II: THE CHARACTER 021

SECTION III: ELEMENTS OF DESIGN 033

SECTION VI: THE EXPANDED CAST 111

SECTION VII: KNOWING YOUR AUDIENCE 131

FOREWORD:

NAME OF THE ROSE

Even though I use it to describe the books that I write and draw, the term "graphic novel" is inadequate and misleading. "Graphic," with its connotations of both commercial art and explicit pornographic images, is followed by "novel," suggesting that it's a bastard offspring of another art form, that of text fiction, which it patently isn't. The comic medium has its own distinct history, traditions, and grammar, and predates the novel form. "Novel" also indicates a length that many graphic novels don't have; most graphic novels are actually novellas or short stories, such as Alan Moore and Brian Bolland's *The Killing Joke* (DC Comics; 1988).

Moore simply calls his books "big comics," partly to deflate any claims of pretension, but chiefly to irritate proponents of the "graphic novel" label. But this is also problematic. For one thing, "comics" describes the entire medium, from the three-panel gag strip to Moore and Eddie Campbell's scholarly epic *From Hell* (now published by Top Shelf Productions), so a "big comic" could just as easily mean a sequential mural. Secondly, the word itself is a misnomer, dating back to the mid-nineteenth century's "comic (meaning funny) papers" and "comic companions" to newspapers, and as we know, graphic novels often deal with tragedy. Like "comics," "sequential art" is unspecific and also a bit of a mouthful, as is "pictorial narrative." So it looks as if we're stuck with the phrase "graphic novels," or its equally unsatisfactory and even less descriptive abbreviation, "GNs." What's needed is a word that simply means GNs in the way that "novel," originally indicating a new form of literature, now means a substantial piece of text fiction.

It's needed because we are living in a golden age of GNs, and it's time they had a proper identity of their own. There are now more and better-quality graphic novels being produced in an incredibly wide gamut of genres and styles than ever before. From Joe Sacco's reportage to Jeff Smith's comedy adventure, from Frank Miller's macho noir to Marjane Satrapi's poignancy, from the realism of Harvey Pekar to the fantasy of Neil Gaiman. Much to the awe of creators who knew the insular boys'-locker-room world of comics prior to the "revolution," public libraries and mainstream bookstores now have graphic novel sections, and according to the marketing director of Barnes & Noble, the GN is the fastest growing area of book sales in the last hundred years. With this in mind, Steven Withrow and Alexander Danner's *Character Design for Graphic Novels* becomes very timely indeed. The key to the survival and growth of the graphic novel is quality, and with more writers and artists entering the field, the need for expert advice couldn't be greater.

In the mid-1980s, the first boom of GNs, spearheaded by Art Spiegelman's *Maus: A Survivor's Tale* (Pantheon, 1986), Moore and Gibbons' *Watchmen* (DC Comics, 1986/1987), and Miller's *The Dark Knight Returns* (DC Comics, 1986), seemed like the dawn of a new age. Respectable newspapers and grown-up magazines ran features on them. Comics were cool. But it didn't last. There simply wasn't the quantity and range of quality books to build on the nascent public interest. Instead, capitalizing on the growing demand, opportunistic comic-book publishers compiled monthly production-line titles and released them as "graphic novels." Duped readers expecting another *Watchmen* were predictably disappointed, and the books confirmed their old prejudices about comics.

Slapping together half a dozen issues of *Superdork* doesn't make a quality graphic novel. As with text fiction, movies, and plays, graphic novels must be created as such—and created as a whole: quality writing and artwork coming together to create something unique, a novel in both substance and structure.

Character Design for Graphic Novels is not just about character design but provides an in-depth examination of the creative process behind the graphic novel.

Now, if only Withrow and Danner would come up with a different name for it...

Bryan Talbot
Sunderland, June 2006

(See pages 142–145 for more about Talbot and his work.)

Right:
An intricate and well-crafted character design from Bryan Talbot's *Heart of Empire: The Legacy of Luther Arkwright* (Dark Horse Comics, 1999).

GRAPHIC NOVEL CHARACTERS & SEVEN PRECEPTS

The graphic novel is a personal, idiosyncratic medium. Other related art forms, including animation, computer games, and monthly comic books, require more standardized processes than graphic novels, due mostly to the larger number of people involved. Also, the particular markets for such products demand that more precise expectations are met, whereas most graphic novel readers enjoy the indivisible peculiarities of an individual vision.

Rather than make pronouncements about how to draw or what tools and techniques are best, we will explore character design as a function of *storytelling*, as each design should follow the unique requirements of each story. We will focus more on the story-driven decisions that specific authors make—and how individual authors *think* when they're crafting characters—than on the steps they take and how their characters look when completed. In short, this is a book as much about the *why* of character design as the *how*.

Other books take a much more comprehensive look at the tools and techniques of comics art, so if you're looking for additional nuts-and-bolts content, we've listed many in the reference guide on pages 185 and 186.

Here are seven basic precepts to consider, and perhaps even challenge, before reading the subsequent sections of this book.

Left:
Character sketch of Elle, the lead character in Matt Kindt's graphic novel *2 Sisters* (Top Shelf Productions; 2004).

Above:
Flashback scene featuring the scar-faced assassin from Matt Kindt's *2 Sisters*.

ONE: CHARACTER DESIGN IS NOT AN END IN ITSELF

The goal of character design for graphic novels is *storytelling*, not image creation. (That said, there is an aesthetic appeal to looking at character designs as visual objects, but that really shouldn't concern the graphic novelist in the moments of creation.)

TWO: COMICS CHARACTERS ARE SEQUENTIAL BEINGS

They are meant to be drawn hundreds if not thousands of times, and often don't (and shouldn't) stay perfectly consistent from drawing to drawing. Unnecessary complexity and disparity, however, can be cumbersome and distracting. And, as we'll emphasize throughout the book, characters can have more than one level or aspect of detail.

THREE: THE "APPEAL" OF A CHARACTER IS CONTEXT-SPECIFIC

Put simply, what works for one author, in one story, for one audience, will not necessarily work for another. Hergé's world-famous design of the boy reporter Tintin, for example, is brilliant in its context, but would be ludicrous for a character in Kazuo Koike and Goseki Kojima's poignant yet violent manga *Lone Wolf and Cub* (except perhaps in an ironic context). Also, it should be noted that readers rarely see exactly what the author sees. (*Lone Wolf and Cub* is now reprinted in English by Dark Horse Comics.)

FOUR: "BAD DESIGNS" CAN BE VERY EFFECTIVE

Some designs lacking in the finer points of visual art—symmetry, consistency, proportion, etc.—are actually perfect for the story they illustrate. If it's done purposefully and serves the story without being too distracting, then no design is truly *bad.* A certain rawness can often be the key to real substance, whereas a slick, schematic surface can sometimes be quite hollow. (Again, it's context-specific.)

FIVE: MEMORABILITY IS NOT ALWAYS A GOOD THING

For minor and background characters, it's often effective to strive for "bland" designs so as not to steal attention away from the main players.

SIX: WRITERS ARE CHARACTER DESIGNERS TOO

In a writer–artist collaboration, the *content* if not the *look* of a character often stems from, or draws upon, the writer's concepts and script work. For example, the characters in *Sandman* (DC Comics/Vertigo, 1988–1996) owe their fictional lives to writer Neil Gaiman's vivid descriptions, dialogue, and story lines.

SEVEN: NO CHARACTER DESIGN EXISTS IN A VACUUM

It is *always* beneficial to study the work of others—other artists, art forms, subjects, cultures, and historical eras. Both influence and comparison are fundamental parts of a graphic novelist and character designer's education.

We've structured this book so that you can read it cover to cover or sample it by section, in order to maximize your opportunities for in-depth investigation, which should *begin* and not end when you've stopped reading.

And so, let us begin.

SECTION I

THE GRAPHIC NOVEL

For much of the twentieth century, in North America and Britain, the very idea of book-length comics were viewed at best as a compelling novelty for young people, and at worst as an affront to all art and literature. Other European countries and Japan, however, had for a long time granted the best comics the same status as serious films, literary novels, and other "fine" arts. Fortunately during the past two decades or so, a new respect for comics has taken hold in those countries formerly opposed to "legitimate" graphic novels, spurring on a massive new publishing phenomenon that shows little sign of abating. And here in the twenty-first century, with emerging technologies and shifting economies, the rest of the world, from India to Brazil and South Africa, seems poised to join the field.

In this section, we attempt to define the graphic novel, offer a brief history and global overview of the form, and introduce the various roles of the creators. ■

Left:
A page from Jeff Nicholson's darkly humorous graphic novel *Through the Habitrails* (first published in 1994), which was developed as a series of short stories intended to form a greater whole. Nicholson says they are interrelated and fluid, but not an oversized or open-ended "epic," as most comics are. (See more of Nicholson's work on pages 84 and 85.)

WHAT IS A GRAPHIC NOVEL?

Left:
Cover to the graphic novel *Hello, Again* by Max Estes (Top Shelf Productions, 2005).

"A graphic novel has to be structured as a novel, as a whole with a beginning, middle, and end, with its own themes and concepts unique to that book and not just as an episodic series of strips that's been thrown together to make a book."

Bryan Talbot

A graphic novel is at once a movement, a format, and a form. Other terms—long-form comic, graphic album, picture novel—have been suggested, but "graphic novel" is currently the front runner in the labeling race.

The term "graphic novel" is often used as an expedient marketing, packaging, or shelving classification for a range of comics publications, including trade paperback collections, short-story anthologies, manga digests, annuals, and non-narrative, nonfiction comics.

The foundation for a "graphic novel movement" was well expressed by Eddie Campbell (see pages 58–63) in his "Graphic Novel Manifesto." We define "graphic novel" simply as a form of *unified comics narrative*— in other words, a storytelling tool.

We remove any restriction of length, structure, complexity, quality, audience, and number of creators, as well as the idea that a graphic novel must be published in a specific medium. While most graphic novels are bound in printed "book" format, many serialized print comics (or specified story arcs within), as well as webcomics and photocomics (comics that use photographs rather than drawn pictures; also called fumetti), also deserve the title. Narrative nonfiction comics—biography, autobiography, comics journalism, and narrative essays—also fit our description. Many minicomics, and even some newspaper-style comic strips, can be counted as graphic novels, whether collected in book format or not, as long as they are clearly unified narratives. ■

"Graphic novel is a necessary term: it pigeonholes things, which can be as dangerous as a definition as it is useful. Obviously, labeling things makes them easier to describe, explain, or understand, but it can at the same time stultify or engender staleness. The novel part, as with the term applied to literature, really refers to the originality or newness of the aesthetic structure. Literary worth depends on many things, but the novelty is paramount. Generally, if something contains pictures as well as text, it is either an illustrated novel or a graphic novel. The latter has more inner dynamics within its workings."

Metaphrog's
John Chalmers

"The interaction and relation of the text to the image is a specific one, and we try to play with that in our books. In some cases, the text will say something that the picture is not saying, thus creating a contrast or shift, but also giving a whole new meaning to the entirety of the panel (and also in turn in relation to the panels around it). Sometimes the text reinforces the picture, like a tautology. In comics and graphic novels, an equal amount of the narration happens in the closure, that is in the mind of the reader, outside of a panel, something suggested, or left to the imagination, or between panels, and also in the rhythm. All these things interacting with each other make the reading of graphic novels a unique experience."

Metaphrog's
Sandra Marrs

Above: Ted Slampyak's *Jazz Age* is both a webcomic (www.jazzagecomics.com, ongoing) and a Sunday-paper-style strip that is structured as a unified graphic novel.

Left: A rustic setting from Bryan Talbot's *The Tale of One Bad Rat*, first published in 1996 (see pages 142–145).

HISTORY & GEOGRAPHY

Far left:
Joe Casey and Tom Scioli's *GØDLAND* (Image Comics) pays homage to Jack Kirby's earlier *New Gods.*

Left:
Will Eisner's story collection marked the transition from "formative" to "contemporary" graphic novels.

The graphic novel is an amalgam of culture, commerce, and the occasional quirk of genius. Looking back on the form's evolution, it's easy to ascribe a linear or cyclical progression of innovation and influence: Artist A's experiment begat Artist B's prototype begat Artist C's masterpiece begat Artist D's imitation begat Artist E's experiment, and so on. However, the reality is messier and far more interesting, as outlined in Paul Gravett's *Graphic Novels: Stories to Change Your Life* (Aurum Press; 2005) and *Manga: 60 Years of Japanese Comics* (Collins Design; 2004).

Some critics say comics are as ancient as the earliest cave etchings; others argue it's a stretch to compare Egyptian hieroglyphics with today's sequential graphics. Regardless of these disputes, many scholars recognize the ambitious nineteenth-century books of Switzerland's Rodolphe Töpffer (*Monsieur Jabot*; 1832) and France's Gustave Doré (*History of Holy Russia*; 1854) as what Gravett calls "pioneering antecedents of graphic novels." Works of such sophistication were rarely seen again until the early twentieth century, when American newspaper comics exploded in quantity and eventually quality, as evidenced by the works of Winsor McCay (*Little Nemo in Slumberland*) and George Herriman (*Krazy Kat*), among others.

Newspaper strips gave rise to comic books (and later comics annuals in the UK) in the 1930s—around the time that American artist Lynd Ward created wordless woodcut novels including *God's Man* (1929). Comic books were nearly annihilated by self-censorship in the 1950s, made a huge comeback in popularity with Marvel Comics' re-emergence in the early 1960s, and became a training ground for such luminaries as Jack Kirby (one of the primary architects of the Marvel Universe), Carl Barks (*Uncle Scrooge*), Neal Adams (*Batman*; *Green Lantern/Green Arrow*), Gil Kane (whose 1971 Bantam paperback *Blackmark* is arguably the first American graphic novel), and Jim Steranko (*Nick Fury, Agent of S.H.I.E.L.D.*). The cultural revolutions of the late 1960s and early 1970s were chronicled by "underground" comics artists such as Robert Crumb, Vaughn Bode, Kim Deitch, Justin Green, and Trina Robbins, who moved away from traditional "assembly-line" processes to celebrate the solo artist, or auteur.

But nothing as serious as a fully-fledged movement, or as unified as a unique art form, had emerged until 1978, when Will Eisner published *A Contract with God and Other Tenement Stories*, for which he used the term "graphic novel," coined by publisher Richard Kyle in 1964. Meanwhile, in England, Bryan Talbot had begun serializing *Luther Arkwright*, and Raymond Briggs would soon publish *When the Wind Blows* in 1982.

Beginning in the 1960s, writes Gravett, Richard Kyle was "among the first to import and champion European comics, especially French *bandes dessinées* in color hardback albums, and thick Japanese paperbacks of manga." The most highly regarded European graphic albums include those of Hergé (*Tintin*), Franquin (*Spirou et Fantasio*), Goscinny and Uderzo (*Asterix*), Hugo Pratt (*Corto Maltese*), Jacques Tardi (*Adèle Blanc-Sec*), and Moebius (*The Airtight Garage*). The Japanese manga of equivalent status include works by Osamu Tezuka (*Astro Boy; Phoenix; Buddha*), Keiji Nakazawa (*Barefoot Gen*), Kazuo Koike and Goseki Kojima (*Lone Wolf and Cub*), Katsuhiro Otomo (*Akira*), and Hayao Miyazaki (*Nausicaä of the Valley of the Wind*). ▸

In the mid-1980s, the American media focused attention on three books: Alan Moore and Dave Gibbons' *Watchmen*, Frank Miller's *Batman: The Dark Night Returns* (both from DC Comics), and Art Spiegelman's Pulitzer Prize–winning, two-part autobiographical novel *Maus: A Survivor's Tale* (Pantheon). Another standout work of the period is *Love & Rockets* by Los Bros Hernandez (Fantagraphics).

The past 20 years, arguably, have wrought more revolutions than the preceding half-century. Bookstores and libraries house GN sections. Art museums showcase GN exhibits. The Internet has spurred new artistic techniques and methods for collaboration and distribution. Women and minorities have sprung to the creative forefront. Small presses and large trade houses vie for a growing pool of talent. University degree programs in sequential art have emerged. GNs have launched successful films. And hope is high that the youngest readers will become the next generation of innovators.

How to capture the breadth and depth, struggle and strife, spirit and speed of the contemporary scene? Just as in studying character design, it can only be done one small piece at a time. ■

Below:
In 2006, Gene Luen Yang's *American Born Chinese* was selected as a finalist for The National Book Awards, in the category of Young People's Literature. It was the first graphic novel to be honored by this prestigious American award. Art copyright Gene Yang, used with permission of First Second Books.

Right:
Inspired by Walt Disney, Osamu Tezuka guided generations of Japanese creators, who in turn influenced the aesthetics and mechanics of comics globally.

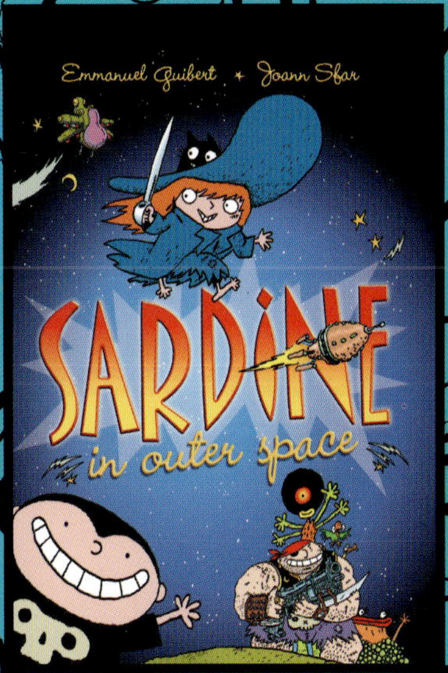

Center left:
In addition to being a respected creator in both Europe and America, Lewis Trondheim is a founding member of L'Association, a prominent publisher of European comics. Art copyright Lewis Trondheim, used with permission of First Second Books.

Left:
French creators Emmanuel Guibert and Joann Sfar have collaborated for years, each taking turns writing and illustrating their projects. *Sardine in Outer Space* copyright Emmanuel Guibert and Joann Sfar, used with permission of First Second Books.

THE GRAPHIC NOVELIST: SINGULAR VISION

Within the idea of the graphic novel as a singular and cohesive work of substance is the concept of the "graphic novelist"—an independent creator responsible for all, or at least most, of the work of creating the graphic novel, including character design. While some creators work solo purely as a matter of practicality (finding a talented and reliable collaborator can be difficult), for others it is a conscious aesthetic choice. Many creators find the strict oversight and mandatory collaboration common in the commercial comics industry stifling, and the artistic results unsatisfying.

Such dissatisfaction, among other factors, has led to the idealization among independent creators of the "pure artistic vision"—the model where a graphic novel is, as much as possible, the work of one mind, free from both editorial "meddling" and an "assembly line" process where creative vision is fragmented or obliterated as it is passed from one "production stage" to the next. According to this aesthetic, only the individual graphic novelist can achieve untrammeled artistic expression. After all, one of the allures of graphic novels is that they can often be "one-person shows," unlike most films, plays, and computer games.

Some graphic novelists known primarily for their solo work include Chynna Clugston-Major, Will Eisner, Jenn Manley Lee (see pages 94–99), Marjane Satrapi, Seth, Bryan Talbot (see pages 142–145), Craig Thompson, Art Spiegelman, and Chris Ware, among others.

In Japan, the collaborative model has never dominated the comics industry in the way it dominates commercial comics in the West. Following in the tradition of the revered Osamu Tezuka, most manga works are credited to a single creator. Although it is not uncommon for creators to have several assistants, it is still the rule that the originator owns and oversees the work, completing the bulk of the creative tasks and leaving only peripheral details, such as backgrounds, to the assistants. ■

Above left:
Although *Good-bye, Chunky Rice* is not overtly autobiographical, the nuances of tone and mood strongly suggest that the themes are drawn from personal experience—these notes of personal revelation might not have been so clearly present if the work had been created as part of a collaboration.

Above:
Craig Thompson's debut graphic novel, *Good-bye, Chunky Rice* (Pantheon, 1999), tells a story of loneliness and wanderlust.

DRAWBACKS TO SOLO CREATION

The clearest drawback to the paradigm of the graphic novelist is that it requires the would-be creator to be an artistic polymath, capable of writing, illustrating, art directing, and editing their comic work competently. If a creator is a brilliant writer but a poor illustrator, or vice versa, that creator will be hard-pressed to produce satisfying work if he or she adheres to the ideal of solo creation. Also, when tight deadlines are involved, it is often helpful to share the more time- and manual-labor-intensive aspects of the creative process without sacrificing storytelling control and the unique vision.

What's more, art is never created in a true vacuum; by walling off outside input, the solo creator is often deprived of the ongoing critical feedback that might help to ensure that the ideas actually come across clearly in the work—without this, creators risk producing final products that are inconsistent, unclear, or at the very least, not quite as successful as they might have been. ■

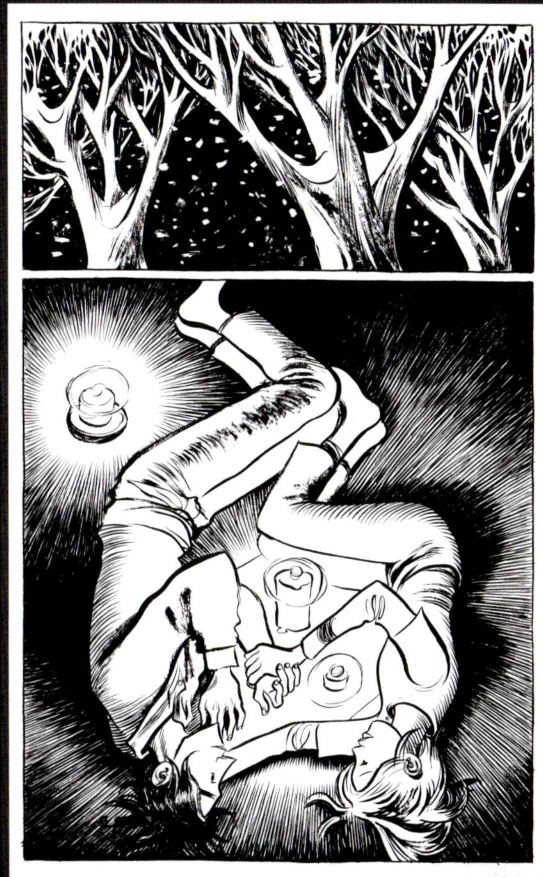

Above & left:
Many consider Craig Thompson's second book, *Blankets* (Top Shelf Productions, 2003), to be a landmark work in the graphic novel form. Being an autobiographical story, it is appropriate that Thompson chooses to work independently. It is rare for creators to seek collaborative partners for autobiographical works. (Harvey Pekar, creator of *American Splendor*, is a notable exception.)

Above:
Another advantage of solo creation is the potential for unity in both narrative and visual vocabulary across works. Note, for instance, that the intricate quilts used to denote intimacy and false security in *Blankets* appeared in a similar context in *Good-bye, Chunky Rice.*

THE DESIGN TEAM:

COLLABORATION & OVERSIGHT

While solo creation currently dominates the graphic novel format, collaboration is far from a thing of the past. Some of the most critically and commercially successful graphic novels—*Sandman* (Vertigo, collected edition, 1991–1997), *From Hell* (Eddie Campbell Comics, collected edition, 1999), and *Astro City* (Homage/DC collected edition, 1999–present)—are the result of collaborations where a unified vision emerged from multiple abilities and sensibilities. Even in Japan, where single authors called "manga-ka" have always been more common, the manga series *Chobits* (published in English by Tokyopop, 2002–2003) and *xxxHOLiC* (published in English by Del Rey, beginning in 2004), created by a team of four women collectively known as CLAMP, are incredibly popular.

Team-based collaborations, with an editor at the helm and a clear division of labor among a revolving cast of five or six creators—still the mainstay of monthly superhero comics—are not as prevalent in graphic novels from independent and trade publishers. Having a small, cohesive team, usually with a lead storyteller or two, is generally held as the best solution.

In writer–artist pairings, the writer is integral to the character design process and sometimes takes the lead role. The balance of decision-making varies with every collaboration. Anything is possible, even, for example, illustrator-driven collaborations and studio-style projects that mimic animation houses (see pages 164–169).

INSIGHT & OVERSIGHT

Graphic novel editors and art directors play important, behind-the-scenes roles in the character design process. In an interview with Tom Spurgeon, Mark Siegel, the editorial director of First Second Books, observed, "There's so much work produced both [in the United States] and in Europe full of incredible artistry, brilliant characters, a totally dazzling premise, and then halfway through the novel, the story falls apart. That's the kind of stuff where a novelist would expect a good editor to ask tough questions and have that fine balance of not meddling with someone's vision, but still coaching alongside and sometimes being unpopular. In the second draft the editor might become the most hated person in the novelist's life. It's not the same with all creators, though. Some people take to [the coaching], while others really want to be left alone."

Janna Morishima, editor-at-large for Scholastic's Graphix imprint, agrees with Siegel, adding that an editor's role is to "refine and polish and make the storytelling even more *economical* and powerful." Her colleague at Scholastic, executive editor Sheila Keenan, says an editor should be adaptable to different working methods with individual artists/authors and serves as a kind of "ideal reader." "You see things that visual artists might take for granted, and can help the artist/author to keep track of minor details, since often they're doing it all—writing, sketching, inking, etc.—by themselves." She regularly reviews character sketches—and for a multi-volume series, would expect an annotated "character bible" to establish consistency of design for characters who will appear in multiple books across the series. "Pick your details carefully," Keenan advises. "You'll end up drawing them hundreds or thousands of times."

In Japan, editors play an even more hands-on role, generating story ideas and providing some artistic assistance. An editor might even stay in a creator's home for days at a time to help meet a deadline! ■

"I like to give a detailed vignette of every character; I type up two pages of description for each important person in a story. I'm the most intimately familiar with the characters, and I have a clear idea inside my head of how they look. I'm obliged to communicate that to the artist [Juan Ferreyra]. At the same time, I try to allow Juan as much freedom as possible. An artist must be able to capture a character's essential nature. The details aren't so important. It's just not possible for an artist to draw a character exactly as I envision them. I've learned to let go. Besides, the more input an artist gives, the better. The artist, after all, is the one doing the drawing, and I have to be conscious of that at all times."

Arvid Nelson, writer of *Rex Mundi*

This page & opposite: Pages from *Rex Mundi*, by Arvid Nelson and Juan Ferreyra (Dark Horse Comics, collected edition, 2004 to time of writing).

Raina?
Is somethin wrong?
I'm just so tired.
Exhausted and tired.

SECTION II

THE CHARACTER

A story, whether fictional or factual, can function without a specified time or place, without a definable plot or theme, without even a significant conflict or climax. But every story needs at least one character—the special someone whom the story is about, and in many cases, the person (not always a human being) whose perceptions or consciousness are at the root of the narrative. Story is about change in character—sometimes evident, sometimes subtle—and this section introduces the many elements that make a comics character work, collectively called characterization, and how more than one character might work together to propel the tale. ■

Left:
This cover image from Stan Sakai's *Usagi Yojimbo*, volume 3, number 92 (2006), features Usagi (the *ronin* rabbit) and Tomoe (who plays a much greater role than "love interest"), two of the anthropomorphic leads from the two-decades-and-still-going-strong comics series set in feudal Japan and now published by Dark Horse Comics. Note the patterning (stippling or hatching) on the clothing, which helps in distinguishing and drawing the eye to the central characters. (See pages 126–129 for more about Stan Sakai's work.)

STORY & ARCHETYPE

Story is, on one level at least, a narrative framework for revealing change in character. Why is character so important? Let's say a comet strikes Jupiter, causing enormous physical and chemical disturbance, but nothing living exists there and no mind registers that it has happened. This is not a story, or even an event. We have setting (time and place) and a simple plot with a rudimentary conflict (nature vs. nature); we could even add tone or thematic significance to the telling. But we have no character.

The imaginative appeal of such a cosmic collision might lead a science-fiction writer to posit futuristic Jovian colonizers or even sentient gaseous entities that experience and respond to the circumstances. Another author might cast the comet and the planet as characters, granting consciousness to each, if not free will. Yet another might eschew individuality altogether and give to the solar system a collective awareness; the total setting, in effect, acts as a single character. No approach is wrong; but each can be enhanced by an understanding of the principles of character.

CHARACTER ARCHETYPES

Central story patterns or archetypes stretching back to the earliest myths and folk tales underlie each character role. Like members of an Olympian pantheon or Tarot deck, characters all have countless aspects, and hybrids of archetypes abound. The classic or mythic hero—the one who saves the day, fights the monsters, and restores order from chaos—is the most recognizable archetype, as the hero's quest is present across all human cultures. Heroes can be male, female, or androgynous; brute (brawn over brains—Hercules or Conan the Barbarian), trickster (brains over brawn—Odysseus or Br'er Rabbit), or both (brains and brawn—Spider-Man or Batman); tragic (motivated toward ruin by fatal flaws—Oedipus or Hamlet), or comedic (a hapless, mostly humorous pawn of greater forces—Charlie Chaplin's Little Tramp or Charles Schulz's Charlie Brown).

Two additional spins on the hero pattern are the messiah and the antihero. The messiah is an incarnation of the ancient "vegetable god" archetype: a promised savior is born, achieves enlightenment, dies, and is reborn in the manner of natural cycles or seasons. In graphic novels, the characters of Morpheus and Daniel from Neil Gaiman's *Sandman* (DC Comics/Vertigo) are messianic counterparts—two avatars of the same endlessly regenerating character. ▶

Left:
Kitsune the trickster fox-thief from Stan Sakai's *Usagi Yojimbo* (see pages 126–129).

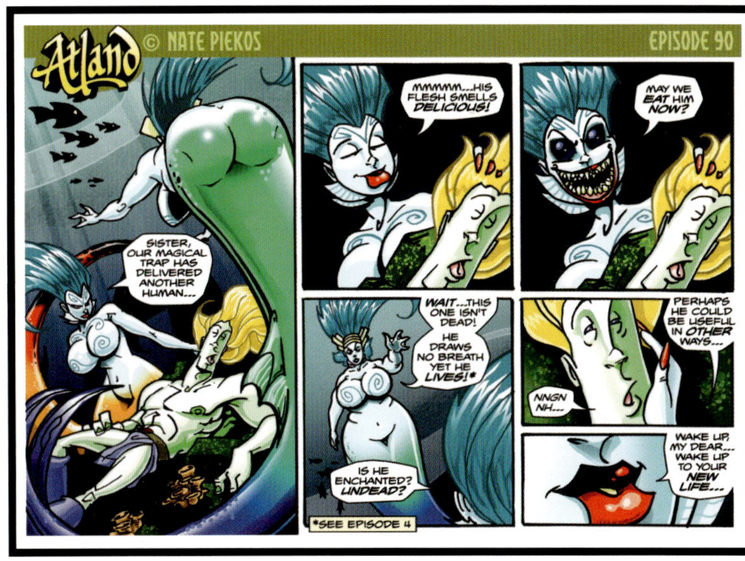

Left:
The young hero, Colby, and adversary/dark mentor, Esurio, from Jim Zubkavich's *The Makeshift Miracle* (www.makeshiftmiracle.com).

The antihero is arguably a melding of the classic hero pattern with a more cynical modern perception of human complexity and weakness—a fusion of the comedic (farce, satire, absurdity, and irony) and the wholly tragic. Though the antihero combats external demons, often using ethically troubling methods, it is the inner demons that bite most brutally. The central characters of *Watchmen* by Alan Moore and Dave Gibbons (DC Comics; 1986–1987), as well as those of *Lone Wolf and Cub* by Kazuo Koike and Goseki Kojima (reprinted in English by Dark Horse Comics) exemplify this increasingly common character type, granting nobility to clearly conflicted protagonists.

Heroes or heroines rarely act alone. Like planets orbiting the sun, the hero/heroine is the gravitational nexus for the adversary, the gods, the king, the monster, the mentor, the grail, the lover, the fool, the pariah, the thief, the wizard, the renegade, and the rabble. These are known by many other names, or a character fills more than one role, but nearly every story and graphic novel references these models and others either directly or indirectly. ■

Above left:
Joe Theseus and Ginny, Queen of the Amazons—late-twentieth-century-styled gods—from Eddie Campbell's *Bacchus* (see pages 58–63).

Above:
Modern monsters from Nate Piekos' *Atland* (see pages 46 and 47).

THE CENTRAL CHARACTER & THE OPPOSITION

Left: Metaphrog's Louis has a round and cute appearance that reflects his earnest, yet gullible nature (see pages 104–109).

THE CENTRAL CHARACTER

At the heart of most narratives is a single character whose actions and passions drive the story. Supporting characters may have their own agendas, but those will often be influenced by the central character. Be it Monkey D. Luffy's quest for the fabled pirate treasure (*One Piece*, reprinted in English by VIZ Media, beginning in 1997), Peter Parker's efforts to live up to the ideals of his murdered uncle (Marvel Comics' *Spider-Man*), or Marjane Satrapi's search for understanding amidst the chaos of revolutionary Iran (*Persepolis*, 2003), it is the central character who binds all the elements of the story into a cohesive whole.

Furthermore, the central character serves as the reader's entry point into the story, providing the primary point of view on the events that unfold. Therefore, more than any other character, it is vital to keep the central character grounded in the story itself. A character is more than a collection of cool clothes and dynamic poses—even a superhero. If the costume is given greater attention than the person wearing it, the resulting character will be shallow and forgettable. This is the true core of character design—crafting a personality. To capture the reader's attention, the character must have sufficient motivation to keep him or her moving forward, making decisions that change the course of events.

This isn't to say the central character must always make the *right* decisions. The most believable characters usually blend enough admirable qualities to make them sympathetic, with enough flaws to keep them real. A character who is too perfect will be difficult for readers to identify with. (The phenomenon of superhero sidekicks was largely a response to the fact that nearly indomitable characters such as the early Batman were difficult to relate to. Less experienced sidekicks were added to give readers a viewpoint more akin to their own.) As characters who are too flawed are difficult to sympathize with, even antiheroes often have some noble intent at the root of their mission.

With a clear understanding of who the character is, the visual design should then extend from the character's own personality. Leading characters can be beautiful or ugly, smart or foolish, exceptional or perfectly average. There are no requirements in any of those regards, so long as your choice makes sense within the context of the story. ▸

THE OPPOSITION

The chief object to the central character's goals isn't always a person—the protagonist's chief obstacle can be nature, technology, or even his or her own personal weakness, such as in the case of a character struggling with addiction. In most stories, however, there will be other characters standing in the way of the central character's aims, often personified by a central antagonist who must be overcome by the story's end.

The opposition may be a constant presence in the story, sticking close to the lead and the events that transpire. At other times, the opposition may linger on the horizon, a mysterious threat toward which the lead is progressing. Whether the opposition is an evil tyrant bent on destroying the world or simply a rival suitor for the affection of the lead's love interest, making the opposition interesting and memorable can be nearly as important as creating a believable, strong lead. After all, the chief measure of a protagonist's worth is often the obstacles he or she overcomes. If the opposition is trivial or unoriginal, the protagonist can be similarly diminished. ■

Left: An alternate-reality John F. Kennedy stars in Diana R. Sassé's *Antique White House* (www.kennedy-tales.com).

CONTRAST & COMMONALITY

In most instances, a story's central opposition is defined in terms of what the protagonist is *not*—if the protagonist is a hero, then the opposition is a villain; if the protagonist is clever, the opposition is strong. Other contrasts include: the outcast versus the charismatic; the poor versus the rich; the humble versus the arrogant. This contrast often extends to the visual design as well; at its most basic, the good guys wear white while the bad guys wear black. Other common contrasts include small versus large, beautiful versus ugly, and simple versus sophisticated. In many stories, these contrasts have become conventions, especially in adventure stories where the contrasts are particularly exaggerated within grand battles of good versus evil. But design by contrast can work on subtler levels as well, and often serves to stress the central themes of the story. A story of class struggle, for instance, certainly requires a degree of contrast, usually pitting a humble working-class character against a slick and well-dressed businessperson or politician.

Useful as contrast can be, the central character and the opposition need not be polar opposites. A degree of commonality between the protagonist and the antagonist can make the struggle much more complicated and interesting, especially as it often serves to externalize the lead character's own internal struggles. In such instances, it is often only by overcoming the lead and the opposition's shared fatal character flaw that the protagonist can succeed. The most obvious instance of this is the classic "evil twin" convention, though the theme need not always be presented in such an overt fashion: a businessman might triumph over a rival businessman by conquering his own greed; a politician might defeat a campaign opponent by refusing to lie.

And, of course, it is not uncommon for the lead and the opposition to have in common the people they love—such is the foundation for traditional love-triangle rivalry. The lead and opposition characters can even be alike in acting with good intentions; just because two characters oppose each other doesn't mean one of them must be evil. Indeed, when the opposition is nearly as sympathetic as the protagonist, it deepens the conflict beyond a simple matter of winning or losing, and gives both characters an opportunity to grow even richer and more complex. ■

Left:
In Metaphrog's *Louis* series, Louis' secret tormentors, Clean and Jerk, are distinguished from Louis by visual details such as their more self-important clothing, as well as by their mean-spirited humor.

This page:
In *Night Fisher* (Fantagraphics, 2005), R. Kikuo Johnson uses the universal aspects of the students' uniform in order to stress subtler characteristics. In his words, "The fact that all the students are issued the same set of clothes becomes a great opportunity to accent their different personalities through subtle variation in the way each character wears the uniform. Loren, a repressed do-gooder, is consistently buttoned up and neatly tied, while Jem, a rebel, wears his collar up and his tie loose."

THE SUPPORTING CAST

Left:
This creepy, but harmless mortician from Jason Little's *Shutterbug Follies* (Doubleday, 2002; see pages 114 and 115) is based on a stereotype, with just enough detail added to make him memorable when he turns up a second time later in the story.

Like the opposition, prominent members of the supporting cast are often designed around contrasts and comparisons with the lead character, though usually in a more complementary way. They may provide the lead with skills they lack, such as a physical power or special knowledge. They might represent maturity that the lead has yet to achieve. They may even serve as unintentional foils, as bad influences who lead the protagonist into conflicts they might otherwise avoid.

Sometimes supporting cast can play very prominent roles, almost rivaling the lead—this shouldn't be confused with the true ensemble, however. Ultimately, the supporting cast must balance the lead, providing a mix of aid and hindrance that keeps the lead's path through the story interesting.

THE LOVE INTEREST

Often, the most prominent member of any story's supporting cast is the love interest—the beautiful man or woman whose mere presence leaves the central character confused and acting irrationally. The love interest often serves as a primary motivation for choices the central character makes throughout the story. Naturally, this is true of romances, but many adventure stories begin with the hero setting out to protect, rescue, or merely impress a beautiful woman. But the love interest isn't just a device for motivating the hero before conveniently falling in love with him at the end. Male or female, the love interest is just as much a character, with unique aims and ideas that might not fit with the protagonist's plans. And it shouldn't be taken for granted that the love interest will eventually return the lead's affections. What's more, knowing what sort of person attracts the interest of the central character reveals a good deal about the lead's own values and personality. As a result, an underdeveloped love interest isn't just a hollow character—it also reflects poorly on the protagonist, whose affections will appear equally shallow, inspired as they are by superficiality.

Not every story needs a love interest. Much as romantic subplots are a staple of modern storytelling, they're certainly not indispensable. People aren't obligated to fall in love with each other just because they happen to be fighting for a common cause. Nor is a hero automatically entitled to the love of the woman of his choice just by virtue of being a hero. In fact, an underdeveloped love interest is frequently an indication that the romantic subplot doesn't work in the story as a whole. ▸

INCIDENTAL CHARACTERS & STEREOTYPES

Not every character warrants close attention. The incidental store clerks, pedestrians, police officers, and such who fill out the background against which the story is set don't all need detailed histories or complex motivations. Often the most straightforward way to develop these roles is by appealing to simple stereotypes—easily recognized, even clichéd characters, such as the gruff bartender, the sleazy lawyer, or the rookie cop. Unsatisfying as these clichés can be when passed off as primary characters, in minor roles, they can be a useful shorthand to explain the motivations of a character who will probably never be seen again. The motivations of such characters can often be gleaned from a single image before a line of dialogue is even uttered. This can certainly be overdone; some genres allow for it more than others, but if every minor character is stereotypical, it will begin to detract from the reality of any story. In moderation, however, there's nothing wrong with including the occasional stereotypical character (barring hurtful racial stereotypes) who is immediately recognizable in design, personality, or role. ■

This page: Craig Thompson explores an early romance in his semi-autobiographical *Blankets* (Top Shelf Productions, 2003). Understanding why one character loves another can reveal a great deal about his or her personality.

CHARACTER HISTORIES:
MOTIVATION & CONFLICT

Some storytellers develop characters on the page as they go along. Others chart out detailed character histories or biographies. These can be useful in clarifying character outlook, motivations, and desires; they can help to establish behavioral patterns that will affect the character's decisions, and ensure consistent behavior throughout longer works. What's more, a detailed history can provide the foundation for conflict between characters, since exploring the ways different characters view the world will reveal vital differences between those views.

There is no set structure or formula for writing a character history. On the facing page is the beginning of a sample history for a hypothetical protagonist in a "Generation Y" romantic drama. It is the result of asking and answering a series of well-defined questions about the character. By asking these sorts of questions about your own major characters and supplying your own answers, you will come to know the world of your story and the dramatic need of your character. This makes it easier to set up relationships and conflicts. It also serves as a primary resource for making visual design choices. A good rule-of-thumb is to move from general to specific, from context to content, with your questions. ►

Right:
If your character is running from the past, then it is especially important to develop the character's history, as Spike has done for Ben Kowolski, protagonist of her online series, *Templar, Arizona* (www.webcomicsnation.com/spike/Templar).

NAME:
Spencer Blake

DATE OF BIRTH/AGE:
March 28, 1980 (26 years old at start of story)

SEX/GENDER:
Male; heterosexual

RACE/ETHNICITY:
Caucasian; mix of French-Canadian and Scottish heritage

RELIGION:
Roman Catholic; very much lapsed

MARITAL STATUS:
Single; one bad breakup in college (caught his girlfriend cheating with his roommate); about to meet the girl of his dreams

OCCUPATION:
Starving artist; aspiring jazz composer; plays piano in a hotel lobby most nights; sees job as a "stepping stone"

HOMETOWN:
Grew up in rural northern Maine, in a depressed logging town called Bettany; now lives in a studio apartment in Boston, Massachusetts; no plans to visit home any time soon

FAMILY:
Youngest of five brothers—all twice his size; now considered something of a "black sheep" by siblings and parents who don't understand or appreciate his ambitions

EDUCATION:
Two years at Berklee College of Music; major in jazz composition; dropped out due to lack of finances (parents stopped helping with tuition after an argument about Spencer's choice of careers)

FINANCIAL HISTORY:
Solid blue-collar family; barely scraping by in an expensive city; considers money a "necessary evil" but gets self-conscious about his shabby clothes and lack of "real job"—especially around women ▸

Above right:
In addition to character histories, Spike even knows how each of her characters will eventually die. For instance, in an online interview, Spike recently revealed that Reagan will die of a heart attack years after the end of the story.

Right:
Templar, Arizona, is an outlandish city populated by outlandish people, like the kilt-clad Scipio. How long a character has actually lived in Templar can make a big difference to how they react to the locals.

That's enough about Spencer. Here are some other questions you could ask about your own characters.

HOBBIES:
What pastimes does the character enjoy? How does he/she spend leisure time? Does he/she prefer physical or mental activity?

SOCIAL BEHAVIOR:
Is the character comfortable in large groups? Does he/she prefer big parties or intimate gatherings? Is he/she comfortable spending time alone? When in groups, does he/she tend to observe quietly, engage in conversation, or become the life of the party? Is he/she popular? Do others enjoy being with him/her?

SOCIETAL OUTLOOK:
How does the character feel about society in general? Is he or she essentially an optimist, pessimist, realist, or idealist?

POLITICS:
Is the character politically active? Does he/she have strong beliefs or pet causes? Is he/she liberal or conservative, or independent?

VIEW OF AUTHORITY:
How does the character view authority figures, like cops or employers? Does he/she respect authority or rebel against it? Is he/she law-abiding or prone to criminal behavior? Has he/she ever broken the law? What was the crime? What was the punishment?

TRAUMA:
Has the character ever suffered a trauma, such as a violent crime or the premature death of a loved one? How long ago was it, and what did he/she do to cope? Is there any lingering guilt or fear about the event?

This is just some of the information that can go into a character history. Useful information can come from surprising places; even minor details can shed light on how a character thinks. Some creators find it useful to work out character *futures* as well, planning out the course of the character's life from the time the official story ends until the day the character dies. Understanding where a character eventually ends up can help to clarify the emotional journey they take through the course of the story at hand. ■

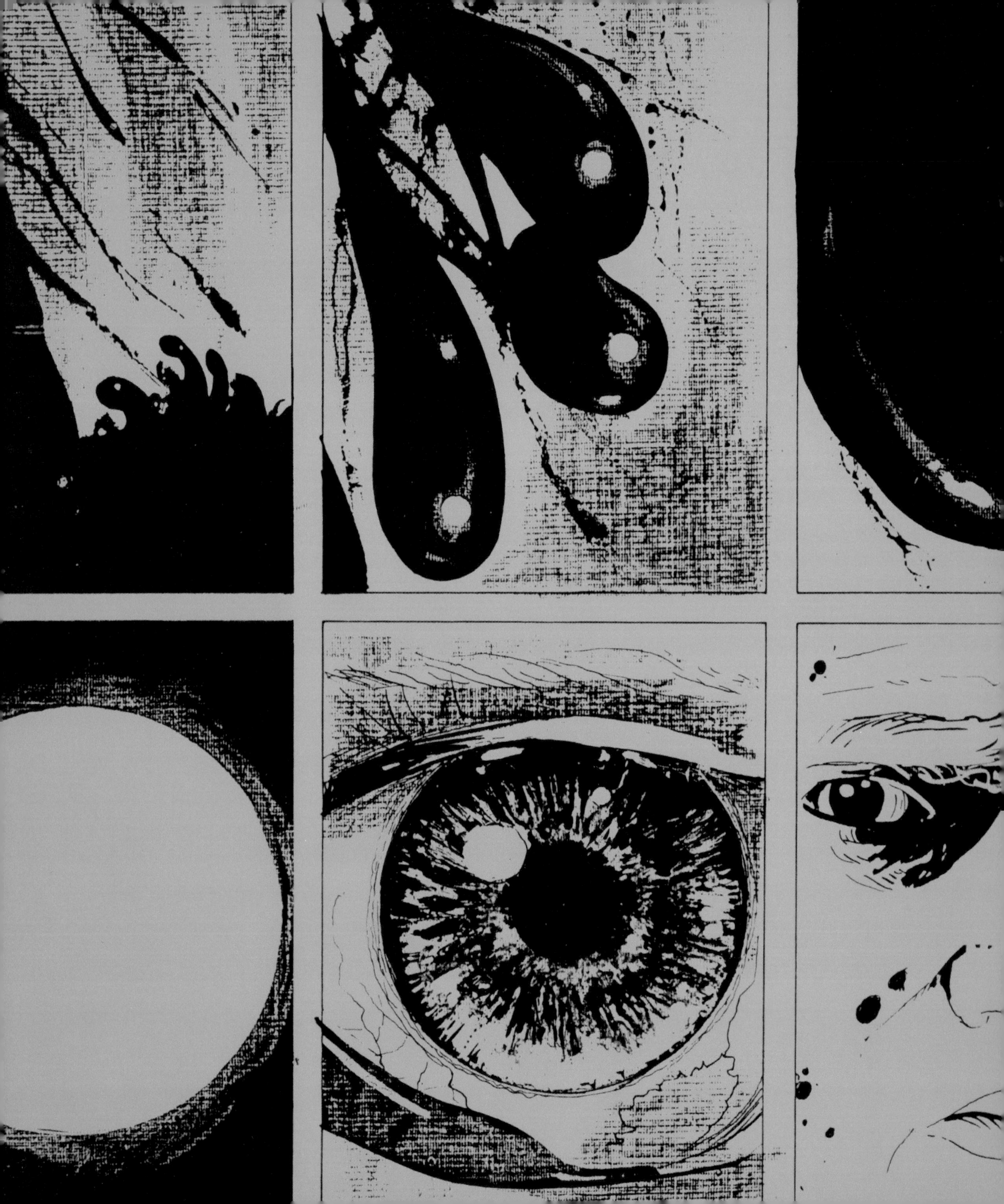

SECTION III

ELEMENTS OF DESIGN

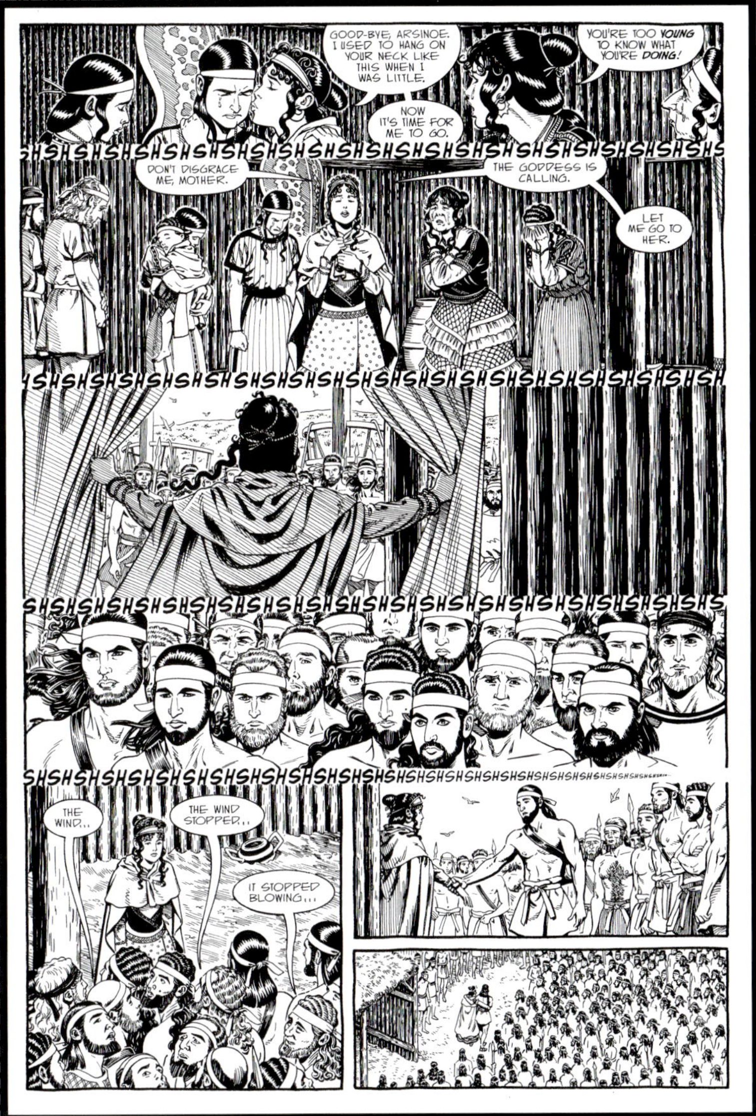

Every artist at every skill level draws to some degree on the fundamentals of visual art—line, form, composition, symmetry, proportion, perspective, color, value—and these formative elements apply directly to comics-character design. While other books about art theory or drawing and painting cover this material in far more depth and breadth than our book, we will introduce a working "visual vocabulary" that is not so much specific to, but certainly appropriate for, the comics form: unity and sequence, panel and gutter, face and figure, tag and icon, and so forth. We will also begin our series of case studies, which are designed to show the character work of individual artists or creative teams. ■

Above:
Pages 10 and 11 from issue 19 of Eric Shanower's *Age of Bronze*, "Sacrifice" (published by Image Comics; see pages 48–53) reveal both the exacting level of historical detail and the elegant storytelling.

UNITY & SEQUENCE

Unity of design/story/vision is perhaps the highest principle of art. And in the sequential art of graphic novels, design and story are inextricably linked. No element of a character design is merely decorative or isolated; everything in the story is functional and interrelated.

Characters in comics are analogous to characters in all other narrative art forms, but there are three distinct areas, in terms of how they affect unity and sequence, worth introducing and emphasizing at this point.

STATIC & DYNAMIC

One way of looking at comics-character designs is to explore the spectrum from *static* to *dynamic*. "Static" does not mean immobile or unchanging in this context, but rather that a character possesses a fundamental (i.e., prototypical) visual design or model. "Dynamic," by contrast, means that a character has no single *ideal* design; the author determines the character's appearance moment by moment, panel by panel. Neither type is superior, and there is a lot of crossover within the spectrum.

Static designs are a crucial part of daily comic strips, monthly comic books, and animated films, where often a collaborative team must strive for visual consistency. Another aspect is what we call "the restart method" of serialized storytelling. At the beginning of each new issue or story arc, the protagonist or antagonist reverts to his or her "default" look, no matter what alterations in appearance (especially costuming) might have occurred previously. Tied to this idea is the issue of corporate branding and packaging—the use of a character's "image" to generate and sell products—which is less prevalent (so far) in the contemporary graphic novel marketplace.

Static design is rarely concerned with the precise passage of time, and many static characters do not age or suffer the effects of weather or physical violence. When used in a more realistic context or contrasted with more dynamically designed characters, static designs call attention to the unreality and conceptual elasticity of the comics form, which can be a positive thing. For instance, in Jeff Smith's *Bone* series (Cartoon Books/Scholastic Graphix), the comedic lead, Fone Bone, is a visually static, cartoony character who contrasts sharply with the more dynamically rendered dramatic lead, Thorn, whose appearance transforms considerably—and not always consistently—throughout the series. Says Smith, "There are two worlds in *Bone*: one has an animated-cartoon flavor, the other is more realistic and researched. To bridge these two drawing styles, I had a few bridging characters, including the dragons and Gran'ma Ben. Thorn is fairly realistically drawn, while Gran'ma is halfway between the two worlds, a bit like Popeye. I made a stylistic decision to make her character a little stepping-stone between the two worlds so there's a sense of unity." ▸

Top left: Visually static, but appealing characters from Jef Czekaj's *Grampa and Julie: Shark Hunters* (Top Shelf Productions, 2004, originally published in *Nickelodeon Magazine*, October 1999; see page 74.)

Bottom left: Jeff Smith's Gran'ma Ben is a bridging character who unites the cartoony and realistic worlds in *Bone* (Cartoon Books/Scholastic Graphix; BONE® is ©2006 Jeff Smith).

ICONIC & SYMBOLIC

The spectrum from *iconic* to *symbolic* is another useful mode of exploration. "Icon" has many connotations, but we take it to mean "a pictorial image simplified for the purposes of recognition by a large audience without losing some resemblance to the physical object the image signifies." A symbol, on the other hand, is a type of visual metaphor (a literary device for comparison), related to the icon, in which the pictorial image stands for an intangible quality without a corresponding physical object. The silhouette of Mickey Mouse's circular head and ears is iconic; Frodo's ring in *The Lord of the Rings* is symbolic.

Alex Ross, famed artist of *Marvels* (1994), *Kingdom Come* (1996), and cover artist and character designer for *Astro City* (see pages 120–125), defines iconic. "You catch the perfect snapshot of the most identifiable form of that character. Fairly simple, fairly direct. You look at [an iconic character], and you know immediately what it's supposed to be and what it represents. It must be readable so that you understand it and believe in it immediately." ▸

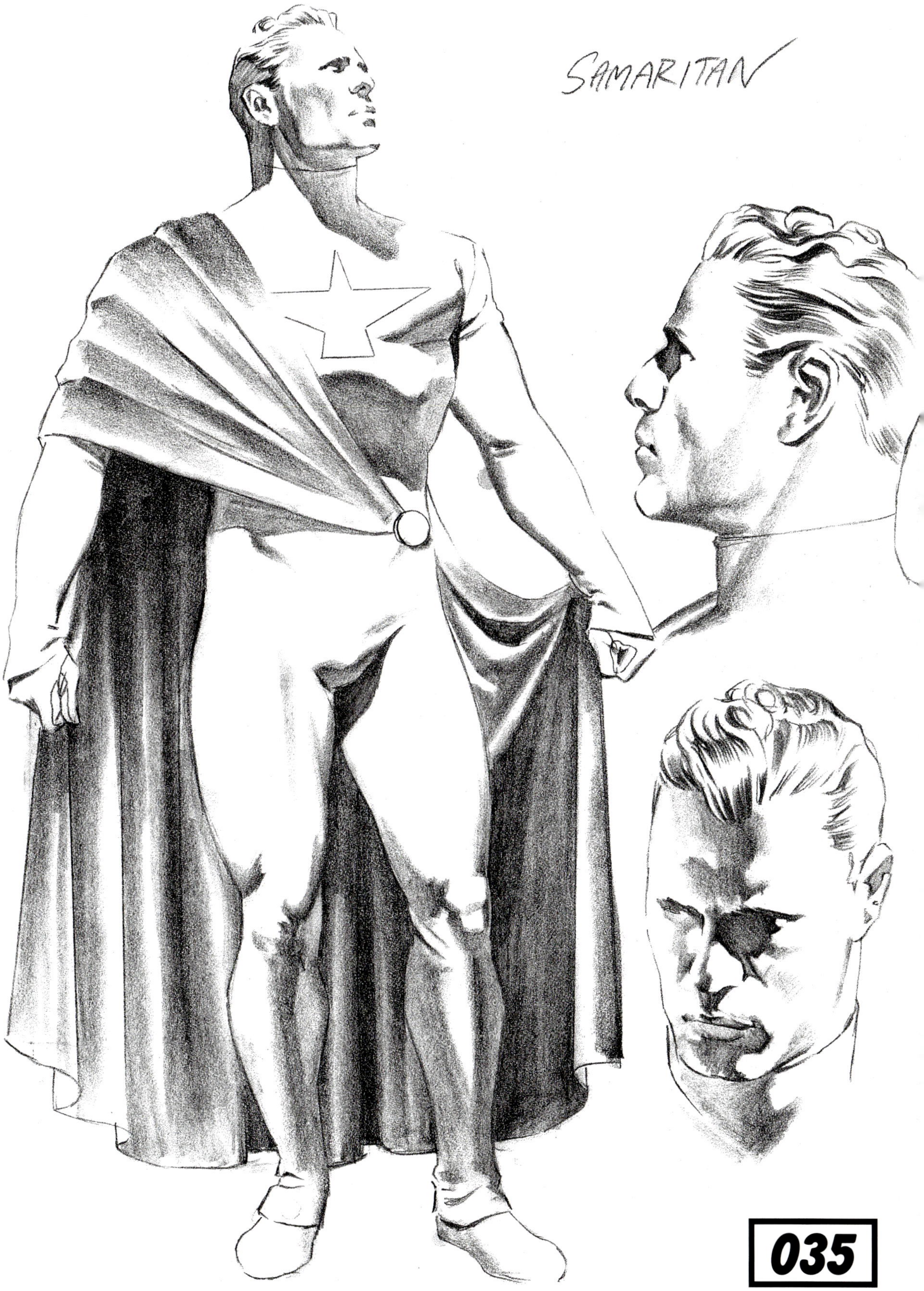

This page: Samaritan, one of Alex Ross' most iconic visual designs, from *Astro City*.

While characters can possess symbolic attributes and objects, the term "symbolic character" is a difficult one to justify. Characters in any story with more depth than the most straightforward allegory do not *symbolize* heroism, unconditional love, jealousy, or corrupted absolute power so much as they *embody* physical and behavioral traits that the reader associates with. To clarify, symbolism is not a direct, one-to-one comparison, but an implied (and hopefully subtle) suggestion of likeness. Hammering the reader over the head with overt symbols is a quick way to lose an audience.

SEQUENTIAL PRESENCE

Unlike a stationary figure in an advertising illustration, or an animated character in a TV cartoon, comics characters exist as part of a visual sequence arranged in space rather than across time—in a sort of map of moments. Each moment (or union of closely related moments) is often framed by a panel border. The author arranges the panels purposefully according to the available space and the story requirements. Theorist Neil Cohn calls a panel an "attention unit," as each box is, in effect, a device for inviting and directing attention. ▸

Left:
Page from issue 3 of Root Nibot and Colleen Coover's *Banana Sunday* (Oni Press; see page 75).

Far left: Dynamic page design from Miriam Katin's "Eucalyptus Nights." "All the characters on this page are Jewish and Israeli. All except one are soldiers," Katin says (see page 76).

Left: Page 14 from Don MacDonald's *Machiavelli.* "A crowd becomes a shape of its own without devolving into its component parts," MacDonald says (see page 77).

Since comics and graphic novels are meant to be *read,* not just looked at, page design that encourages clarity and left-to-right, top-to-bottom forward movement (the opposite for traditional manga) is of paramount importance—except when those are not the author's intentions.

Page design, therefore, exerts a strong influence on character design. Pages packed with panels dictate a different set of "shots"—angles, distances, scales, perspectives—than a more "airy" design with numerous open frames. A "talking-head" story composed of medium shots and close-ups might merit more constrained physical proportions, for example, and also a greater or lesser amount of visual detail as compared with a more cinematic or panoramic layout.

Whatever the format, character designers should know their character from every angle, at every scale, and from every distance.

Also important is the location of characters in relation to one another within each panel—making use of background, middle ground, and foreground to guide the eye and "direct" the action.

The shapes characters strike in space are also essential for helping the reader to navigate the page, and helping the author to "pace" the story for maximum dramatic effect. As critic Tom Spurgeon pointed out, visual cues can increase the sense of motion and action—creating visual starts, stops, and pauses. The precise placement and positioning of the bodies, the shapes of faces and props, can move the reader from one side of the panel to the other, and from one panel to the next. A dominant structural element such as a panel border or a wall is a clear stop, and an element breaking the border can cause the reader to move out of the panel, giving the work a careening or carefully controlled energy. ■

TOOLS & TECHNIQUES:

CHARACTER MODEL SHEETS

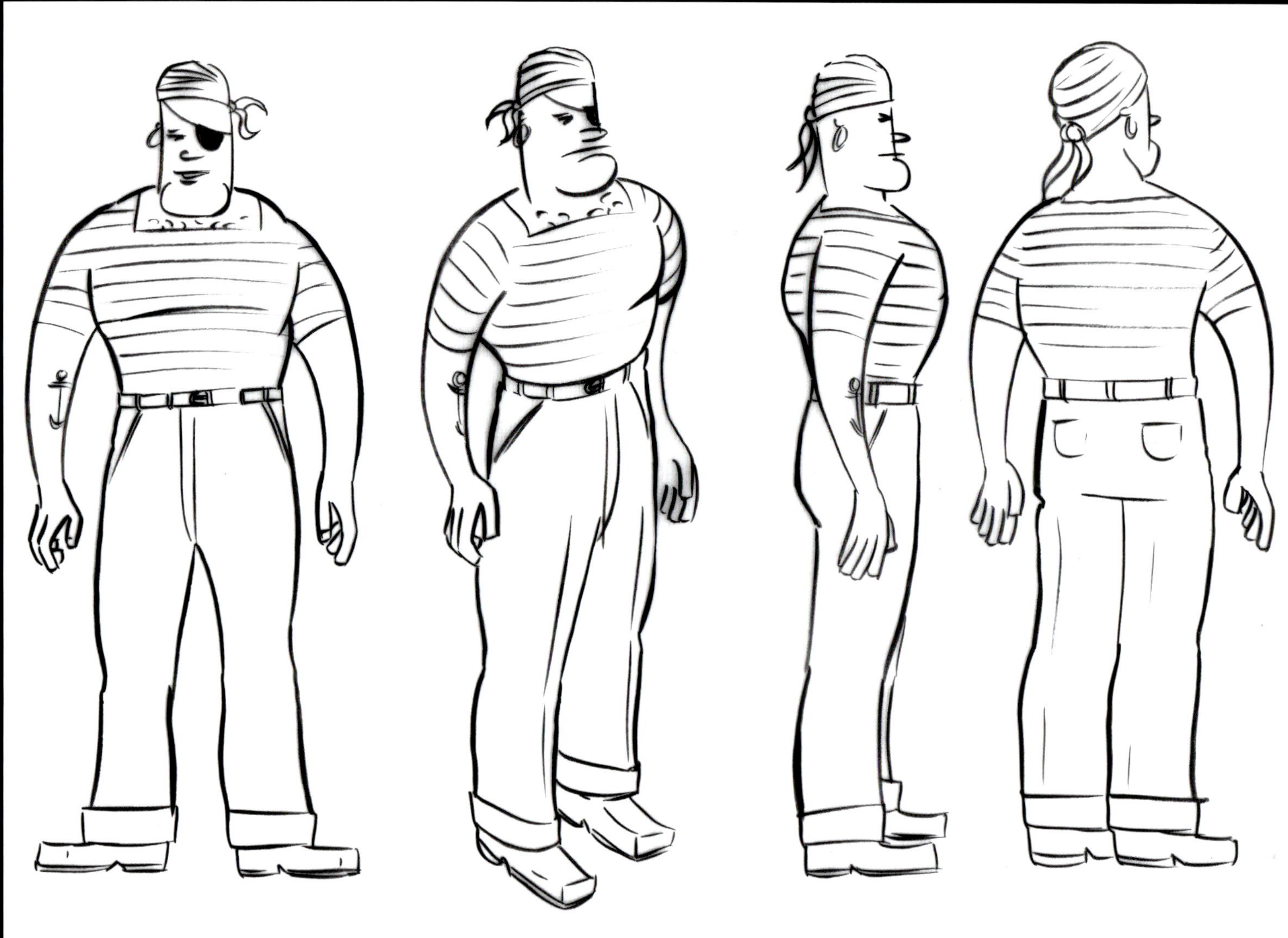

Graphic novelists are free to use any artistic means at their disposal—from pencil and paper, to acrylics and watercolors on canvas, to collaged photographs and 3-D rendering software—so we will merely recommend that you do not let your choice and mastery of those tools dominate your aesthetic decisions. Your storytelling vision is primary; your artistic methods are secondary.

Whatever your approach, the most essential tool for a comics artist is a good working sketchbook. In your sketchbook, you can try *anything*, the most radical designs or soon-to-be-abandoned scribbles, and never show another soul. The sketchbook is where you record your impressions of the outside world as well as the musings of your imagination.

When you're working with a team or with an editor—or planning a series of stories with the same characters—a character model sheet is often a useful tool. A model sheet is a more formal distillation of your sketches and serves as a functional reference for composition, character likeness, poses, and accuracy and consistency of detail. Unless otherwise required, a model sheet can be as quick and loose as you like, and completely cryptic to anyone but you, the artist. The most common types of model sheet are given on the facing page. ▸

Above:
Turnaround for a pirate character from Matt Kindt and Jason Hall's *Pistolwhip* (Top Shelf Productions, 2001).

Left & below: Photo references and live models are also useful tools. This *Super Spy* weekly comic strip for Top Shelf's website (art and writing by Matt Kindt) is based on a found photo (circa 1940s) from an estate sale. Photographer and subject unknown.

CHARACTER SHEET

This contains mostly text, but can include sketches or be combined with other visual sheets. It can include notes about the character's vital statistics—background, present situation, relationships, motivations, obstacles (internal and external), strengths and abilities, etc. Here you should ask yourself questions about, or even "interview," your character.

CONCEPT SHEET

This is the most common type of model sheet. It includes a full visual shot of the character (from head to toe), with some smaller details enlarged, for example, a single element such as a character's face, costuming, props, and logo, with the signature, distinguishing features (also called "tags") recorded.

TURNAROUND

This is sometimes called a "three-view" in its simplest form. It provides views of the character from every useful angle, and can show a 360-degree picture drawn to precise scale.

ACTION SHEET

This presents the range of motion and the most common movements for a character, usually minus the details of setting and dialogue.

EXPRESSION SHEET

Related to the action sheet, this generally shows a series of heads and faces expressing the spectrum of different emotions appropriate to the character and the story.

VALUE STUDY

This is a useful tool for composing an image, in order to establish the dominant pattern and structure—negative and positive space; range of lights and darks; effects of differing distances and light sources (including "reading" the character's silhouette for "legibility"); shading and tonality (including hatching and stippling).

COLOR STUDY

Related to the value study, this establishes the signature "palette" and highlights complements and contrasts. Of color and composition, *Bone* creator and graphic novelist Jeff Smith says, "Make sure certain compositions are favored by the color choices. So from a storytelling perspective, lead the eye to the right thing. Color can overwhelm. Color should step back and hide behind the lines and not jump forward. The drawing has to do its work; the depth has to be there in the line work. Use blacks to determine how close an object is from the camera."

Other variations of the model sheet include the storyboard (designing the character directly in thumbnail drawings of the actual pages and panels; the character line-up (showing relative proportions and scale of a group of characters); and the fully fledged character bible (which incorporates any or all of the above types of model sheet). Also see the case studies throughout this book, especially the model sheets of Scott Christian Sava on pages 164–169. ■

SPEECH PATTERNS:

DIALOGUE, BALLOONS & LETTERING

DIALOGUE

Few elements of character design are as revealing as a character's spoken words—not just *what* is said, but *how*—each character has an individual vocabulary, syntax, and style or inflection. Understanding speech patterns is an essential step in understanding your characters: eloquent or tongue-tied, literal or metaphorical, confident or cautious, flowing or stuttering. Ask yourself: Is my character's speech consistent with his or her background and present circumstances? How much of themselves do they reveal in their speech? Character design is a holistic process; presentation and identity are directly linked.

BALLOONS

Word balloons and first-person captions are common tools for presenting dialogue in comics. But they can easily clutter up an otherwise attractive page of artwork. As Dylan Meconis points out, "Word balloons can be very obnoxious things, taking up space that could be devoted to better visual information. But if you use them as a vessel for the character's personality, rather than just 'text dumps,' they become much more useful." By tailoring balloons to the moods of the characters, you tie the words being spoken more intimately to the character.

DIGITAL LETTERING

Whether you letter by hand or by computer, it's important to choose your letterforms or typefaces carefully. Some creators create their own typefaces, often based on their own handwriting. Typefaces designed specifically for comic speech are also available at sites such as Blambot.com.

Digital lettering allows an artist to choose typefaces specific to characters or situations. Of course, as designer Nate Piekos points out, this can be overdone. "Using a multitude of fonts for dialogue is one of those things in the lettering world that generally denotes an amateur. It's a mistake made when a creator is more concerned with using a bunch of cool typefaces and less concerned with readability. If every character has a different font for his or her 'voice,' it tends to be a distraction, pulling the reader just that much farther out of the story. This is not to say that it doesn't have its place. It just needs to be used sparingly. Save that spooky font for when you've got a character who really benefits from it. If the reader isn't used to seeing several different fonts in your comic, the impact will be greater when that zombie speaks in a diseased-looking typeface!" ■

Above:
According to creator and font designer Nate Piekos, "Picking a style of word balloons should be based on how it couples with the art in question. I use a manga-style shape for the balloons in *Atland* (www.realmofatland.com) for three reasons: it saves space, it's rarely seen in American comics, and it looks neat with my particular style of drawing."

Left:
Ted Slampyak's *Jazz Age* (www.jazzagecomics.com) uses boldface type, italics, and varied type size to capture speech inflections.

Below:
Claire the vampire demonstrates her mastery of High German in *Bite Me!* by Dylan Meconis.

DYLAN MECONIS ON INDICATING DIALECT

The characters in Dylan Meconis' comedic vampire tale, *Bite Me!*, (Girlamatic.com, 2001–2004) speak in a variety of languages and dialects, which she represents by varying the appearance of her hand-rendered text and balloons without sacrificing the visual unity of the page.

"Luther's distinctive balloons and lettering gave him the sense of having a sharper accent than the other characters, without reducing me to 'I vass chust followink orderz' dialect writing. It also drove home his more cynical, practical attitude. His speech is boxy and straightforward, which echoes his character design. The most diametrically opposed character to him in the story, Audric, speaks in curlicues and swishes. It also allows for some jokes that wouldn't work in any other medium. At one point a character surprises Luther by suddenly speaking to him in very aristocratic German. Rather than just adopting his angular letters, she speaks in a very elaborate, black-letter script style with beveled balloon corners. Just to rub it in." (See pages 116–119.) ■

THE FACE

We cannot escape images of faces in everyday life. We envision and fashion faces on every surface. Look around; try *not* to see a face in an electrical socket, manual clock, the bark of a tree trunk, the grinning patch of cloud hovering overhead. This tendency, psychologists say, relates to the newborn baby's need to recognize its mother, as well as expressing our lifelong desire to communicate with everything else in existence. It is part of our greater inclination to "anthropomorphize"—or make things seem more human.

The face is our primary tool for expression and connection, but for the graphic novelist, faces are more than tools; they are windows that reveal entire universes, mirrors on which we reflect identities, sometimes radically different from our own. Not surprisingly, the face is the foremost aspect of character design, and most artists concentrate their energy on getting a face to look "right," because the face is the part of the character the reader identifies with the most. In reading a graphic novel, it's almost as if the characters' faces are a series of carnival masks we try on and wear for a short while.

THE GRAPHICAL FACE

What's the minimum number of elements needed to represent a pictorial image that is recognizable as a face? A basic answer is four: marks signifying two eyes, a nose, and a mouth—for example, the popular e-mail smiley, :-). But it is possible to dispense with any of those features and still see a face.

Some critics argue that it's the arrangement, a particular spatial relationship between at least two elements, that tells the brain it is seeing a face, and that this arrangement is the foundation of how we read facial expression. But how about a single element—an eye, a slant of brow or jaw line, an amorphous cast of shadow, an open space where a face ought to be?

The most important factor is not how we *see* faces visually, but how our minds *construct* them.

Armed with this dual knowledge of minimalism and anthropomorphism, the graphic novelist is able to choose a broad range of facial features, varying them subtly for emphasis or exaggerating them wildly to show intense emotional reaction. ▸

This page: Four faces of coauthor Steven Withrow (counter-clockwise from right): Photograph by kristin studio inc.; 3-D to 2-D rendering by Gil Agudín; *Astronaut Elementary*–style by Dave Roman; and *Picture Story Theatre*–style by Bill Duncan.

THE MASKED OR FACELESS CHARACTER

Sometimes a character has, and indeed needs, no face, or wears a mask that supplants the face beneath. Many Marvel Comics artists of Spider-Man, including co-creator Steve Ditko and fan favorites John Romita Sr. and Jr., make Spidey as expressive in his customary webbed mask as in his unmasked alter ego, Peter Parker. (One of Spider-Man's villains, Mysterio, upholds his name by wearing an opaque dome over his head.) Writer Alan Moore is fond of more ominous masked characters, bringing expressionless life to the psychopathic, inkblotted Rorschach from *Watchmen* and the renegade V, in Guy Fawkes guise, from *V for Vendetta* (both from DC Comics).

A SENSE OF ORDER (EVEN IN DISORDER)

A running theme in this book is unity, and the characters pictured here show how close attention to symmetry, proportion, balance and precise placement of features, understatement and exaggeration, likeness and contrast, can help bring about memorable, recognizable, *living* characters. ■

Above left: Agamemnon, High King of the Achaeans, in Eric Shanower's *Age of Bronze* (see pages 48–53) is memorable and distinguishable for the visual tag of his curved beard.

Left: Examples of unmasked and masked faces from Hope Larson's novels *Salamander Dream* (AdHouse Books, 2005) and *Gray Horses* (Oni Press, 2006).

THE HUMAN FORM

Mastering human anatomy is widely considered the Holy Grail of visual art, and even the most successful abstract and nonrepresentational artists have made it a priority to study the male and female figure. Examining anatomy books and drawing from photographs and from live models (or even a mirrored self-portrait) are invaluable skill boosters and mind openers for the graphic novelist. (See pages 185 and 186 for some useful reference books.)

The shapes and interrelationships of bones, muscles, skin, hair, facial features—the effects of postures and gestures and expressions, the fall of light and the cast of shadow—can be modified, simplified, or transmogrified to your heart's content. But without a good sense of how the human form is actually composed, in all its great variety, and the realistic range of its movement, your abstractions and distortions will most likely seem flat, immobile, and implausible.

Aside from learning the difference between the metacarpals and the metatarsals, the abdominals and the obliques, drawing the human body is a wonderful training ground for mastering perspective, proportion, and symmetry.

WEIGHT & MOMENTUM

Writer Kurt Busiek (see pages 120–125) points out a key idea behind many comics character designs: *weight establishes momentum.* While this principle applies to any type of character in any genre, rendered in any drawing style, the idealized and exaggerated world of the superhero is a great place to see it in action. According to Busiek, "What the character does is expressed in what parts of the body—which gravity points—are emphasized." For example, the bigger, stronger, more monstrous the character is, the lower the head is—with eye line below shoulder line and no neck—giving the character the appearance of being ▸

Left:
Mike Mignola's *Hellboy* (Dark Horse Comics) is one of comics' most acclaimed character designs. The figure is so elegant, refined, and rooted in realistic anatomy (though amplified and morphed by Mignola's myth-inspired imagination), that it translated remarkably well into feature-film format in 2004.

Above left:
Female torso study, rendered in colored pencil, by Jenn Manley Lee (see pages 94–99).

anchored to the earth and possibly suggesting a grounded, stubborn, or indomitable personality. Conversely, an artist drawing a flying or leaping character, such as Superman or Spider-Man, often lengthens or diminishes the legs and feet, while amplifying the breadth of the shoulders for a higher center of gravity, to communicate upward momentum. Mike Mignola's demonic character Hellboy is, Busiek says, "one big arc of motion across the shoulders; massive hands; goat legs trailing off; horns sawed off. He looks great leaping down on somebody."

A sense of balance is essential to any successful character design; the weight relationship between the head and the body mass is important. The heavy boots and broad shoulders of Marvel's Captain America (co-created by Jack Kirby and Joe Simon) are separated by a balancing band of red and white stripes, granting him both solidity and agility.

To highlight contrasts, an artist might choose drastic differences in proportion among characters, or go for more classically realistic differences. He or she can also subvert the reader's expectations—for instance, we might see a hulking monster and predict plodding stupidity but instead we find the character has quite the opposite qualities (for example, the title character from Paul Chadwick's *Concrete*; Dark Horse Comics). And finally, body language and brilliant physical acting can enhance and distinguish even the most overused design (more on these subjects and others in Section V). ■

Left & above: Paul Chadwick's character Concrete (Dark Horse Comics) was previously called Ron Lithgow, a normal man whose psyche was transplanted by aliens into a massive stone body. While this type of design is generally used for slower, less intelligent characters, Chadwick trumps our expectations at every turn with his character's adventures.

THE NONHUMAN FORM

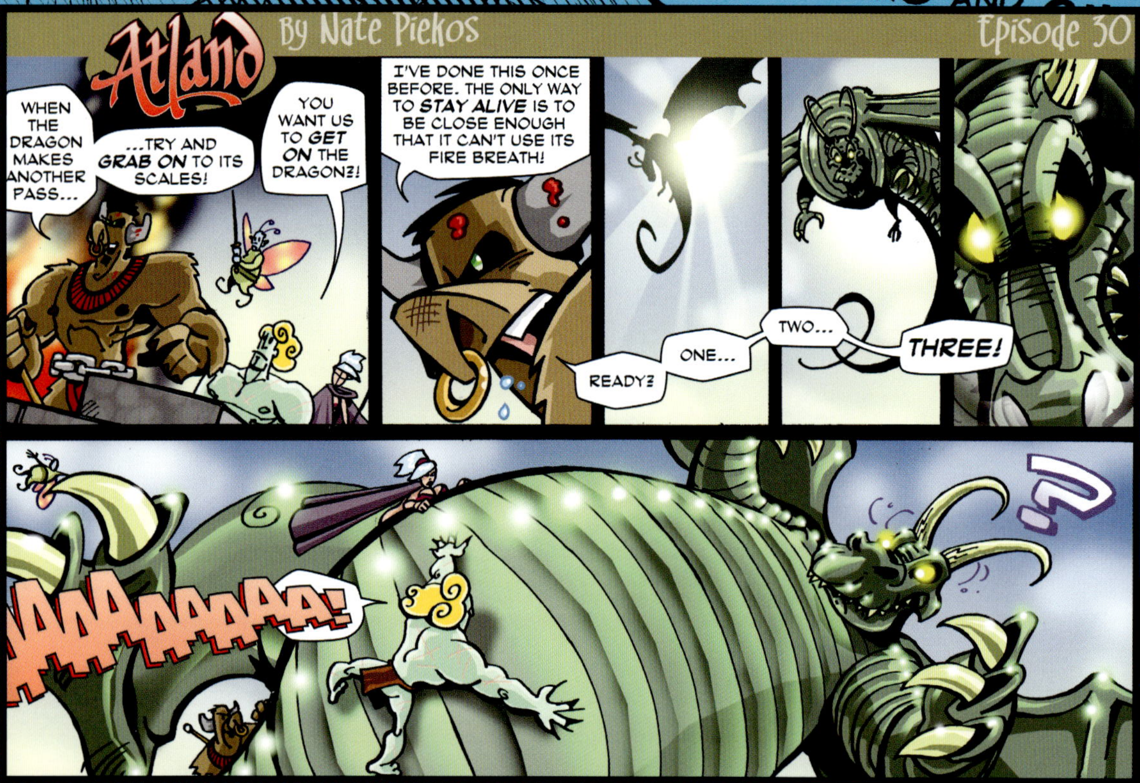

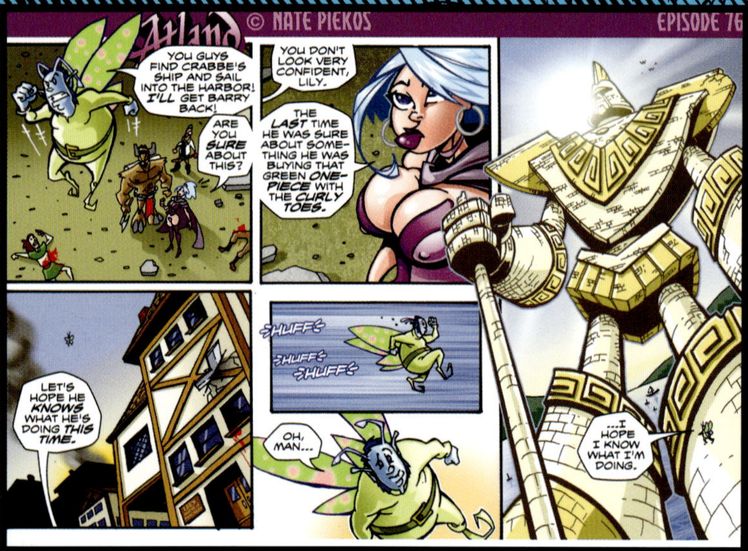

Top:
A display of death-defying derring-do in Nate Piekos' *Atland* (self-published comics series).

Above:
The realm of Atland teems with organic/inorganic hybrids.

Human and humanoid characters dominate graphic novels, but the simple truth is that comics characters can take any form imaginable, as long as they can be rendered visually. Some, like Bigby Wolf in Bill Willingham's *Fables* series (DC Comics/Vertigo), shift shape at will. Others, most notably Alan Moore and colleagues' elemental incarnation of Swamp Thing (DC Comics; first appeared in comics in 1971), seem to be in a constant state of transition from animal to vegetable to mineral to spiritual.

While we have touched on the many benefits of studying human anatomy, we believe it is also useful to study organic forms (all things zoological, botanical, and geological) as well as human-fashioned forms—machinery, vehicles, architecture, household appliances, etc. These can provide the basis for, or be the actual embodiment of, your character.

The individual artist decides the level of anthropomorphism appropriate to the story, which could be none at all. A theme of otherness or alienation, for example, might be enhanced by crafting a character that defies human comparison. Some characters can even be abstractions with little or no likeness or reference to human beings—for example, the character/setting of Fiddler's Green in Neil Gaiman's *Sandman* (DC Comics/Vertigo), a shape-shifting, sentient location that is part of Gaiman's fictional universe, The Dreaming. Or an artist might simply want to tell a story about real animals without any imposed human qualities. Masashi Tanaka employs both anthropomorphic and real animal characters masterfully in his wild, wordless manga, *Gon* (reprinted in English in 1996 by DC Comics). ■

CREATURE CREATION TUTORIAL: NATE PIEKOS

Two kinds of creatures appear in *Atland*: established and new. Established creatures are things from mythology such as minotaurs or dragons—accepted standards in fantasy fauna. For these animals, I put my own spin on a common theme, which can be fun, but is not as rewarding as creating from scratch. The second type of creature is wholly new, both to *Atland* and, hopefully, fantasy in general. There's no creative satisfaction in referring to a *Dungeons & Dragons Monster Manual* for ideas.

In any fantasy, everybody seems to ride around on horses. Why not consider an alternative? Many concept artists take inspiration from real-life animals, and I agree with that approach, as long as the end result is *not* simply a reproduction of the source material.

During a morning walk, I noticed a man walking two dogs—a huge retriever mix and a rambunctious pug. I had found my starting point: the goofy face of the pug, with the big body and even temperament of the retriever. When I got home, I Googled "pugs" and started sketching. Since I didn't want the animal to end up being too dog-like, I decided to find another creature that I associated with an even temperament and large size. This led me to three more source animals: the camel, the tortoise, and the brontosaurus. Now I had four concepts to mix, and I started to draw some heads. ▸

1. I liked the idea of a long chicken neck and nostrils set between the eyes. For the body, I decided it should be pretty large. Not fast like a horse, but powerful—the ultimate pack animal. ▸

2. I made up a story for these creatures in my head to give the drawings more life. I then took my favorite head and finished a body for it. ▸

3. Now I was happy. Essentially it's a dinosaur with the personality and features I wanted to capture. That was my beast. I scanned in a quick sketch of Barry (the unfortunate comedic hero of *Atland*) and Photoshopped him in there to create a scale reference. ▸

4. Now it was time to do a final version. I broke out the inks and then scanned it into Photoshop for coloring. I ended up with this. ■

CASE STUDY:

ERIC SHANOWER

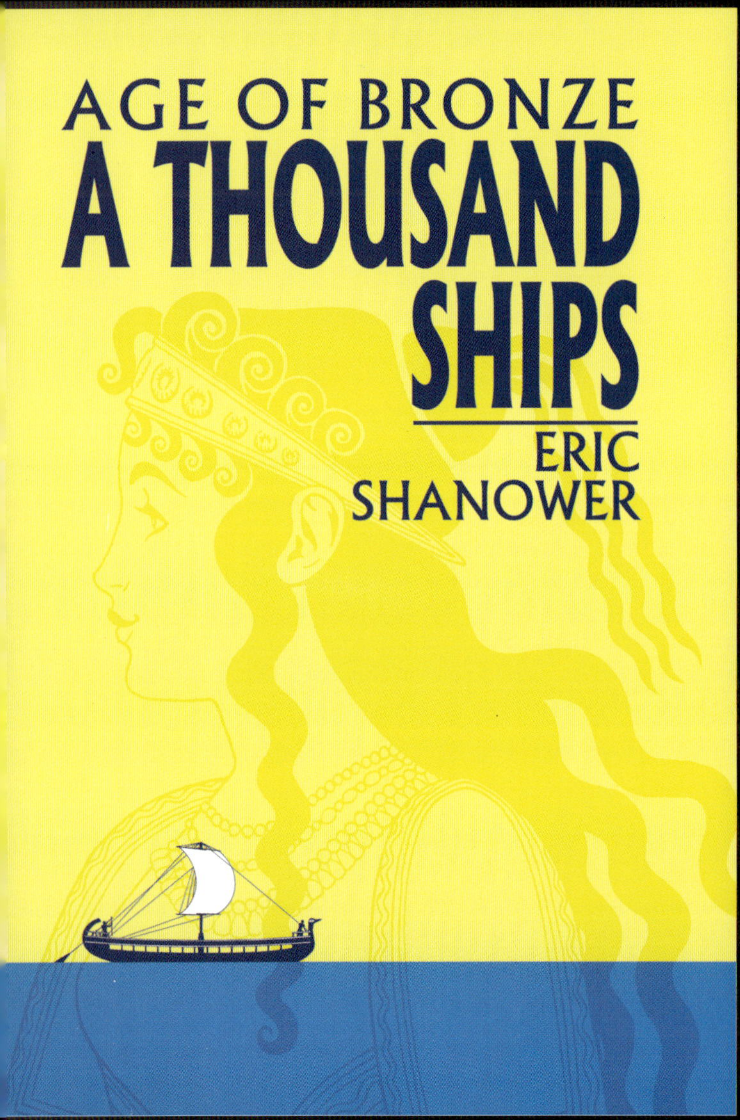

Above:
Cover of Shanower's first collection, *A Thousand Ships.*

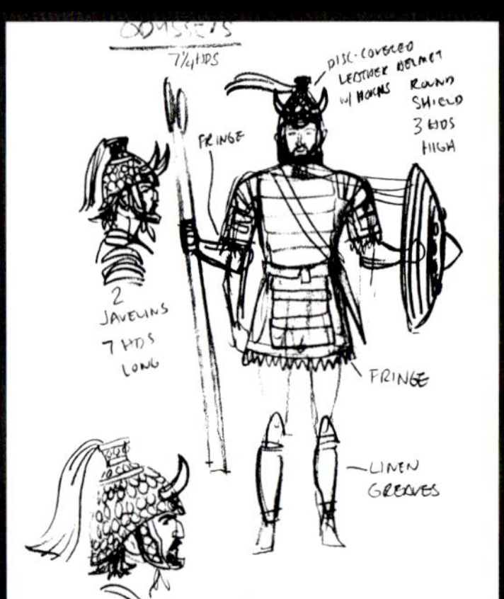

Right & opposite page:
Character model sheets from *Age of Bronze.*

Early in life, Eric Shanower showed an interest in drawing and creating stories. At the age of six, he discovered the series of Oz books by L. Frank Baum (and others) and decided to continue the Oz series with his own books. As a young man, on the day after graduation from the Joe Kubert School of Cartoon and Graphic Art, he received his first professional comics assignment, lettering (writing the words into the speech bubbles) an issue of *Warp* (First Comics). In 1986, First Comics published *The Enchanted Apples of Oz.* Four more volumes in the Oz series followed. In 1991, Shanower began meticulous research for *Age of Bronze*, his comics-retelling of the Trojan War legend. *Age of Bronze* began publication from Image Comics in 1998. It won an Eisner Award for Best Writer/Artist in 2001 and 2003, and was nominated in 2006. The series has also been nominated for an Ignatz Award and a National Cartoonists Society Division Award. In 2004, *Publishers Weekly* selected the second collected volume, *Age of Bronze: Sacrifice*, as one of the Best Books of the Year. Meanwhile, Shanower published *An Accidental Death* and *Prez: Smells Like Teen President* with writer Ed Brubaker; *The Elsewhere Prince* with Moebius (Jean Giraud) and Randy and Jean-Marc Lofficier; and illustrations from Harlan Ellison's *Dream Corridor.* He also founded Hungry Tiger Press (www.hungrytigerpress.com and www.age-of-bronze.com) with his partner David Maxine. Shanower currently lives in San Diego, California.

Shanower uses various sources to design his characters. Most of the time, he begins simply by sketching until he arrives at an appearance he's satisfied with. Once in a while, he'll think of an actual person and use his idea of that person as a basis for the character's design. Sometimes he'll find a photograph that looks like his idea of a particular character. For the characters in *Age of Bronze*, he sometimes uses Bronze-Age artifacts—such as a death mask for Agamemnon's face and a sculpture of a goddess for Thetis's face—or a previous artist's conception of a particular character—such as a Roman painting from Herculaneum for Cheiron's face—as the basis for his design.

When Shanower first picks up a pencil to "find" the appearance of a new character, he tries to hold the idea of that character's function and personality in his mind while doing his best to banish any preconceived notions or habits of drawing that might be trying to assert themselves. Sometimes, he says, it's fun to play deliberately against preconceived notions of a character's looks, and he likes to be surprised by the results. He wants to think, "That's not what I thought that character would look like." Shanower says, "That doesn't always happen, but when it does, it's gratifying because it creates the illusion that the character has a life separate from mine. What's important is to be able to see that the face I've sketched can encompass all the character's backstory as well as the events of the particular story I'll be drawing—that the entire 'life' of the character is hinted at in their face." ▸

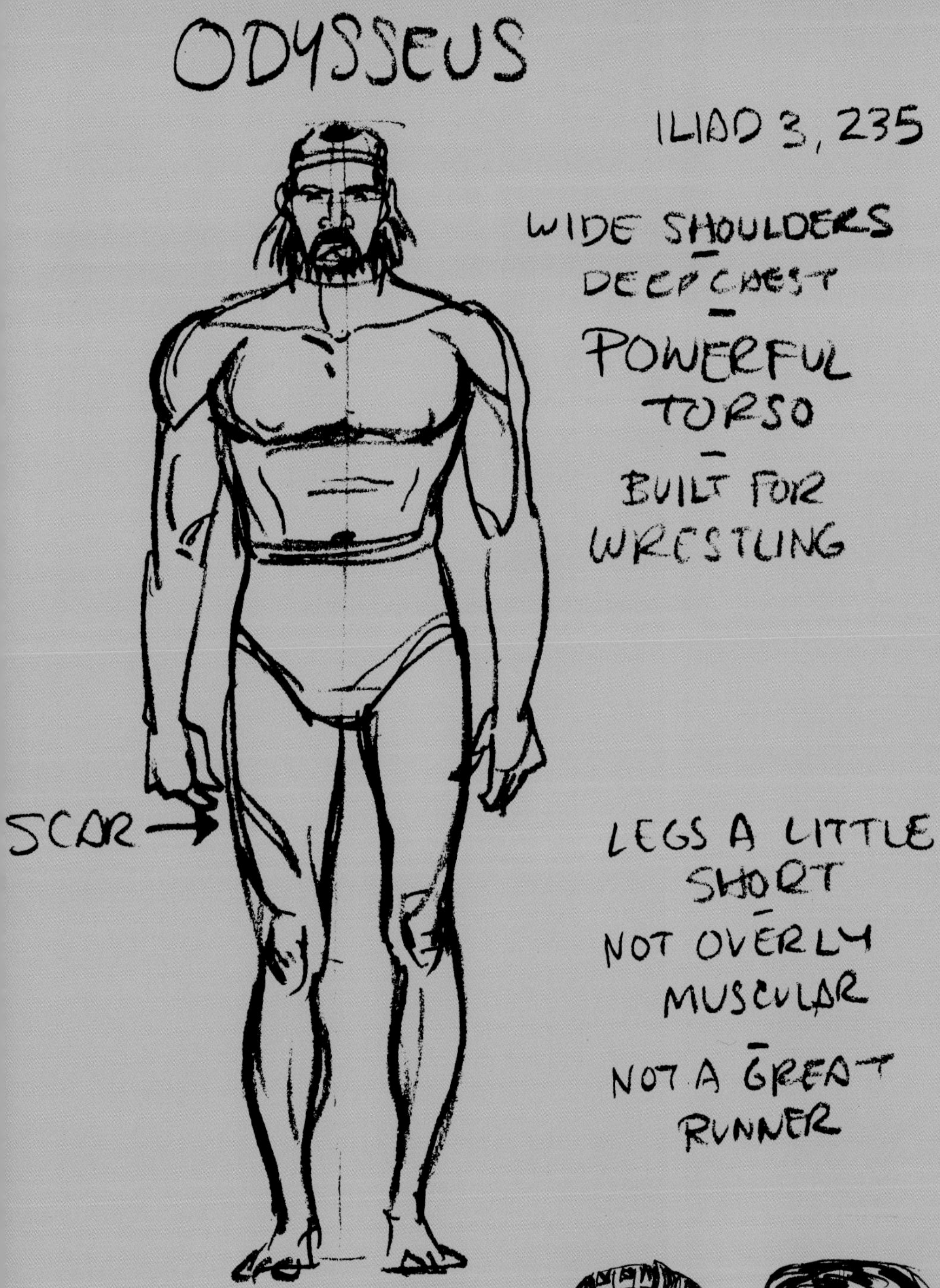

Model sheets are extremely important for *Age of Bronze*. Types of clothing and hairstyles often don't vary much—for instance, most of the Trojan men wear a single braid, and all the Trojan women wear headscarves in public—so facial features are often Shanower's primary way to differentiate between characters. When he designs a character, he also assigns him or her a height and, usually, an age. It's important to Shanower to keep these characteristics consistent.

Since *Age of Bronze* is a very long project, Shanower expects the way he draws the characters to change over time. "What I don't want to change," he says, "is the ability of the reader to recognize the characters, so I still go back to the model sheet for nearly every character I draw."

Shanower sees each of his characters as unique, so his process is different for each one. When drawing an established character, he tries to stay as close to the "model" as he can. "When I've drawn superhero projects, it's usually enough just to get the costume right; facial structure doesn't really matter much as long as it's generically attractive, and body type doesn't vary much from one superhero to the next," he says. "I view this 'cookie-cutter' approach to drawing comics with a little distaste, since in fiction, individuals are more interesting than types. But I understand the economic structure that created this situation, and it has become the convention." ▸

Left and right: Model sheets for Iphigenia, daughter of Agamemnon.

Designing such a large cast of characters who change clothes and hairstyles and age up to 14 years (sometimes more if they're in flashbacks) is a challenge for Shanower. Keeping each recognizable and distinguishable from the rest is often a problem. Early in the project, he designed many Trojan princes who happen to be brothers. He wanted to keep them looking related to each other, yet recognizably different. "Readers told me it was hard to tell them apart, so I obviously didn't succeed with those characters," he says. "I've kept that lesson in mind as I've continued with the project and continued to design more characters. And I've since tried to emphasize the Trojan princes' differences when I draw them. They age in the context of the story, so I have opportunities to modify their characteristics."

Now eight years into the project, Shanower sometimes finds it difficult to come up with unique character designs. "But I remember that the human face is unendingly variable, so I take heart," he says. "Sometimes the literature of the Trojan War specifies features; broad features such as hair color, or small ones such as dimples or squints. I take these into consideration, although there are instances when I've decided to ignore an established specification for one reason or another, usually archaeological."

Drawing the Trojan women with headscarves is also a major challenge because half of each head is hidden. That makes almost everything dependent on facial features, especially in close-ups where the reader won't see much costume. Shanower says he's afraid he's not a good enough artist to keep facial features perfectly consistent, so he finds himself working really hard to make a character recognizable, then thinks he's failed when he sees the drawing finally published.

There are so many variables in what bodies look like that Shanower says it's sometimes overwhelming with such a large cast, and he finds himself forgetting details of scar placement and body and facial hair. How fat one character is or how wide another's shoulders are can change from panel to panel, although he tries to keep these details consistent. He keeps notes of the personal characteristics of individual characters, but has found that written notes aren't the most successful technique for him. "I draw a character more consistently when I've managed to fix their attributes in my mind so that I carry a clear concept of him or her as a whole before I turn to my model sheet and notes."

Sometimes he has to rely on the script and insert names often enough to keep the reader clear about who's who. ▶

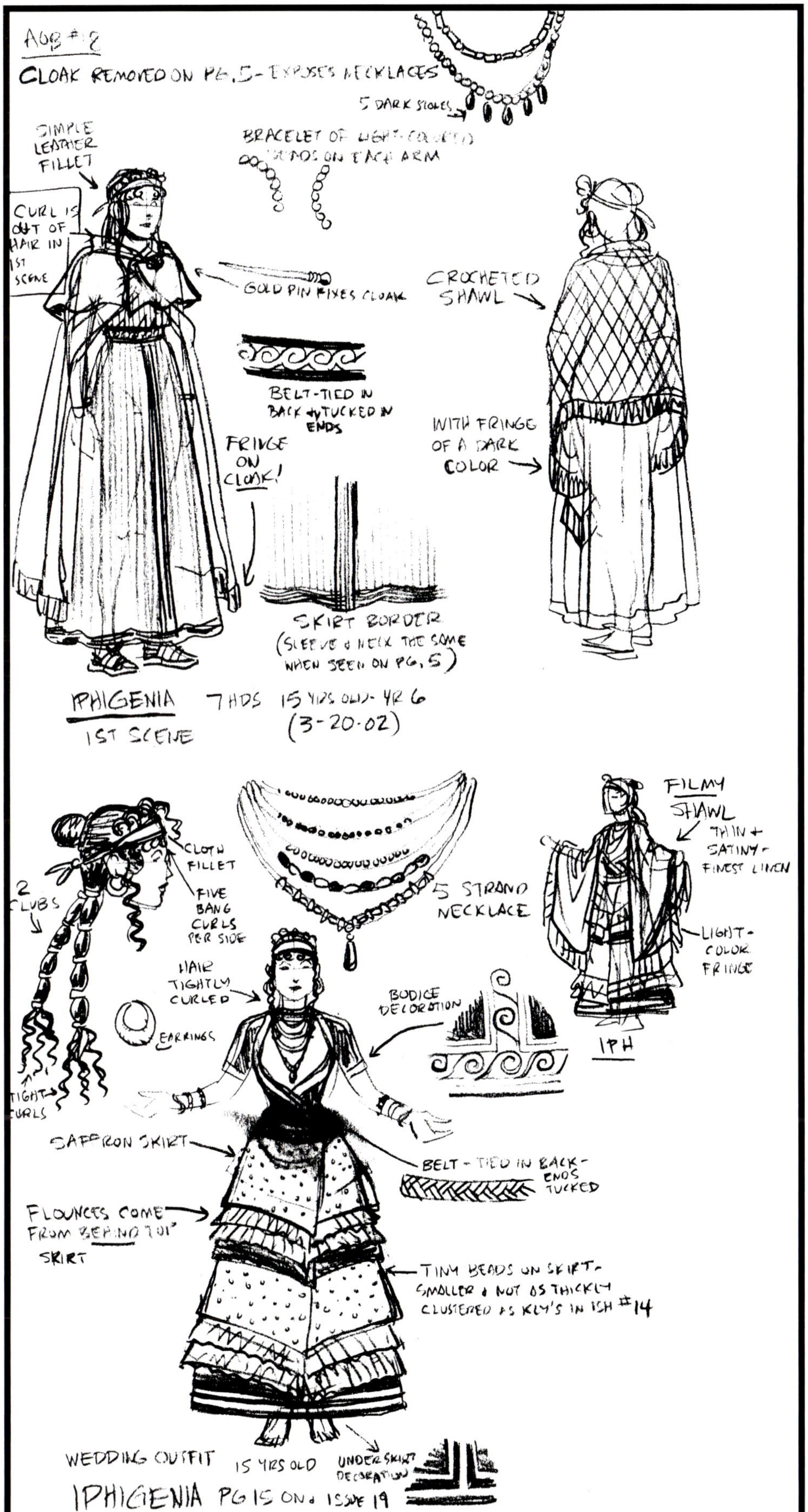

Above:
Eric Shanower's rendition of L. Frank Baum's much-loved character Scarecrow. His continuing tales of *Oz* show his ability to breathe new life into already existing characters.

The story of *Age of Bronze*, Shanower points out, takes place in what we now call Greece and Turkey in the thirteenth century BC, the Late Bronze Age of the Aegean world. The civilization in Greece at that time is called Mycenaean. The civilization in Turkey at that time is called the Hittite Empire. Since Shanower has set the story during this period, he's had to research these civilizations and become familiar with the existing artifacts. Both civilizations left representations of human beings in paintings and sculpture, so that is where Shanower discovered what the people looked like and what they wore. He has also looked at photos of modern people from those areas in an attempt to capture an eastern Mediterranean look. He has used some of these contemporary people as models for characters in *Age of Bronze*, but overall, the faces of modern Greece and Turkey seem to him as varied as anywhere else in the world. He notes that so far, however, there are no blondes in *Age of Bronze*.

"We have recovered skeletons from the Aegean Late Bronze Age. Reconstructions of faces have been made from the skulls. But I haven't found these particularly helpful in providing a 'Bronze Age' look, since the reconstructions look to me as individual as any random group of people of today," Shanower says. "I don't know of any cloth that's survived from the period, but we do have armor and jewelry. In conjunction with paintings and sculpture, we have a pretty good idea of how people dressed, at least in the wealthy classes." ▸

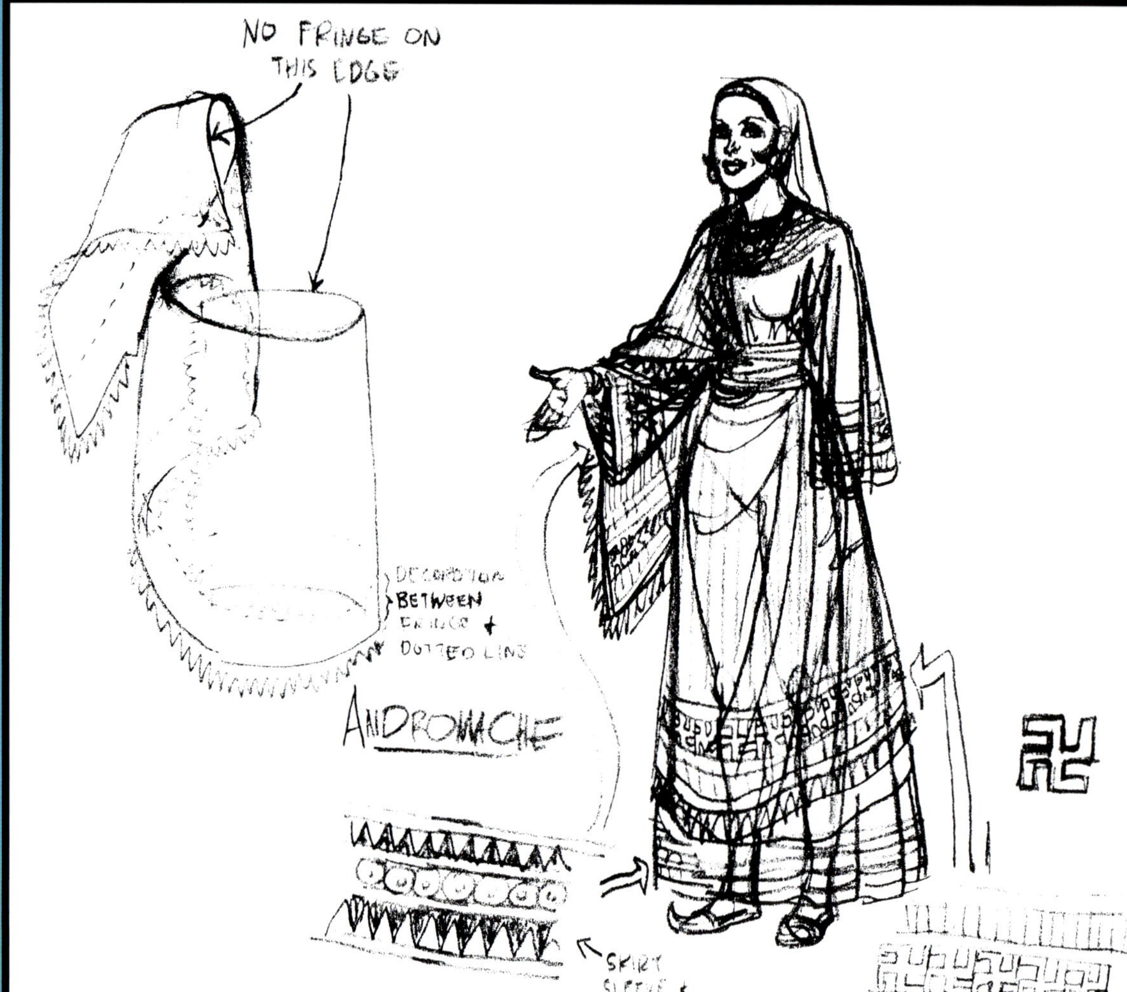

Above right & right:
Model sheets for Andromache, wife of Hektor.

As for interactions between people, that's trickier for Shanower. "Social customs are much more difficult to deduce from archaeological remains. We do have written records, lists and letters, but these only provide a small part of the picture of these societies. Since archaeology really doesn't give much helpful detail about individual interactions, I have to look elsewhere—to my story sources," he says. The story in *Age of Bronze* is based on the entire literary and artistic tradition of the Trojan War, so Shanower is provided with a basic structure for the relationships and actions of the characters. The sources of this structure range over a period of about 2,800 years, so they're all informed by the culture of their various periods. Says Shanower, "I've got to distill what's constant about human nature in each of them and fit that into what I know about the culture of the late Bronze Age while remaining true to the outlines of the Trojan War story. Sometimes it's easy, sometimes not so easy. Every facet of the story presents a different challenge." ■

Left & opposite page, right: Pages 12 and 13 from issue 10 of *Age of Bronze* are remarkable in their orderly arrangement of more than a dozen disparate yet unified characters. Note how the density of visual detail recedes from precise likenesses to vague figures as the eye moves from foreground to background.

LINE, CONTOUR & SEQUENCE

Some artists move directly from mental concept to final drawing, but most find that preparatory sketches are invaluable for generating and refining ideas. In a quick doodle you can solve problems of anatomy, expression, proportion, perspective, and composition efficiently.

BEGINNING WITH GESTURE DRAWINGS

In *Exploring Drawing for Animation* (Thomson Delmar Learning; 2004), Kevin Hedgpeth and Stephen Missal write, "Gesture drawings, or quick sketches—simple diagrammatic versions of the object being drawn—are done in a variety of styles and are the most effective means of translating the 3-D object into a 2-D drawing with the most important information intact."

The two types of line most common in gesture drawings are *construction* and *action.* Construction lines—which vary in weight (visual density) and character (emotional quality)—are the set of lines that compose a figure. They help to position anatomical elements correctly in space relative to one another. Extraneous lines that detract or distract from the basic form are easily erased, leaving only the essential marks on the page.

Related to line drawing is *modular drawing*; arranging simple shapes or forms—modules—in order to construct the figure. Graphic novelist Wendy Pini shows how basic shapes can be applied in character design on pages 136–141.

Action lines (not to be confused with motion lines, which are a type of visual shorthand in comics), while most prevalent in animation, are equally valuable in designing and posing characters for graphic novels. According to Hedgpeth and Missal, "In some styles, an imaginary line running through the axis (line) of motion or action leads the early process of drawing the figure. This line of action indicates the dominant direction of action as it 'flows' through the figure, often centering on the spine or centerline." If it helps you to visualize the direction of the motion, you can draw in action lines and erase them later, or simply see them in your mind.

Many artists try at this stage to capture the most fitting combinations of body posture, hand gesture, and facial expression—elements that signal a character's emotional state—leaving the finer details like hairstyle and costume until later in the design process. (For more detail on expression, motion, and gesture see pages 92 and 93.) ▶

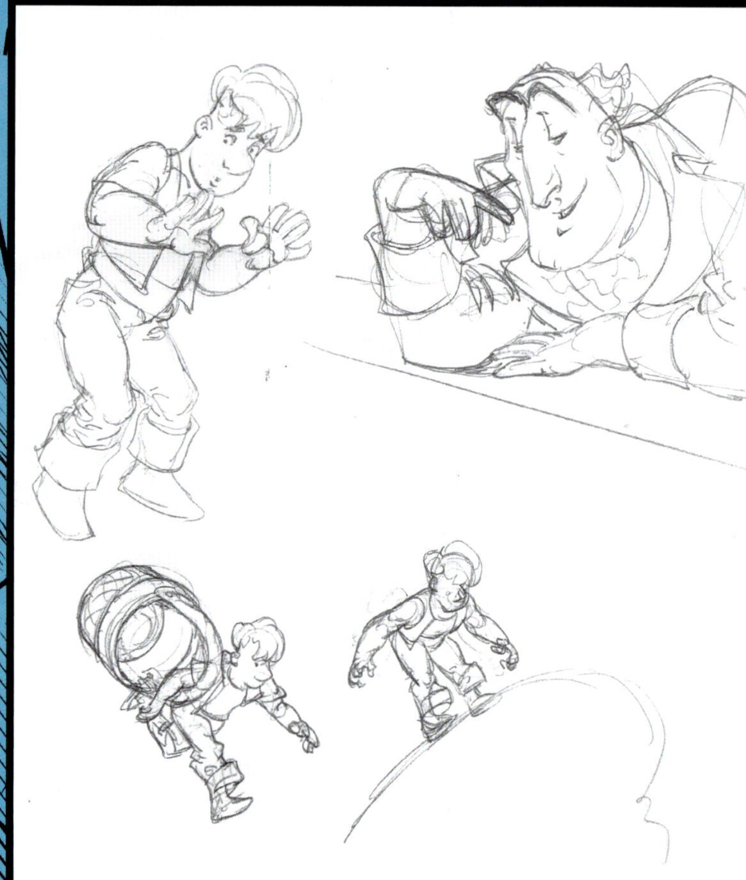

Opposite page: Character studies in watercolor and pen from Don MacDonald's *Machiavelli* (Vendome Press; 2007) based on paintings from Italian Renaissance artists Maso Finiguerra and Federico Zuccari.

This page: Gesture drawings of Hans, the miller, and the water-rat from P. Craig Russell's adaptation of "The Devoted Friend" in *Fairy Tales of Oscar Wilde: The Devoted Friend & The Nightingale and the Rose* (Nantier Beall Minoustchine Publishing; 2004).

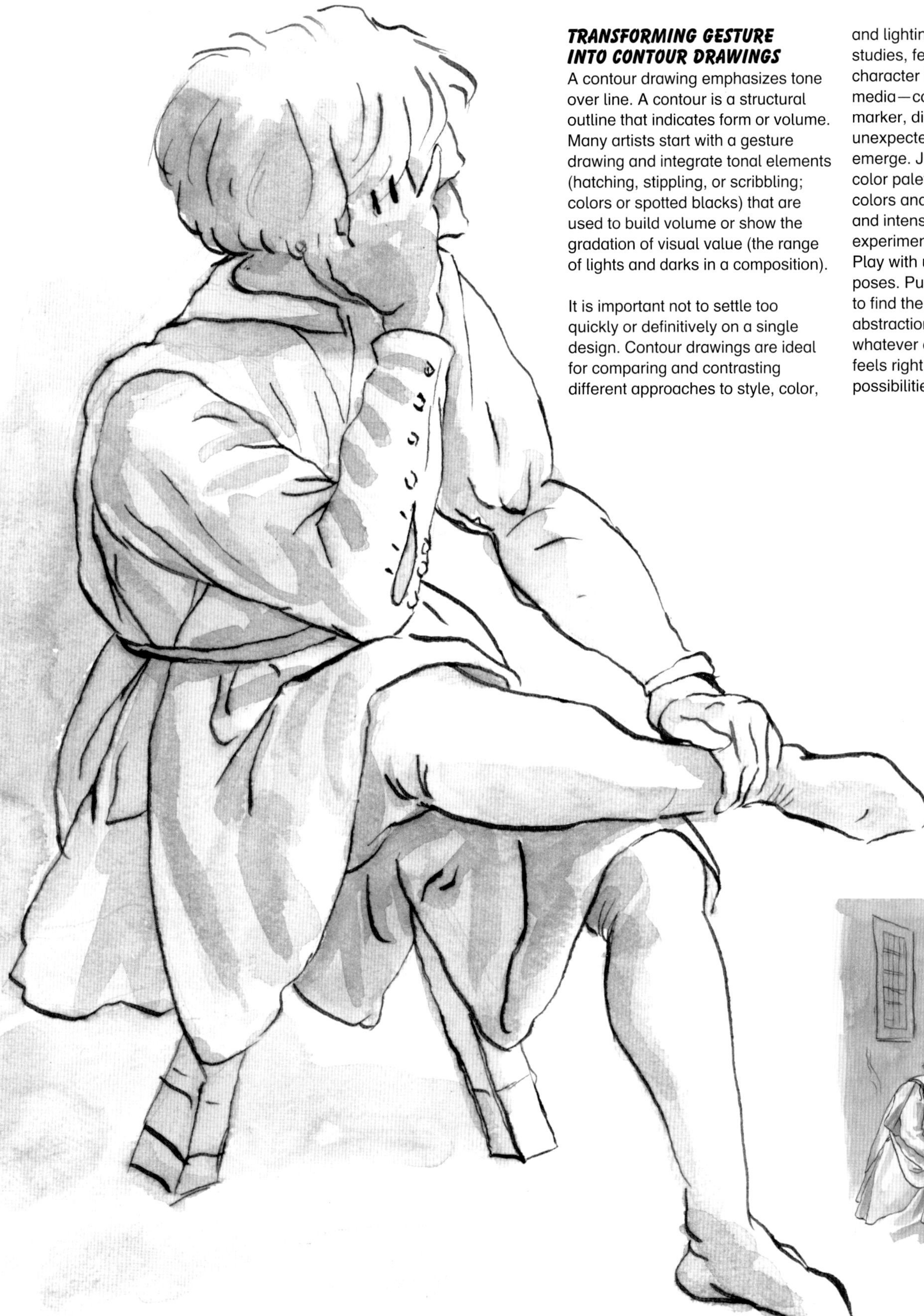

TRANSFORMING GESTURE INTO CONTOUR DRAWINGS

A contour drawing emphasizes tone over line. A contour is a structural outline that indicates form or volume. Many artists start with a gesture drawing and integrate tonal elements (hatching, stippling, or scribbling; colors or spotted blacks) that are used to build volume or show the gradation of visual value (the range of lights and darks in a composition).

It is important not to settle too quickly or definitively on a single design. Contour drawings are ideal for comparing and contrasting different approaches to style, color, and lighting. Since these are only studies, feel free to render your character in multiple techniques or media—colored pencil, watercolor, marker, digital collage—to see what unexpected combinations might emerge. Juxtapose vastly different color palettes, try out divergent base colors and highlights. Alter the angle and intensity of the light sources to experiment with mood and shadow. Play with unique proportions and poses. Push them to the extreme to find the best balance between abstraction and realism. Simply, do whatever comes to mind, whatever feels right, to explore the visual possibilities of your character. ▸

055

SEQUENTIAL DESIGN: THE FIGURE IN ACTION

Characters in graphic novels don't actually appear to move as they do in animated films. However, critics often compare the "key frames" in animation to the sequential panels (also called frames) of a graphic novel. In comics, we might not see all of the minute movements in between the extremes, but there is implied or suggested motion, or dramatic action, within and across the panels.

Knowing just how your character stands, walks, runs, stoops to pick up an object, bends, twists, jumps, falls, flies perhaps, flashes a smile, waves goodbye—the whole range of animal locomotion—is as important as knowing what he or she looks like. If each movement isn't believable and specific to the character and the moment, the flow of action can be broken and the reader's sense of the story's reality disturbed.

As comics tend to be a minimalist art form, rarely do graphic novelists include the full, exhaustive sequence of a complicated, multistep action in a given scene. They usually select the most significant, or meaningful, component movements and draw our attention to those centers of visual impact through effective page and panel composition.

Sequential drawing, also called stop-action drawing, is a series of gesture drawings placed in chronological order to demonstrate a complete action. Sequence drawing has as much to do with page and panel design as it does with character design—and matters of distance, perspective, and pacing come immediately into play.

Unlike animation sequences, in which a character's body position is plotted over time, comics sequences track a character's position across space. Consistency of proportion and placement is not quite as important in graphic novels as it is in animation, but it does help to pay close attention to the flow of invisible action lines from one panel to the next. A clear, continuous flow can speed up the reading experience, while interruptions and visual pauses can slow down the pace. Both of these devices are tremendously useful in storytelling. ■

Above:
Page from Todd Dezago and Craig Rousseau's *The Perhapanauts* (Dark Horse Comics), illustrating the carefully choreographed flow of action from panel to panel.

Right:
A page from David Petersen's *Mouse Guard* (Archaia Studios Press) demonstrating the awkward movement of a collapse.

Far right:
A page from demian.5's short story "Life Code." Developing the way characters with unusual anatomies move may require extra consideration.

CASE STUDY:

EDDIE CAMPBELL

Born in Scotland and now residing in Australia, Eddie Campbell has been a formidable presence in graphic novels since the late 1970s and early 1980s, when he began to publish semi-autobiographical comics in British fanzines and reviews such as *Escape* and *Knockabout.* These early attempts evolved into stories about Alec McGarry, a sort of stand-in for Campbell, who has appeared in several collections since 1984, most recently *Alec: How to Be an Artist* (2000) and *After the Snooter* (2002). Another of his series, *Eddie Campbell's Bacchus*, published or self-published from 1986 to 1998, transplants the Greek gods to the late twentieth century. The graphic novel *From Hell*, Campbell's best-known collaboration with writer Alan Moore, is an exploration of the darkest attributes of Victorian English culture that centers on a hypothetical account of the Jack the Ripper murders. The book, now published by Top Shelf Productions, was also made into a feature film in 2001. First Second Books published Campbell's most recent graphic novel, *The Fate of the Artist*, in May 2006. ■

This page:
A page from *Alec: How to Be an Artist* (2000), featuring Alan Moore.

Opposite page:
A page from *After the Snooter* (2002), featuring Campbell's "imaginary nemesis" the Snooter.

ON CHARACTER DESIGN FOR GRAPHIC NOVELS

I've been making pronouncements about what exactly "graphic novel" means, and while I'm not so naive as to presume there could ever be a consensus, I think it's useful to ally the word with a new sensibility in the world of comics. In getting a clear mental picture of this "sensibility," I have suggested that it should be contrasted against the older "comic book culture." A term that I would attribute to the older culture rather than the new is "character design." In the new sensibility, the author is more like a literary author (though I am always careful to say that the graphic novel is not just a pictorial version of the literary one), and I do not imagine that a writer "designs" his or her characters. To "design" a character makes it sound like a product, a chair, or a new toothpaste flavor. Certainly in animation, where several people have to work on a character, designing it at the outset is logical. But the literary author figures the character out on the page as things go along. It's a person that he or she is getting to know, developing with each word and deed.

I don't practice "character design" or "character creation" and loathe the expression. I do not consider myself an illustrator in the traditional sense, and I have no art materials that in any way reflect how I would go about making a character work on the page, apart from the finished works themselves. When I draw my books, I feel that I am attempting to reach into the heart of the human experience and drag out some small but important part of it and cause it to leave its imprint on the page. I'm usually partially successful, but probably not in any way that could be used as an example to others. ■

Above:
Page from the Appendix of *From Hell* by Campbell and Alan Moore.

ON HIS "HOLISTIC" PROCESS

The most important thing in a work for me is authenticity. Anything that looks fabricated should be shunned. In seeking authenticity, a quality that tends to come to the fore is spontaneity. Too much consideration can undermine authenticity. For instance, I'll often get exactly what I wanted to put down in my first sketch, and if that is in a sketchbook or on a scrap of paper, no amount of copying can convey that to the board I'm doing the finished work on. The finished work would then be a secondhand copy rather than a firsthand drawing, and whether I look at it for 10 seconds or a half hour, all I will see is that it's not the genuine authentic statement, the understanding of people and their presence rather than of marks on paper. So it's unusual for me to do preparatory sketching for a piece of work. There are exceptions, of course, but as a rule I work everything out on the page as I go along, and if it all goes wrong I just have to start again or correct it as best I can. My original art used to have the look of an inky battlefield, though inevitably, with experience, I've reduced a lot of the false starts and misdirections.

The next important quality is observation. I do not have standard figure types that I dress up like store-window dummies. Each character is unique. I'm usually trying to harness memories of an actual individual, wrestling with the fleeting wisps of memory until I start to see what I'm looking for among the pencil scribbles. I try to fasten on personal idiosyncrasies. For example, I might first recall the physical presence of the person that my character of Danny Grey is based upon, and then I will be pleasantly surprised by the clarity of the memory of the way he would roll his cigarette paper so tightly that his cheeks would appear pinched from the effort of drawing the smoke through it. And then he would smoke it so close to the end that he'd have to clutch it out from between his lips rather than employ the more elegant and conventional gesture of taking it between fore and middle finger. You can't make up stuff like that. It is the essence of authenticity.

Naturally, as a memory aid, I keep files of candid photos of friends for the day when they may play a part in one of my narratives. Now, after I get the generality of my character down on paper, I deal with the same problems panel after panel, until my drawing hand becomes familiar with the character and is able to capture it more easily. That is usually when the danger arises of the representation becoming rote. The character starts to be a set of variations on a drawing rather than a new drawing. A little of this I find acceptable. But as soon as I realize I'm doing it, I'm on green alert.

Through the whole of *From Hell*, I never tired of drawing William Gull. He became more interesting to me with every panel he appeared in. By the end of the book, one drawing of Gull shows a fuller and better-understood representation of a human being than any of his earlier appearances possibly could. This seems to be inevitable in the form we're working in, and we should perhaps accept it and deny the temptation to go back and update the earlier conception. Having said that, I am often guilty of such tinkering.

An important rule comes into play once the generality of the character is pinned down. When you reduce a human being to a representation about three inches high, then everything you decide to include will be symbolic whether you mean it to be or not. If a person has a facial scar, it probably wouldn't be visible on a figure three inches tall. If you choose to include it then the reader will presume a reason. Therefore, it would be wise to give one rather than let the reader invent one of their own. The scar may tell us that the character was a street fighter, or that the character blames it for the failure of her social life. If everybody else on the page overlooks it and never mentions it and it has no bearing on the proceedings, it would be as well to leave it out and let the reader overlook it, too. ■

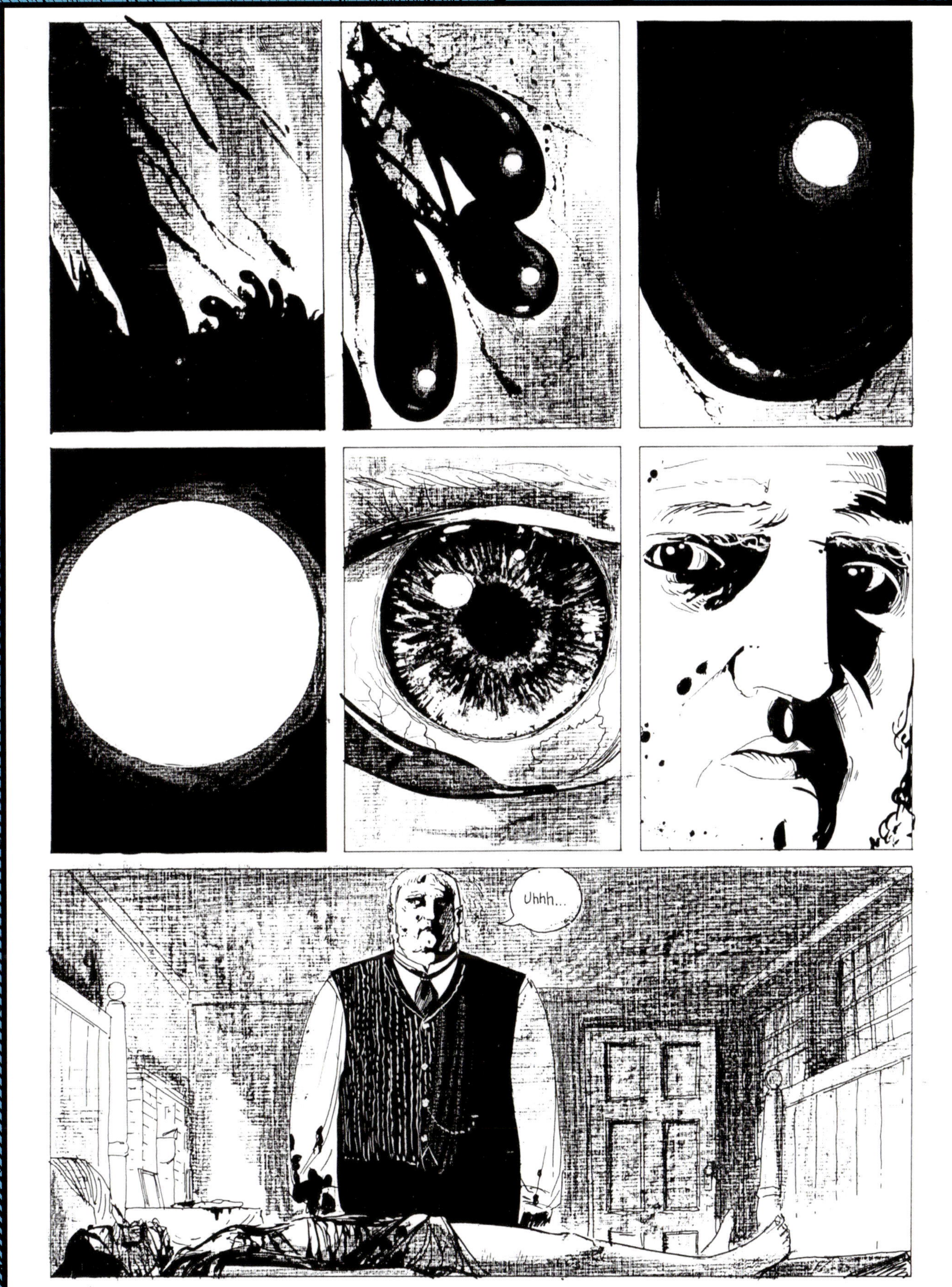

Left: William Gull, the fictional character responsible for the Jack the Ripper murders, in *From Hell*.

Above:
Image of the Eyeball Kid from *Bacchus: The Picture of Dorian Grey*.

ON BACCHUS

Bacchus perhaps doesn't fit within the aesthetic mentioned above, and is closer to the traditional concept of "character design." It's about the Greek gods, or what's left of them. Bacchus is 4,000 years old. Joe Theseus is a mob boss, and the Eyeball Kid is a grandson of Argus of the 100 eyes. Getting 10 sets of eyes on one face in a convincing way was quite a challenge. Earlier renditions look inquisitive and sometimes clumsy. By the time of the image pictured here, quite late in the series, I was quite confident about the character. In a way he represents everything that is chaotic and unpredictable and is a favorite character of mine from that period (1986–1998). ■

ON THE FATE OF THE ARTIST

In *The Fate of the Artist*, I set myself a rather tricky problem. To express the odd notion that I have disappeared and don't want to be Eddie Campbell anymore, I've made an autobiographical novel in which my part is played by a fictitious actor. My plan was that, apart from announcing it up front, the only thing revealing this in the pictures would be subtle differences in body language and of shape and weight. I created rather too much of a difficulty with this, however, in that the actor is a fiction and not clearly based on an actual person, which would be my normal method. Whether it all succeeds is up to the reader. It never gets any easier. I feel any artist worth his salt should always be setting challenges just beyond his abilities. ■

This page:
A page from *The Fate of the Artist.*

I HEREBY CLAIM THIS LAND FOR MY KING AND COUNTRY
OK

DESIGN STYLE

Are you in or out of style? To which "school" of art do you belong? Does style even matter? Here we take the approach that style is a convenient catchall term for the amalgamation of technique, tone, genre, influence, and inspiration. Pinning a single style on an artist is a bit like trying to pin a ribbon on a charging rhinoceros: it's a dangerous business, since no one likes to be reduced to a label. Comparing and contrasting artistic approaches, however, does have its merits, and this section provides some of the common bases for comparison, along with new case studies and galleries. ■

Clean and Jerk scheming with the postman in page 31 of Louis - Red Letter Day (2000)

Right: Clean and Jerk scheming with the postman on page 31 of Metaphrog's *Louis: Red Letter Day* (2000). See pages 104–109 for more about Metaphrog's work, which the duo describes as drawn in a "scary-cute" style that is a mix of emotional realism and cartoon fantasy.

THE CHARACTER DESIGN SPECTRUM: ABSTRACTION TO HYPERREALISM

Graphic novels offer great flexibility in the realism of character designs. Characters can be anything from simple stick figures, to stylistic line drawings, to highly detailed photorealistic representations, and depending on the demands of the story, these approaches can all be equally valid.

It has been argued by comics theorist Scott McCloud, among others, that much of the power of the cartoon character derives from its abstraction. The more abstract a design is, the more universal it becomes, allowing a greater number of readers to identify with a character. Humorous comics and children's comics in particular tend to favor highly abstract designs that evoke an immediate emotional response. This is not to say that abstract designs can't be used for drama; they certainly can, but seeing beyond the "cuteness" of such depictions can be a hurdle for some readers. Still, when used well, abstract character designs can achieve quite evocative dramatic results, such as in Art Spiegelman's use of cartoon animals to represent the characters in his Holocaust story, *Maus*.

At the farthest end of abstraction is the unseen character—whether it's God speaking from the heavens, an artificial intelligence speaking from within a computer, or simply an unseen narrator communicating directly to the reader via captions, the unseen character can be literally anyone or anything. And yet the principles of character design still apply—the way they speak, their values, the actions they take or claim to take, all form a distinct personality. Even the word balloons and typeface used to represent them can tell us something about who they are. ▸

Left:
In Jef Czekaj's *Shark Hunters*, Grampa bears little resemblance to humans, yet immediately projects a warm and cuddly human persona. (See pages 152 and 153 for more about Jef Czekaj.)

Right:
Artist Brett Weldele combines realistic anatomy with abstract touches in proposed projects, as shown in this female character's suggestion of a nose and the male character's single line for a mouth.

Most character designs are more realistic, however. Body proportions mimic those of real people; eyes appear on opposite sides of the nose; hair usually succumbs to the force of gravity. A degree of abstraction may still be employed; physiques may be exaggerated, particularly in adventure stories, and nonessential details such as complex shading or creases in clothing will be hinted at only or left out entirely. Faces are distinct enough to distinguish one character from another, but are not so distinct as to prevent readers from identifying with them. The subtler nuances of realistic designs allow for greater character ambiguity—you can't immediately judge a character by his or her appearance.

Beyond realism is hyperrealism, a technique that attempts to create such detailed and accurate images that they almost look like photographs. The challenge of this style is that even small errors in accuracy will be amplified by the high level of detail. As comic-book artist Alex Ross points out, "Hyperrealism is about 'buying into or not buying into' a character. With realism, you have to compare your characters against an exact model, and that's a challenge that more exaggerated work does not have."

At the farthest end of realism is the fumetto, or photocomic, which utilizes photographs of live models or staged sets instead of illustrations. Though popular in Italy, photography remains an infrequently used method in most other places. Where it does show up, it usually takes the form of goofy humor strips, such as *ToyFare* magazine's *Twisted ToyFare Theatre*, which stars dolls based on superheroes. It can be difficult to capture live models acting out a narrative without the resulting images seeming self-consciously staged, and the unreality of the staging undermining the reality of the models. This can work for parody comics, but usually precludes any genuine dramatic effect or serious character development. Of course, these challenges are not insurmountable. Writer Joey Comeau and photographer Emily Horne regularly achieve dramatic, even chilling results in their online strip, *A Softer World*, at www.asofterworld.com. While they have not attempted a full-length story using these techniques, the tone of their work certainly suggests the possibility.

Finally, it's worth noting that it's not always necessary to commit to a single design style within the body of a work. Manga artists routinely use shifts in the level of abstraction to indicate shifts in mood. Joe Zabel combines digitally rendered 3-D characters with photographic backgrounds for his *Trespassers* mysteries. And Jeff Smith freely mixes highly abstract characters and more realistic characters within the world of *Bone*. ■

Left:
Fantasy stories, such as David Petersen's *Mouse Guard* (Archaia Studios Press), often treat their otherworldly creatures with realistic detail to amplify the sense that such creatures could exist in the real world.

Far left:
This strip from Joey Comeau and Emily Horne's *A Softer World* contains two characters: the girl we see in the photograph and her unseen mother, whose words drive the story.

GENRE & TONE

CHARACTER-SPECIFIC GENRES

Different kinds of stories call for different kinds of characters. Major characters help set the tone of a story, grounding it within or distinguishing it from its primary genre. After all, a romance starring a homicidal maniac isn't likely to work, nor is a crime thriller starring talking animals—unless, of course, you are subverting your chosen genre intentionally, in which case casting untraditional character types may be essential. And while some genres necessarily require that characters have particular traits or professions, other genres are expansive, allowing a no-limits attitude for all characters involved.

Some genres demand certain character types. Cop stories have cops, crime capers have thieves, and war stories have soldiers. Certainly, exceptions are possible if the writer is clever enough, but those stories will be just that—exceptions. You can generally expect readers picking up cop stories to want to read about cops. If creating cop characters doesn't interest you, avoid the cop-story genre.

Character-specific genres can be closely related, with the primary difference being the sort of character they focus on. For instance, the mystery and the psychological thriller often rely on similar plot elements and themes, but are distinguished from each other largely by how the hero perceives and engages with the crime.

The mystery genre makes particularly specific requirements of its lead character. Most mysteries are meant to be solved, and so the lead character must be capable of solving them. This demands a high level of intelligence, or at the very least a command of some useful knowledge. This is not to say that all sleuths must think or behave in the same way—cops, forensic investigators, private eyes, and amateur detectives are all viable mystery leads who think and investigate in very different ways.

A unique facet of the mystery lead is that he or she is almost always involved by choice—either because of a job or natural curiosity. Rarely is the investigator also the intended target of the crime. Thus, it's necessary to explore just why it is that your character is drawn to the investigative life.

The psychological thriller is very closely related. Both genres often begin with a murder or other crime, and revolve around efforts to nab the criminal. But while the mystery usually puts emphasis on deciphering the criminal's plans and identity, the thriller is more concerned with the actual capture or death of the villain, whose ▸

identity may even be known from the start. Intelligence is often still called for on the part of the thriller's lead, but skills like brawling, gunplay, and fast driving are likely to play just as critical a role.

Additionally, in the thriller, the lead character is often at the heart of the criminal's plot—since thrillers tend to aim for a more frightening tone, the lead will often have a clear physical or emotional vulnerability. This character is often fighting for survival or to protect a loved one. Likewise, the opposition in thrillers is likely to be more physically imposing or psychologically frightening compared with the more scheming tendencies of the typical mystery villain.

To summarize, while both mysteries and thrillers revolve around the lead's efforts to bring a criminal to justice, the characters' motivations and methods play an important role in setting the genre and tone of the story. A lead with an emotional distance from events and a clear reliance on intellectual methodologies suggests a mystery, while a more physically vulnerable and emotionally involved lead implies a thriller. ▸

Opposite page: Jeff Mariotte's Western tale *Desperadoes: Banners of Gold* (IDW Publishing; 2005), with art by Jeremy Haun. Some genres require very specific character types. Traditional Westerns are necessarily set in a mythical American West populated by rugged individualists and the ever-popular gunslinger.

Left: *Catching Lucifer's Lunch* by T. J. and Jason May (SUMM Publications; 2006). Horror stories, often similar to thrillers, have a greater emphasis on making the opposition frightening, usually through the addition of supernatural elements.

BROAD GENRES & THE ROLE OF CHARACTERS

Some genres have no limit on character types. Memoir is limited only by the range of people the author knows personally. Romance stories can focus on virtually any two people—the only requirement is that they have the potential for love. Visual essays can be particularly affected by the "face" you put on the narration. Do you choose an erudite professor? A perky tour guide? Yourself?

Like Scott McCloud before him, comics theorist Neil Cohn uses a self-representation as the narrator of his visual essays, though with some reservation. "McCloud turned himself into a character, whereas I wanted to make it more subdued, just a person talking about things. I hoped that removing the personal aspect would place more emphasis on the ideas. This is partially the thinking behind the clothing choice (a common, casual 'look' for me), and whenever I'm out of the context of the main discussion, I've tried to dress myself in different clothes, to make it seem less of a 'costume.'"

SUBGENRES & MIXED GENRES

Science-fiction stories can be set in a far-distant future, like Jenn Manley Lee's *Dicebox* (see pages 94–99), or in any period of history, such as Lea Hernandez's Texas *Steampunk* novels (see pages 80–83). They can involve technological presence and themes, or use the speculative elements in smaller doses. The characters themselves need not have a direct connection to the science of the story; they may be scientists or astronauts, or they may be ordinary folks caught up in extraordinary events.

Science fiction has spawned a great many subgenres, some of which presuppose certain types of characters. Usually, space operas involve swashbuckling rebels and mercenaries; cyberpunk features characters on the fringes of society; and superhero stories contain would-be crime fighters, etc. ▸

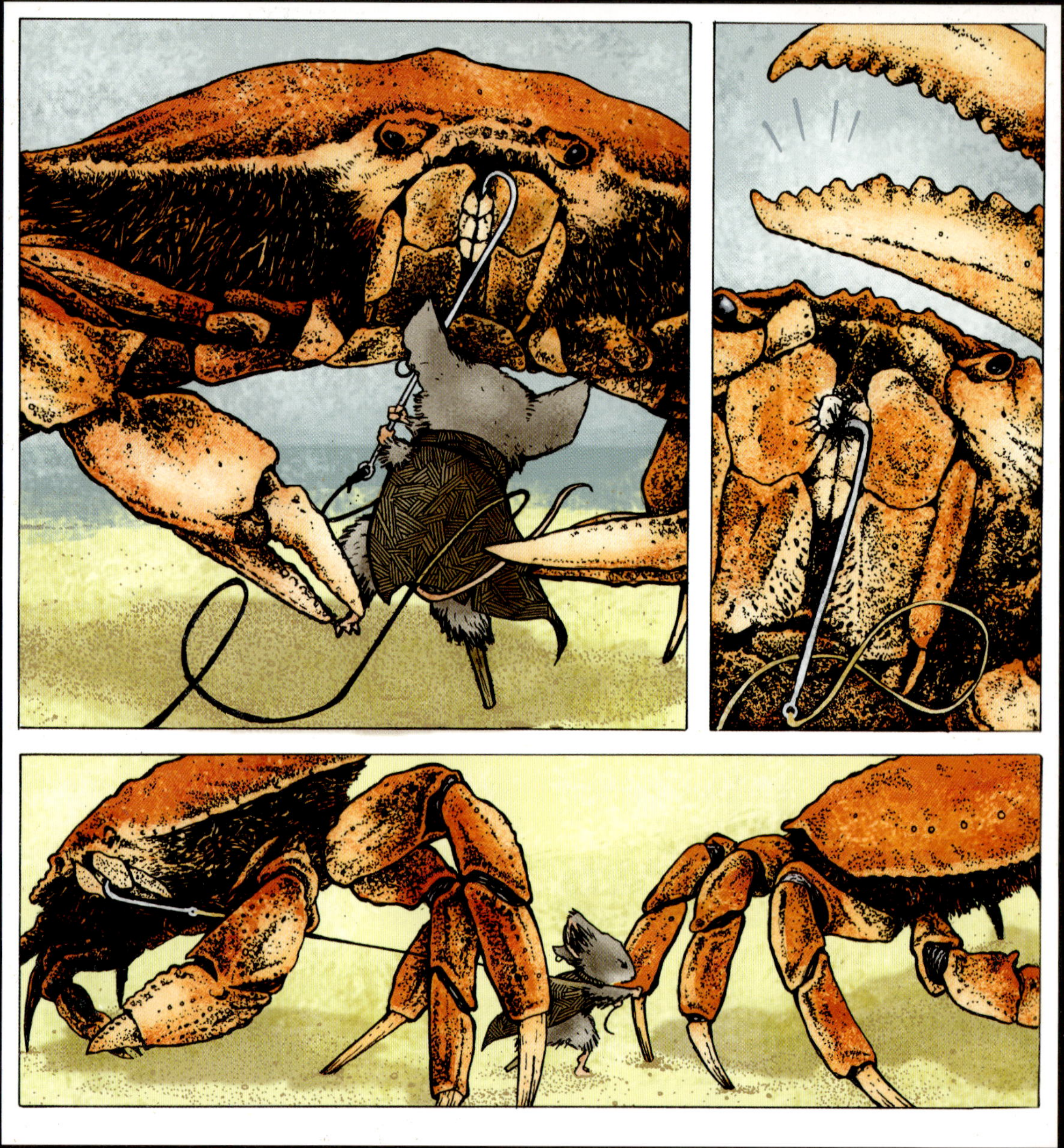

Left:
By presenting himself as friendly and cheerful, Neil Cohn sets a tone that suggests his essays on comics theory will be enjoyable and accessible, even while exploring concepts that may be challenging.

Above:
David Petersen's *Mouse Guard* (Archaia Studios Press) reinvents the ordinary world fantastically, so that even a normal crab seems like a dragon-sized beast.

Above:
In graphic novels, nonhuman character designs may be metaphorical or purely stylistic. For instance, Steve Lafler depicts the patrons of a jazz club as humanoid insects in *Bughouse* (Top Shelf Productions; 2000).

Right:
Jason Little's villain, Oleg, from *Shutterbug Follies* is reminiscent of Hergé's *Tintin* characters—a design motif that can be somewhat incongruous with the book's more grisly imagery (see pages 114–115).

SETTING TONE WITHIN GENRE

A character's personal outlook plays a major role in how a genre is interpreted. For instance, while Alan Moore's Rorschach and Jason Little's Bee are both detectives, they each set very different tones. Rorschach's Machiavellian methods and paranoid outlook set an extremely dark and gritty tone for *Watchmen* (DC Comics; 1986–1987), while Bee's enthusiasm and uninhibited curiosity give *Shutterbug Follies* a slightly odd, upbeat tone, which Little describes as "bubblegum noir."

Little has regretted to some degree his decision to combine graphic images of death with the lighter tone set by his character and art style. "At the time I felt like a suspense story had to have brutal murder in it, even though that's not a primary interest of mine... With comics, the reader can sit there and stare at the disemboweled corpse for as long as they like, which is a problem. Another problem is that I'm taking too much from one creator: clear line like Hergé plus bright colors like Hergé creates expectations that the work will be predictably like Hergé in all ways. Which it almost is, but not entirely." ■

MINIMALISM

According to the online information source Wikipedia, minimalism "describes movements in various forms of art and design ... where the work is stripped down to its most fundamental features. The term 'minimalist' can also refer to anything which is spare, stripped to its essentials, or providing only the outline of structure."

The less-is-more, minimalist aesthetic is quite popular among graphic novelists today, and two comics artists who are particularly adept at minimalist work are Tom Gauld and Jeffrey Brown. Though both aim to simplify, the contrast between their character designs is intriguing and informative. ■

TOM GAULD

Tom Gauld is an illustrator and comic-book artist. He grew up in Scotland and now lives and works in London. He created the comic strips "Move to the City" for *Timeout* and "The Writer at Work" and "Hunter and Painter" for *The Guardian*. He runs Cabanon Press (www.cabanonpress.com) with Simone Lia, and their comics *First* and *Second* were republished as *Both* by Bloomsbury in 2003. His most recent book, *Hunter and Painter*, was published in 2006 by Buenaventura Press.

Gauld's two characters in *Invasion*, a 16-page minicomic first published in 2004 at pleasingly pocket-sized dimensions, were inspired in part by the Lewis Chessmen at the British Museum, who have, according to Gauld, "lovely simple faces and a great expression of slightly sad acceptance. I think this suits the mood of the tale."

"I think that creating a believable, cohesive world is one of the most important parts of making a comic," he says. "The Soldier in the story is supposed to be quite innocent, so I had to work to make him look a bit like this, while still having a beard and helmet, which at first made him look a bit fierce. I wanted the Soldier and the Farmer characters to look quite alike so that neither is the villain or hero. They're more or less the same character dressed differently. There's nothing ostentatious about either of the characters. I wanted them to be simple, ordinary figures." ■

Left: Pages from Gauld's *Invasion* minicomic. Note the use of silhouettes to define the essential natures of the characters when seen from a distance. Nothing is lost, even printed at such a small size.

Above left: *Invasion's* characters, world, and story all developed in Gauld's sketchbook.

JEFFREY BROWN

Jeffrey Brown is the author of the autobiographical novels *Clumsy* (2003), *Unlikely* (2003), and *AEIOU* or *Any Easy Intimacy* (2005), as well as the collection of satirical superhero stories, *Bighead* (2004), all of which are published by Top Shelf Productions. Top Shelf also published his most recent work, a collection of gag cartoons titled *I Am Going to Be Small*, in 2006. His illustrations have featured in a range of media, from *McSweeney's* magazine to an animated video for the band *Death Cab for Cutie*.

Brown avoids "fictionalizing" the characters in his autobiographical stories, and his simplified style plays an important role in drawing out the particular traits he hopes to capture. "The character of 'me' in my books is designed with spindly arms, generic shirts, wide eyes, and a scruffy beard. The basic design is an attempt at simplicity and trying to echo the manner of drawing like a child; because my autobiographical stories attempt to get at some kind of essential humanity, having a childlike quality to the drawing reinforces the sense of honesty and sincerity I try to portray. The wide eyes and spindly arms let me imbue the sometimes-serious stories with a lot of humor. Although these are real people, so to speak, they're also still cartoon characters, and so I'm able to make even simple actions, like handing a mug to someone, look funny. Humor is important, even in drama, and I feel that having such goofy, flawed characters gives more warmth to the stories." ■

Left:
Jeffrey experiences a moment of anxiety in *Clumsy*, the first book in the *Girlfriends* trilogy.

Above left:
Jeffrey and his girlfriend Theresa return from a trip in *Clumsy*. When depicting real people, Brown tries "to be fair and balanced, and never do things like make someone look bad."

Above:
Jeffrey and a later girlfriend, Sophia, enjoy a movie in *AEIOU*, book three of the *Girlfriends* Trilogy. Here, even the dialogue is abstracted; a sense of connection overrides the details of what is said.

Left:
The cute softness of Brown's designs in *AEIOU* heightens the pathos of an upsetting exchange.

CARTOONING

In *Understanding Comics*, Scott McCloud defines cartooning as "amplification through simplification"—abstracting an image to its essential "meaning." Under cartooning's umbrella—broader than minimalism and more expansive than realism—is a loosely connected set of styles labeled "cartoony," often possessing a comedic or childlike flair, with elements of caricature and iconic design. ■

JEF CZEKAJ

Jef Czekaj (www.czekaj.com) is a cartoonist, illustrator, printmaker, and musician who lives in Somerville, Massachusetts.

"Plots, settings, characters, bad jokes, all evolve together. Sometimes a character comes first; sometimes a bad joke. Both are equally important," says Czekaj. "I draw a lot of doodles in my spiral notebook, and some have more life than others. They seem to want to do things, so I let them." Czekaj says of *Grampa and Julie: Shark Hunters*, his two-page adventure/comedy strips for Nickelodeon (Top Shelf Productions published the first collection in 2004), "Some recurring characters have a little room for development, but many don't get much more personality than 'funny-looking' and 'wants to eat Grampa.'"

Of graphic novels, Czekaj says, "This push for legitimacy in the art world, while great and important and necessary, is leading younger artists away from what comics are great at: being funny."

(These pages incorporate work that was originally published in *Nickelodeon Magazine*.) ■

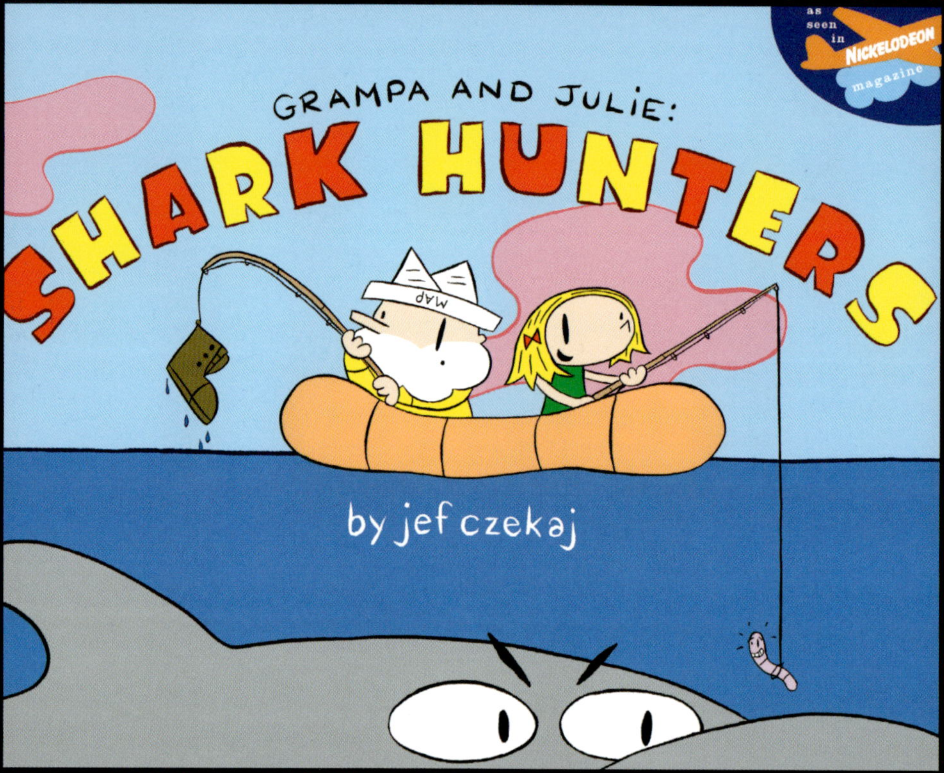

Left:
The cover of *Grampa and Julie: Shark Hunters*.

Below left and below:
A page from the *Shark Hunters* pitch, along with a sketchbook page.

Right:
About his "one big eye" feature Czekaj says, "Just a happy accident. Kids always ask, and I say I don't know. Almost always one of them says it's because of perspective (the eye closest to the 'camera' is always bigger). That's not intentional, but it could be."

COLLEEN COOVER

Colleen Coover (http://cooverart.livejournal.com) is a comic-book artist and illustrator living in Portland, Oregon. She is the creator of the erotic romance *Small Favors* (Eros Comix; 2002) and the artist for *Banana Sunday*, a comedy for young readers written by Root Nibot (Oni Press; 2006).

"I don't draw from life much at all; I use what are pretty traditional cartoon techniques to design my characters," says Coover. "I've learned a lot from my rather dog-eared copy of Jack Hamm's book *Cartooning the Head & Figure*, which addresses the construction of human cartoon anatomy and how different cartooning techniques can lend personality to a character, whether in 'big nose' humor cartoons or editorial caricatures," says Coover, whose biggest influences in comics are Los Bros Hernandez and Milton Caniff.

Her characters tend to emerge fully formed and then become more defined as she gets to know them better. The exception tends to be animal characters, like the monkeys in *Banana Sunday*, because she has to think more about how their bodies are constructed and adjust her style to their nonhuman physiques. Her animal characters bear little resemblance to the actual apes they represent.

She makes no formal model sheets, but when she's working from a script, she'll doodle the characters in the margins—"especially when a strong emotion or tricky bit of action is going on in a panel." She also draws rough costume sketches on scrap paper. "But certainly the characters wind up dictating their design to me as we go along," she says.

Banana Sunday's main character, a high-school girl named Kirby Steinberg, is new to her school, just starting to make friends, and is responsible for keeping control of three chaotic monkeys. Coover designed her to be "cute, but not extraordinary." She dresses in T-shirts, skirts, and flat shoes, and to distinguish her visually, even in a crowd scene, Coover gave her a plain pair of pigtails. By contrast, her friend Nickels—"a school-paper reporter with a hero complex"—is confident, outgoing, and nosey. "She dresses with more flash in shirts with logos, Western wear, and geek chic. If Kirby is Everygirl, I wanted Nickels to be the type of person every girl would want for her best friend." ■

Left:
Layout page from *Banana Sunday*.

Bottom left & middle:
Banana Sunday, from issues 1 and 2.

Bottom right:
Kirby and Nickels from *Banana Sunday*, issue 3.

VERISIMILITUDE

Verisimilitude is the appearance of truth or the quality of seeming to be true. A "true" image possesses *emotional* authenticity, and a character should have a genuine *presence* on the page. This quality is important across all genres, but especially in "life stories": autobiography, biography, memoir, and historical fiction. ■

Left:
Katin's favorite character is "a Russian soldier who speaks some Hungarian. He is to me the embodiment of the Red Army soldiers that we learned about in communist Hungary."

MIRIAM KATIN

Illustrator and animator Miriam Katin was born in Hungary in 1942 and now lives in the United States. Her comics stories have appeared in various anthologies, and Drawn & Quarterly published her graphic memoir, *We Are On Our Own*, in 2006. "In 1944, the Hungarian government decided to participate in the Final Solution and enter the war on the side of Germany. At this late date, there was a great rush to achieve quickly what they had been doing in other countries all along," Katin says. "When orders came to go to the ghetto in Budapest, my mother decided to escape with me. Many other Jews had found various ways to disappear. This story is about that year, our living in hiding until 1945, the liberation." ■

Left & above:
"The characters are so alive for me, from faces to the clothes they wear, and how they speak and act and think, that there are no revisions and, because of my rather sketchy style, there [is little] refining work," Katin says.

DON MACDONALD

Don MacDonald, an accomplished painter, first conceived *Machiavelli*—closer to historical fiction than true biography—in 1996 after a trip to Italy. After arduous historical research, he published a "prologue" in the 2002 Small Press Expo anthology. The Vendome Press published the 150-page graphic novel in 2007.

"I want the reader to feel like they are spending a day with Machiavelli," says MacDonald. "I want to modernize the characters as much as I can. I'm modernizing their language, though not the spirit of the words."

MacDonald's art—pen-and-ink over pencil, with watercolor washes for value, shading, and shaping—is drawn in the style of Renaissance "cartoons," which were painter's sketches or studies. "Using photographs too closely can look very stilted," MacDonald says. "I don't use a lot of photo references for my characters; mostly for backgrounds."

MacDonald doesn't want the viewer to be bogged down by a lot of detail, and his art tends toward organic rather than iconic forms. "I don't want the reader to linger on the buttons or the cut of a doublet. You should be listening to what they're saying, looking at the faces or the hands. Where it's appropriate, I'll put in the detail, but I want it to be able to melt away. The challenge is to keep the art from being needlessly complex without overly simplifying. It's a balancing act." ■

Top left:
MacDonald likes to "riff," producing variations on actual paintings, and introduces two of his characters through portraits.

Top right:
MacDonald's style is drawn from Renaissance painter's studies.

Bottom left:
Note the two levels of realism between the living characters and the figures in the tapestries. Here MacDonald presents a picture within a picture.

Bottom middle & right:
MacDonald experiments with distance and levels of detail. His scenes reflecting the internal world are often more realistically drawn, where his external world is more impressionistic.

REALITY & IMAGINATION

JEFF PARKER

The Interman is Jeff Parker's standout, self-published graphic novel (Octopus Books; 2003). Parker had wanted to create an adventure book with lots of global intrigue years ago. As he was reading Stephen Jay Gould's Natural History essays, "the notion of a human who could adapt his body to extreme situations seemed like an interesting way to go with a comic," he says. "Car chases and that kind of action don't work as well in comics, but character-based dynamics do."

Sketching from life, Parker says, is crucial for good character design. "When you stare at people's faces you realize how genetic traits repeat themselves, and it helps in designing believable characters who convey particular personas. I like artists who embrace bold skull and body shapes, people ranging from Alex Toth to Jamie Hewlett."

Parker tries to work out different angles on his characters and get to a strong design before he begins drawing pages. He considers at length the characters' wardrobe: "[the hero] Van Meach tends to dress outdoorsy, and rarely has a shirt with a collar. Since he can adapt to any temperature around him, he has to make a conscious effort to dress according to the weather so he doesn't stick out in public. I tried to make him look as if he could be from any number of countries because he was assembled from the genes of thousands of people from around the globe." Parker also creates a "line-up" to determine the relative heights and shapes of the cast. ■

Left:
Parker draws May as a female version of the hero, Van Meach, because they originated from the same Interman Project laboratory.

Right:
Parker looks to genetic types in the sketching of his characters.

Below:
Pages from *The Interman.*

COLLEEN DORAN

Though she is a prolific illustrator for major US comics companies, Colleen Doran's signature work is her creator-owned series, *A Distant Soil*, an epic science-fiction/fantasy tale with four graphic novels in print from Image Comics (series first self-published in 1991). She is also the writer and artist of *Girl to GRRRL Manga*, a how-to art book for shoujo manga enthusiasts (North Light Books; 2006).

Doran tries to keep her characters' faces and body language consistent at all times, and she tries to keep the sense of line consistent. But she says it's difficult to be absolutely consistent in style over the entire course of *A Distant Soil*, a 20-year project she began as a teenager.

To assist her, she draws from life a great deal and keeps extensive reference files on people. She also has models with whom she likes to work. She has thousands of photos and keeps a comprehensive library of information about clothes and costume design as well as ethnic clothes and historical costumes. She frequents museums and studies constantly for inspiration.

Says Doran, "I rarely ever whittle away at a character once he is on paper. I just have it so clearly in my head it never occurs to me to use an eraser later. If I can't picture him in my head, I don't start drawing in the first place. I'm surprised that other people do." ■

COLLEEN DORAN ON NINIRI FROM A DISTANT SOIL

I like Niniri a lot because she is a very deceptive character. She is angelically pretty, and when she was revealed to be an incredibly manipulative villain, most of my readers kept right on waiting for the revelation that she was really a good guy. She has a roundish, sweet face with enormous blue eyes. She looks like Snow White, and has an almost prim manner. It drove the readers batty that this pretty, delicate woman was such a manipulative critter. I love how the character was able to deceive people simply by her appearance. ■

Top left:
Cover art from *A Distant Soil*, issue 34 showing Seren in Ovanan costume.

Top right:
Interior art for *A Distant Soil*, issue 25. Jason and Liana.

Bottom right:
Cover drawing for *A Distant Soil*, issue 37. Niniri and Seren.

Bottom left:
Cover art from *A Distant Soil*, issue 13. Etan and child in Ovanan costumes.

CASE STUDY:

LEA HERNANDEZ

Lea Hernandez's *Texas Steampunk* series includes the books *Cathedral Child* (1998) and *Clockwork Angels* (1999), with a third volume, *Ironclad Petal*, currently being serialized online at www.girlamatic.com. The first volume of her Rumble Girls series, *Silky Warrior Tansie*, was first published online, with a print edition available from NBM Publishing (2003). She illustrated *Killer Princesses* (Oni Press; 2002), written by Gail Simone, as well as the Scott Lobdell–written *The Hardy Boys: The Ocean of Osyria* (Papercutz; 2005).

Hernandez was an early advocate of manga, penning the first manga column published by *Wizard* magazine, as well as the how-to guide *Manga Secrets* (Impact Books; 2005). She is also an ardent proponent of creator-owned works, as well as being very active in promoting women in comics. She was the founding editor of Girlamatic.com, where she remains active as a creator, despite having since passed on the editorial reins. In addition, she recently announced the Women Webcomicker Grant Nan, which serves "to foster women publishing independently, with economy, and as owners of what they create." (The grant is named after the "digital person" Nan 1^1 from *Rumble Girls: Silky Warrior Tansie.*)

PROCESS & METHOD

Hernandez likes to work out her character designs before inserting them into her pages, mostly to avoid making discoveries about a character after she's already well into the work. Sometimes she's able to capture her mental image of a character on the first try; more often it takes a bit more "prodding," as she tries to coax details from her vision of the character's own self-image. "This sounds strange, but I ask the characters to show me what they want to look like and sound like. I know when I've got it right—it's that 'ah-ha!' moment when everything falls into place."

Of course, not everything falls straight into place every time. Hernandez points out that sometimes she's not fully satisfied with a character's design even by the time she finishes the book they feature in. "I think much more about character design than I used to, but I think that's because I learned how important it was for readers." Still, she sees limits to just how much preparatory work should be done. "Character design is crucial when you're going to have a number of different people drawing the character, as in animation. I think it's important for graphic novels ... but not as important as it is for animation. I think too much preparatory work can even be detrimental, and sap creative energy. On DeviantArt [an online portfolio compendium], there are artists who make exquisite, professional-level design sheets for their comics, but never draw page one." ▸

Above left:
In *Cathedral Child*, lead character Glory shares a peach with her lifelong companion Sumner, while the scheming Parrish listens in. While Hernandez' books often feature elaborate settings and exciting action sequences, her plots are always character-driven, with strong romantic overtones.

Above:
Glory, from *Cathedral Child*, turns to her mother for advice on sex and the relative worth of the men in their lives.

This page: Parrish, the villain of *Cathedral Child*, is decked out in his finest clothes as he presents the strange computer, Cathedral, to his financial investors.

This page: The second Texas Steampunk book, *Clockwork Angels*, follows Temperance, a young woman with mental powers, and Amy. Here, the villain Sacerdote mistakes Amy for his missing assistant, Milly. The two women are identical, save that Milly is mute and lacks Amy's freckles.

INSPIRATION & INFLUENCES

Much of Hernandez's early influence comes from *Mad Magazine* illustrators, such as Jack Davis and Paul Coker, as well as the animation she watched growing up, particularly Disney and Rankin/Bass (producer of *The Last Unicorn*, *The Hobbit*, and many classic holiday cartoons). "I grew up in the era of Hanna-Barbera (producer of *Space Ghost*, *Jonny Quest*, *Scooby Doo*, etc.) and Filmation (producer of *Mighty Mouse*, *Fat Albert and the Cosby Kids*, etc.), the late 1960s and 1970s, and the stuff from that era from those two studios (*Jonny Quest* aside), is really pretty awful. But the [Rankin/Bass] stuff was different, and I didn't miss—because I always read the credits—that there were lots of Japanese creators involved ... I'd say my seeking out of Disney cartoons and *anime* [Japanese animation] made me want to draw characters beautifully and with life."

Hernandez frequently draws from life when developing characters, incorporating details of friends and strangers alike. "I am lucky to be surrounded by characters in my friends! Also, when I am out, I am people-watching all the time, looking for interesting hairstyles, interesting outfits, mannerisms. I take pictures when I can, and notes when I can't."

RESEARCH & AUTHENTICITY

Set in the town of Heaven, Texas, in the year 1897, *Cathedral Child* required attention to period dress and social convention in the character designs, even when these elements were blended with bits of fantasy and unreal technology. Written in the early days of the Internet, Hernandez relied primarily on her library, photocopying page after page from costume and historical texts, along with *Eyewitness* books (Dorling Kindersley) for photo reference and interesting details.

"I got fairly close, authenticity-wise. For example, while the women wore shorter skirts than were typical at the time, they kept their legs covered. Their dress was modeled on Annie Oakley's performance costumes [in Buffalo Bill Cody's Wild West Show], which were designed to give a girlish impression and yet be modest. Also, in the harsher conditions of the time, "rules" of proper dress went right out the window. I never drew it, but the women in *Cathedral Child* do wear underclothes, albeit lighter and more practical. They're not well-to-do, and definitely not going to wear corsetry and do hard labor. All that stuff was for women who could afford to be immobile objects. I felt I achieved a fairly authentic look for the men's clothing, but it was hard to find good, detailed men's costume reference."

TYPEFACE

Hernandez is selective in using typeface as an element of character design. Most characters, those with "typical" voices, are all given the same clean but plain typeface. More stylistic typefaces and balloons are reserved for those characters with unique voices, such as Sacerdote in *Clockwork Angels* and the "digital person" Nan 5^5 in *Silky Warrior Tansie*. "Sacerdote, in his second appearance, has a haunting, disturbing voice, and I wanted to show that. The typeface, Ebola [designed by Susan Townsend], with its backwards 'e's' and grungy forms, was perfect. I wanted Nan 5^5 to 'sound' like a normal person whose voice is heard over an electronic connection, so I gave her the four-sided balloons to suggest that mechanical aspect, and rounded their corners to make them look friendlier, and to prevent them looking like caption boxes." ■

Above left:
In manga, it is common for shifts in art style to be used for dramatic effect or to indicate changes in character emotion. Here, Hernandez uses a shift to uninked pencils to indicate that Temperance is drifting into memory, remembering her childhood with Amy.

Above middle:
Set in 1897, *Clockwork Angels* begins in New Orleans, where Temperance and Amy are often in the company of the wealthy, necessitating more elaborate garb than is customary among the women of Heaven.

Above right:
Hernandez captures the creepy and otherworldly tone of Sacerdote's voice in her choice of typeface and the irregularly shaped word balloons.

CASE STUDY:

JEFF NICHOLSON

Hailing from the San Francisco Bay area, multiple Eisner Award–nominee Jeff Nicholson (www.coloniapress.com) is best known for *Colonia*, his self-published fantasy-adventure series set in the New World and conceived in 1997, as well as the graphic novels *Through the Habitrails* (1994; see pages 10 and 11) and *Father & Son* (1995–1996).

Nicholson thinks first of his characters' speech and personality, especially their motivations and how they will react to the story line, before he begins any sketching. Likewise, he daydreams story lines long before attempting a script. For his "more eccentric" earlier comics, his first sketch of a character would most often serve as the template for the entire project. But for *Colonia*, he wanted a solid, animation-like feel and for his sketches to serve as model sheets.

Nicholson struggled most with his main character, Jack. "He is you, the reader. He is your eyes, ears, and shoes as you experience the more colorful characters around you, and therefore he is very neutral. Selfish, angry, or stupid characters are easier, even clichéd, I suppose, but a plain one is tough," Nicholson says. Thinking of the 1960s TV series *Lost in Space*, he modeled Jack after Will Robinson somewhat, with a neutral hairstyle and nonspecific age. As a graphic-design student, Nicholson loathed making dozens of thumbnails for something he felt he had "nailed internally." It takes discipline, he learned, to keep exploring versions of a character with only himself as judge and jury. "You know when they are dead wrong, and you need to keep at it," he says, "but you don't always know when they could be better."

Thumbnailing an entire issue has helped him to clarify the layout and page count and avoid accidentally altering the characters defined in his model sheets. On the final page, Nicholson first draws the characters loosely using a nonreproducible blue pencil, and then tightens these sketches with a lead pencil before inking, so he has two more chances to modify the characters before a design is set in stone.

Nicholson's character Adarro has his roots in folklore. "I wish I could say it was New-World folklore, but I believe it was Greek," Nicholson notes. "It was from a volume of the Dover coloring book series, which offer a great wealth of reference for artists, with its simplified line art covering historical costume, settings, occupations, and architecture, etc. It was here that I saw Adarro, described as a rubbing from a Greek ruin. He had fish hands and feet, and when I saw him I knew it was time to start on *Colonia*. It was very primitive, so I worked him up more like a real fish from an animal reference book, and gave him a period coat based on a portrait of Admiral Anson of HMS *Centurion*." ■

Above right: The cover for Issue 4 of *Colonia*.

Right: Character sketches for *Colonia*.

Above far left:
A scene from *Colonia*, in which the characters are "shanghaied" or forcibly taken aboard ship.

Above middle:
The pirates' duel from *Colonia*. Physical action and conflict are key components of character development.

Above:
For *Colonia*, Nicholson created his initial sketches with animation in mind so that they could be used as model sheets.

Far left:
The characters converse in the ship's galley. Dialogue is also a primary aspect of character development.

Left:
Adarro, the mysterious fish-man, from *Colonia*.

SECTION V

APPEARANCE & REALITY

We are all born into bodies whose appearances are in many ways out of our control. Height, eye color, bone structure—each of these is largely determined before birth, barring harmful environmental influences. Other physical attributes, such as weight or musculature, may be controllable, but only within certain limits. In light of how much of a person's appearance is outside their control, those aspects that can be controlled—such as wardrobe and gesture—take on considerable significance, allowing us to present an elaborate mix of communications and miscommunications about how we perceive ourselves and how we wish to be perceived by others. In this section, we'll discuss the use of these variable physical factors in expressing character personality and purpose, looking at how they function in both realistic and minimalist styles. ■

Right: A page from Jenn Manley Lee's *Dicebox* (self-published; 1999). Locked in a cheap flophouse after curfew, Griffen waits anxiously for morning, while her companion, Molly, undergoes surgery. (For information about *Dicebox*, see pages 94–99.)

SUBTEXT & SYMBOLISM

Left:
In *Night Fisher*, the disconnection the central character Loren feels from his father can be felt in R. Kikuo Johnson's slightly askew compositions when depicting the father.

Below left:
In Jeff Mariotte's *Desperadoes: Banners of Gold* (IDW Publishing; 2005), with art by Jeremy Haun, heavy shadows around a character are a not-so-subtle, but effective indicator of the character's dark mood.

Communication is a messy business. Rarely do the words we say, the meanings we intend, and what our audience perceives perfectly align. Even the most straightforward conversations draw on countless signals—our choice of words, tone of voice, facial expression, body language, and physical appearance. All of these can be used, misused, and misinterpreted to alter the message sent and the message received. And that's without even touching on intentional dishonesty.

This complexity is doubled for the storyteller, since there are at least two layers of communication in any story: between one character and another, and between creator and reader. And while appearances often deceive, appearances in comics must enlighten as well. While characters themselves may not be aware of every message they send, it's vital that creators consider carefully the specific moments and poses they choose to capture in each panel.

SUBTEXT

Subtext is the meaning beneath what is openly expressed, and is arguably the core of good character development. Dialogue is what a character says; subtext is what a character means. Comics artists generally reveal subtext visually. Consider the difference between a character who says "I love you" while looking in his lover's eyes and another who says the same words but with back turned and teeth clenched. Subtext is a suggestion that leads the reader to discern a character's inmost feelings and motivations.

Other tools for revealing character subtext include composition, angle, lighting, and point of view. A close-up can be used to heighten a sense of emotional intensity, while a long shot within a large panel can reveal feelings of loneliness. A ground-level (or worm's eye) point of view, looking up at a character, can reveal feelings of intimidation on the part of the viewer, or feelings of greatness on the part of the character depicted. External elements of setting and atmosphere—traditionally called "pathetic fallacy" when the weather mirrors a character's mood—can also help reveal a character's internal state. Paired with dialogue, these visual cues can add layers of meaning to a character's dialogue, and thus deepen a character's personality. ▸

SYMBOLISM

Symbolism in comics is essentially visual metaphor, wherein a literal object, trait, or event serves to convey nonvisual, usually abstract, information about the character to the reader. For instance, a character with a fiery temperament might have naturally bright red hair. Obviously, the character is not communicating anything simply by possessing a particular hair color, nor is there any real significance to hair color as an indicator of personality. But the symbolic color is able to clearly convey an aspect of personality to the reader.

Symbolism also plays a major role in relating characters to the ideas and themes of the story as a whole. This can be as simple and overt as Art Spiegelman's decision to represent Jews as mice and Nazis as cats in *Maus*, or as subtle as Jenn Manley Lee's use of shared colors to unify closely connected characters within *Dicebox* (see pages 94–99 for more on Lee's use of color symbolism). ■

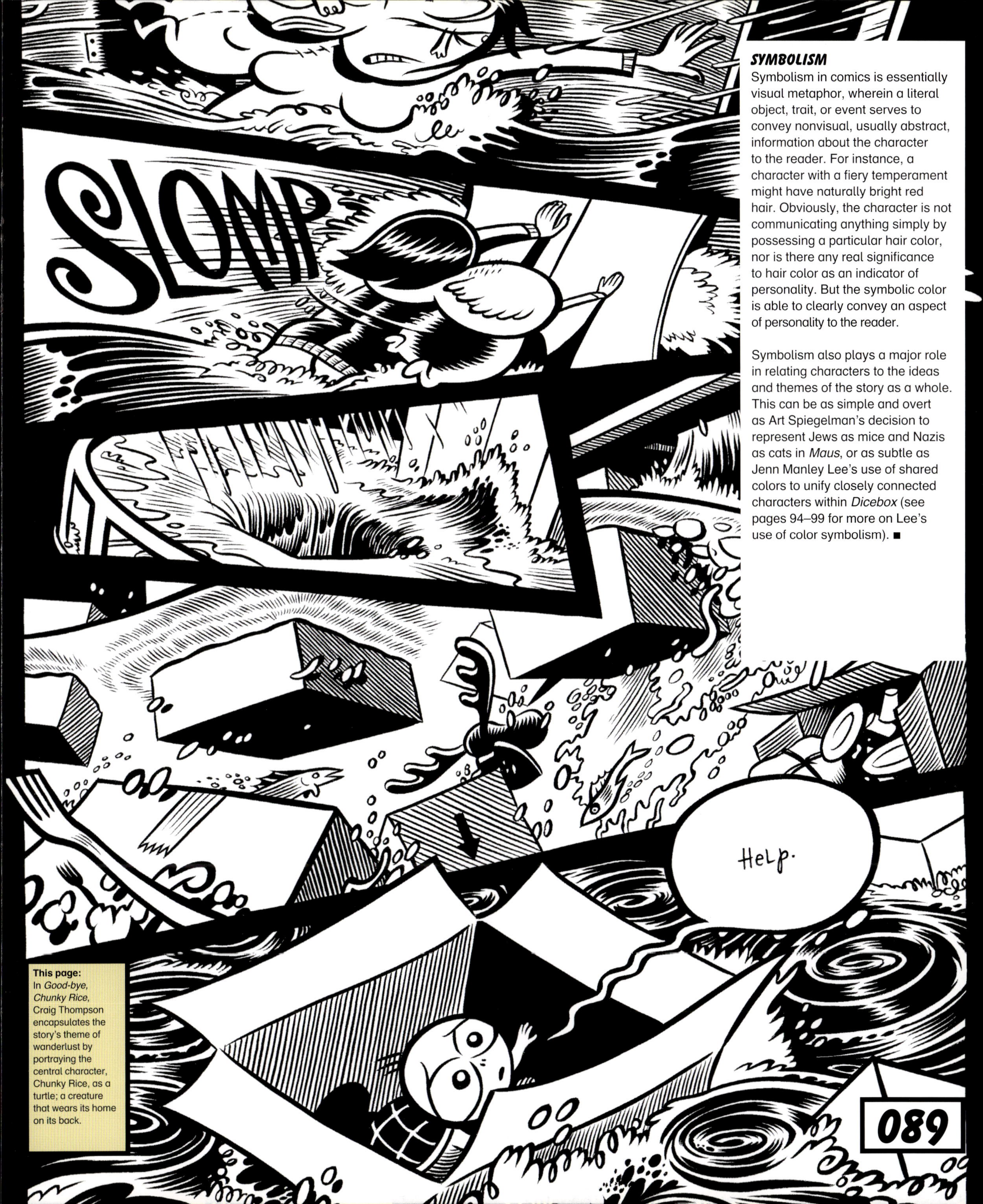

This page: In *Good-bye, Chunky Rice*, Craig Thompson encapsulates the story's theme of wanderlust by portraying the central character, Chunky Rice, as a turtle; a creature that wears its home on its back.

This page: Jenn Manley Lee devotes considerable attention to the clothing worn in *Dicebox* (www.dicebox.net), creating realistic textiles appropriate not only to her futuristic setting, but also to each character's taste.

CLOTHING AS COMMUNICATION

At the most superficial level, clothing may communicate social or professional status. Uniforms clearly announce members of particular professions: the policeman's uniform, the nurse's scrubs, the priest's collar. A yarmulke, cross, or burqa may reveal the wearer's faith. Among teenagers, choice of clothing clearly divides goths from punks, skateboarders from preppies. On this level, clothing is an expression of identity and allegiance. But details can make a big difference—a goth girl in fishnet stockings and a corset sends a very different message than a goth girl in a full-length skirt and high-collared top.

Clothing is also a powerful tool for communicating interpersonal feelings. For instance, a woman might put on a sweater when meeting a man whom she finds particularly unappealing, emphasizing her desire to be distanced from him. A teacher might wear a shirt and tie as a way of projecting authority when addressing a disrespectful group of students. Furthermore, clothing choices are likely to vary with changes in a character's self-image—a man who has gained weight might wear baggier clothing and muted colors, but might celebrate a weight loss by wearing a particularly eye-catching outfit.

It's even common for people who are actively trying to alter their own self-image to make intentional dramatic shifts in their wardrobe as a way of precipitating positive personal change. An unambitious slacker who decides his life needs more direction might decide to replace his torn jeans and old T-shirts with a new suit. The dull office manager who decides he needs to be more fun might buy a Hawaiian shirt. Of course, such efforts don't always succeed—that manager's Hawaiian shirt might serve only to emphasize just how humorless he really is. ▸

EMBLEMATIC COSTUMING

There is a long tradition of creating costumes and accessories that stand as permanent emblems of the characters who wear them, such as Charlie Brown's yellow sweater with the black zigzag or Captain America's red-white-and-blue shield. These items are immediately recognizable, even when seen apart from the characters who wear them.

This tradition continues in many graphic novels today: Tom Hart's homeless revolutionary Hutch Owen consistently wears a black knit hat, while Eiichiro Oda's Monkey D. Luffy (*One Piece*; published in English by VIZ Media, from 2003) always wears the straw hat given to him by his childhood hero. Even authors of nonfiction often use emblematic costuming.

Emblematic costuming can help to make characters immediately recognizable, both in and out of the context of their stories. It can also externalize defining characteristics, such as Charlie Brown's indecisive worrying, or Captain America's steadfast patriotism. Of course, it's all the more important that emblematic costumes accurately reflect an active choice on the part of the character, since it needs to be believable that these are clothes the character is at ease wearing every day. ■

Left:
Loren, the protagonist of R. Kikuo Johnson's *Night Fisher* (Fantagraphics, 2005) suffers in the tropical heat. Johnson points out how wardrobe can play a role in establishing a character's relationship to his or her environment. "Throughout the book Loren is most often in his prep-school uniform: white shirt, black tie, black pants, black wool blazer. The school is presented as an oppressive force in Loren's life, and the excessive heavy clothing in the hot, tropical setting emphasizes this."

Left:
Scott McCloud's self-representation, including the flannel shirt, thick glasses, and lightning-bolt T-shirt, has become a hallmark of his nonfiction works, such as *Making Comics* (2006). The lightning bolt is a reference to yet another of McCloud's characters, the superhero Zot.

EXPRESSION, MOTION & GESTURE

If wardrobe represents the manner by which characters consciously express themselves, then facial expression and body language represent the subconscious and semiconscious portion of physical expression. However we want to be seen, our true emotions have countless ways of bubbling to the surface through the ways we move, stand, or respond physically to the people around us.

As stated earlier, the face is our primary tool for expression and connection. When we want someone to believe we're acting or speaking in earnest, we look directly into their eyes; conversely, when a person won't look us in the eyes, we're inclined to believe they're lying to us. We look for hints of true feeling in each nuance of facial movement: an involuntary smile, a raised eyebrow, a sideward glance.

Not every facial signal means the same thing for every person. Is that person averting their eyes because they're lying to you? Or is it because they're embarrassed about being secretly in love with you? Does a person's scowl indicate anger or merely intense concentration? It's important to know not just what a particular expression means in general, but also what it means coming from your particular character. And, of course, the way other characters interpret facial expressions can be just as revealing as the expressions.

While the facial expressions we make are usually uncalculated, we are generally at least aware of them—if we're smiling, we know we're smiling, and we have a rough idea of what that means to the person we're smiling at. This is often less true of our bodily movement, especially the way we walk or run. A person who walks with their head down and a shuffling gait sends a very different message from a person who looks straight ahead and takes long, even strides, but generally, neither is aware of the messages they're sending.

Finally, there are small movements that usually coincide with verbal communication: the way we nod our heads in agreement, or tilt our heads to speak in confidence; the way we use various hand gestures to emphasize or elaborate what we're saying; or the way we close ourselves off from those around us by keeping our hands in our pockets or arms crossed. Our hands in particular can be inseparable from our sense of communication, as evidenced by the fact that many people will embellish their speech with hand motions even when they're on the telephone and can't be seen by the person to whom they're speaking.

CONSCIOUS BODY LANGUAGE

The fact that body language is both highly revealing and largely involuntary gives many people incentive to exert conscious control over their physical expressiveness. This is especially true of people engaged in occupations of deceit or bluffing, such as a professional poker player with a perfectly blank expression. Of course, this insincerity or inscrutability can be very off-putting; it's no coincidence that the most unreadable character is often the mysterious and malevolent villain.

There are certainly more benign reasons to practice body language as well, such as the eager job applicant who works to perfect his or her handshake, and to develop physical habits that project confidence and resolve. As with our clothing, sometimes people consciously change their body language in the hope of instigating a change in themselves; by behaving with greater confidence, they hope to feel more confident.

In truth, we all do this to some degree. As children, we are unreserved in expressing ourselves physically, but we are taught to rein in those instincts for the sake of dignity and social nicety. Otherwise we might all be inclined to break into a spontaneous dance whenever our favorite food is served or stamp our feet when we have to go to the dentist. But it's important to know the degree to which your characters make conscious choices in their body language, and what truly motivates them to do so. ■

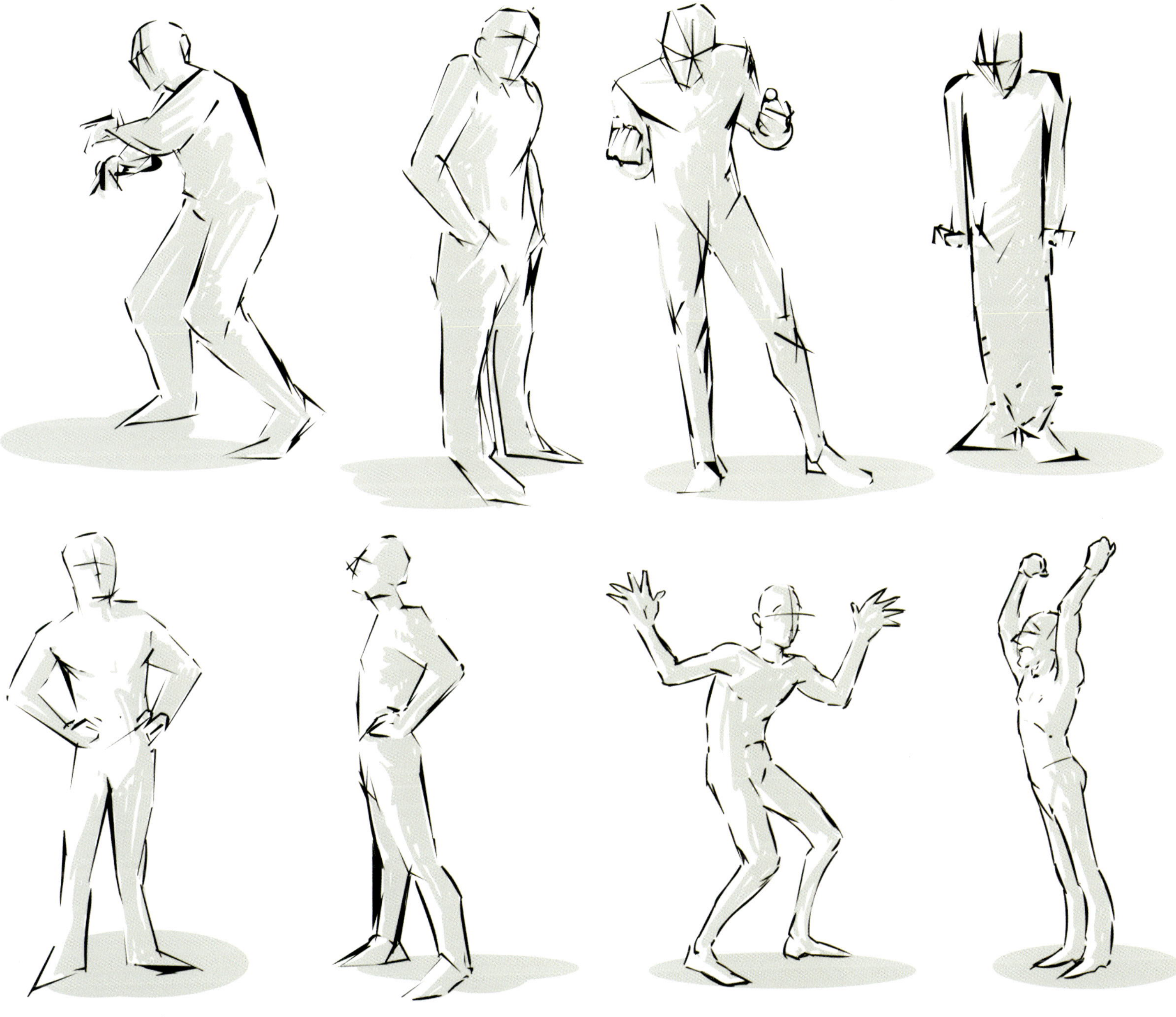

This page:
Body language studies by Neal Von Flue.

CASE STUDY:

JENN MANLEY LEE

Set in a distant future where space travel is commonplace, Jenn Manley Lee's *Dicebox* (www.dicebox.net) follows Molly and Griffen, a pair of itinerant factory workers, as they follow available jobs from planet to planet. Lee began publishing *Dicebox* online in 1999, updating with a new page every week. Currently in the sixth of its projected 36 chapters, the story will eventually span 900 pages, recounting a full year in the lives of its characters. Sophisticated and slow-paced, *Dicebox* is the very definition of character-driven storytelling. The vast majority of Lee's pages are spent exploring the subtle nuances of interpersonal interactions, while crafting a larger picture of culture and society.

MOLLY & GRIFFEN

Visually, the two lead characters are a study in contrasts. Molly: sturdy and voluptuous, dark skin, dark hair often worn in long dreadlocks, usually dressed in practical clothes. Griffen: tall and lanky, short blond hair, ghostly pale skin, given to flashier clothes, most notably her elaborately cut coat. Molly's shape is defined by curves, Griffen's by angles. Readers new to *Dicebox* often mistake Griffen for a somewhat feminine man (a reasonable error, given the recurrent themes of gender ambiguity); readers never make that mistake with Molly. ▸

Far right:
Molly Robbins and Griffen Medea Stoyka are a study in visual contrasts.

Right:
Griffen in her trademark long coat, with a guitar on her back. This is the first time Griffen is seen in full, as she balks at the prospect of a long walk into town, when she and Molly could have stayed on the bus they were already riding.

Left:
Despite pain and profuse bleeding, Molly is reluctant to admit physical distress. Griffen, the less physically sturdy of the pair (note only she wears a hat and sunglasses to protect against the sun's rays), is much more concerned than Molly herself. Salin—a beggar whom Griffen and Molly have been hired to escort—has a direct and calm demeanor, which is often unsettling rather than soothing, especially to Molly. Though he has thus far given no indication of ill intent, he is the only character in *Dicebox* dressed in solid black, emphasizing the discordant note he strikes.

Griffen, a registered troubadour, carries a guitar and a pen-and-ink journal. She is given to dramatic gesture and ostentatious chatter, usually peppered with unnecessary insults; she intentionally irritates nearly everyone she meets. Molly is more restrained, both physically and verbally, providing a stabilizing influence to Griffen's rash and impulsive behavior. She appears to carry no more than she really needs for her travels. Griffen tends to avoid physical exertion and discomfort, while Molly relishes it, never accepting a ride when she can feasibly walk. Given an extra bit of spending money, Griffen prefers to spend it on cushier sleeping arrangements, while Molly happily forgoes a soft bed in favor of higher quality beer.

And yet they share a sense of passion, though they express it differently—Griffen through argument and conversation, Molly through physical exertion. Neither will back down when threatened, nor will either tolerate a threat to the other. Their constant banter, even when one-sided, is affectionate and intimate. Both have their secrets and mysteries (as well as their pseudonyms), kept hidden even from each other, and yet these two women connect on a primal level that they are hard put to explain. ▸

Right:
Body language and simple gestures can be powerful indicators of how characters relate to each other. A simple act such as hair brushing can reveal the intimacy and affection of close friendship. In *Dicebox*, the passage of time is realistically acknowledged through shifts in character appearance; the passing days bring regular changes of clothing and hairstyles.

COLOR SYMBOLISM

The role of color in Lee's artwork and character designs has been profound since *Dicebox's* beginning. The symbolic power of color is particularly important; for instance, Lee associates the color red primarily with blood, especially as a symbol of female energy. As Lee observes in *Webcomics*, "Repeatedly, blood is aligned with women and border places. Death, birth, the river surrounding Faerie, blood on the snow, blood in the shoe. And then there's the whole idea of blood as guilt by association. In other words, you can't trust a woman because they bleed three days a month and don't die of it."

In keeping with this symbolism, Molly and Griffen always wear some piece of red clothing, though Lee does point out "This is a standard I'm setting up so I can break it at an appropriate time."

Color functions as an organizing principle throughout *Dicebox*, not only for character interactions, but for story structure, mood, and pacing. Each character aligns with a particular color, which correlates to particular seasons, elements, and story segments, among other factors. "What this color alignment mostly accomplishes is to give me focus points on my characters and their interactions. It's a structure to build upon or ignore if I wish, but it always gives me a control to base decisions on, and a way to think of the character and their base relation with other characters."

Griffen and Molly, who share both their primary color, red, and secondary color, yellow, along with the aspects of fire and passion, are natural companions. Rande and Grae, another pair of itinerant workers who frequently cross paths with Molly and Griffen, share the colors green and blue, along with aspects of water and spirit, and are similarly matched. Characters sharing only a secondary color—Griffen and Grae or Molly and Rande—tolerate each other, but don't fully connect. And those who share no colors, having perfectly opposite attributes—Griffen and Rande or Molly and Grae—can barely stand to be around each other at all. ■

Right:
Here, a bit of red can be seen in Griffen's shoes, as well as in the lining of her coat.

ON ORGANIZING PRINCIPLES OF DICEBOX

I had surrendered to my fascination with quarters or principles of four in organizing the world … and so split the story of *Dicebox* into four books. Each of these books quickly became associated with a compass point, a season, and an element from the Western set of Earth, Fire, Air, Water. As I found countless examples of color being associated with directions, elements, etc., I was naturally inclined to do the same, especially as color is a good mood setter. Not aligning myself to any particular culture's associations, I spent some time aligning the various aspects to certain quadrants, the placement of any particular aspect dependent on all the others. Fairly quickly, white, blue, yellow, and black were my points on the compass, leaving red and green, which was perfect, as I saw them as colors of the living, of animal and plant, that which exists in all quadrants.

It was only natural that Molly and Griffen were of the red, especially since the element they share is Fire. This left green for Rande and Grae, the other major players in *Dicebox*, which worked perfectly as green is usually the color of blood of the Other and usually positioned as red's partner and/or opposite (stop and go, red and green color blindness, etc.). ■

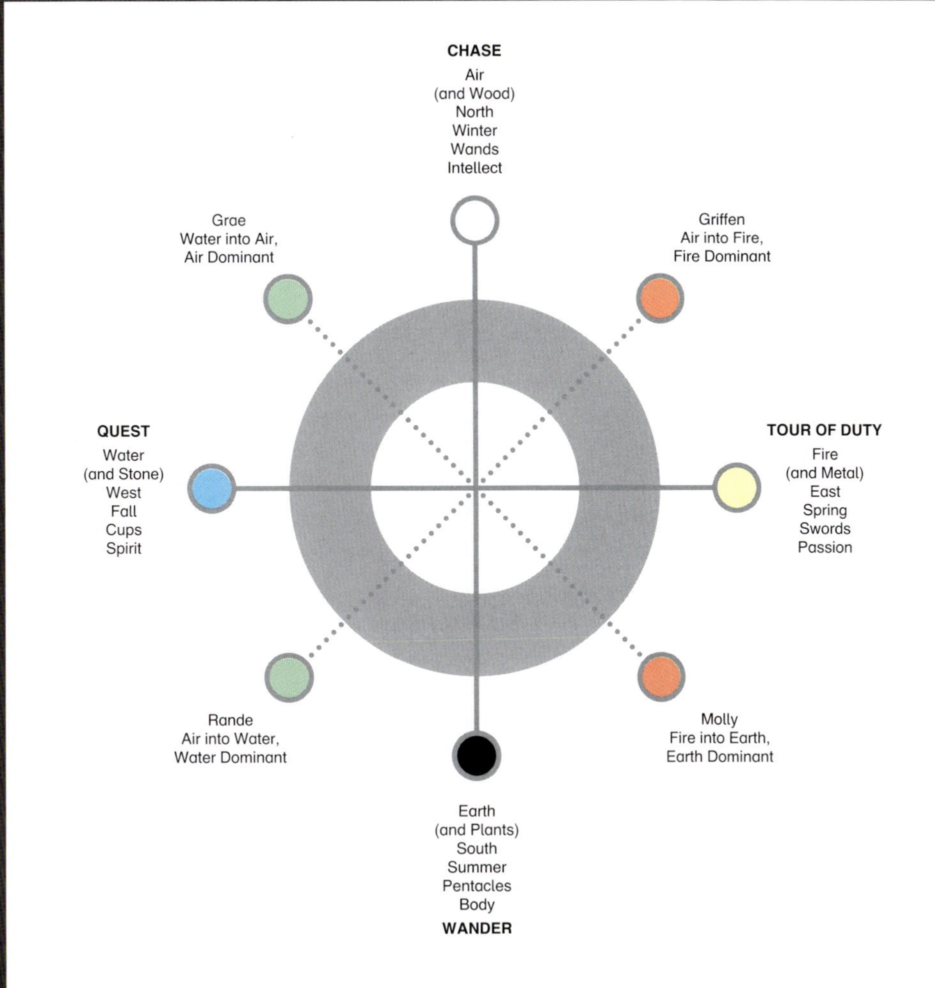

Right:
A simplified version of the chart Manley Lee uses to map relationships, environmental aspects, and personality traits onto her characters. The full chart includes additional aspects (time of day, age of man, etc.) and associations (tastes, humors, etc.).

Right:
Clockwise from top left: Grae, Griffen, Molly, and Rande in a revealing panel that reflects the organization of Lee's color compass. Griffen and Molly in their red clothes are clearly contrasted with Grae and Rande's green, emphasizing the tension between the two pairs of traveling companions.

ON INFLUENCE & INSPIRATION

In my design of characters, I'm influenced by just about everything I encounter: life, my own experience, the life stories and philosophies of family and friends, people on the street (at work, on the bus, etc.), TV shows, advertising art, fine art, illustrations, descriptions of characters in prose, and comics. I can't really point to any particular artist who influences my character designs per se, though I admire and take note of many, either how they write their characters or render their appearance.

All this inspiration goes into clip files—physical, digital, and mental. When the time comes to design a character, I subconsciously draw on mental data I've collected as I rifle through the files.

In terms of art, I often find inspiration in something that looks nothing like my final result. I'm reacting to the art instead of trying to emulate it. For example, my art style could hardly be described as manga, but I'm often inspired by the character designs of manga artists; their approach or the choices they make in capturing a character's essence. I learn a lot by studying their designs that I can then apply to my art, even though my style has nothing in common with theirs. ■

Right:
Griffen, the semiprofessional performer, often wears showier clothes, especially for a night of recreation. Molly, who avoids drawing too much attention to herself, is more likely to wear an unadorned jacket or simple T-shirt. In either case, every item worn is a unique garment, immediately recognizable when worn a second time—a character's choice of clothing is no more generic than body language or facial expressions, giving each a personal style, and a finite wardrobe appropriate to a lifestyle of traveling with all your worldly possessions carried in a backpack. The one exception, again, is Salin, who appears to own only a single outfit, as befits his beggar status.

ON THE DESIGN OF MARY ANNE CATHERINE RAFFERTY XIII (MARE)

All main, recurring characters in *Dicebox* are story archetypes of one sort or another, even if they are only archetypes I acknowledge: the Barkeep, the Fence, the Fool, the Fallen One, the Errant Prince, the Called One, the Spy, etc. Mare is the scout, liaison, or ambassador, the traveler with a purpose not tied to the story, who intersects with it from time to time. She belongs to a clan of Sooners, traveling immigrant workers modeled loosely on the tinkers [itinerants and gypsies] of Ireland.

With just those two aspects, Mare started to form as quick-witted and confident, not necessarily wealthy, but clean, comfortable, and with significant backing. There's a sense of responsibility and a lurking authority that she reports to, while at the same time she has a lot of freedom to make snap decisions and broker her own deals. It seems that people who succeed in this kind of role are friendly, attractive in an approachable way, nonthreatening but not weak. Their word is good but not easily given, and her ultimate loyalty has already been spoken for, however much she might like you.

All of the above were only half-articulated thoughts and intuitions. It was enough to start rapidly forming a visual impression of her: a red-headed Irish Catholic gal, small, and sharp-featured. This is derived from my own life experience of Irish Catholic family and friends, coupled with the Sooners' origins. Red-haired women are typically ascribed certain characteristics that work for Mare: passionate, clever, sexual, and of fiery temperament—Mare certainly is not a calm person. Plus there's the fact that red is Molly and Griffen's color and Mare is their ally, of sorts. ■

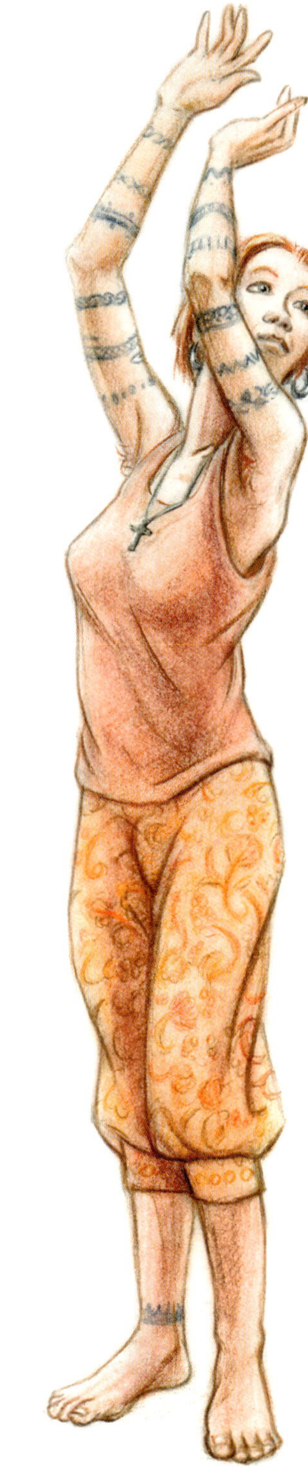

Above:
An early color sketch of Mare. Mare's look is based on a female juggler from Portland, who had red hair and a full beard—hence Mare's sideburns.

Left:
Griffen, Molly, and Mare enjoy a moment of leisure.

CASE STUDY:

BRENDAN CAHILL

Brendan Cahill's online pulpy yet philosophical detective series *Outside the Box* (brendancahill.com) was among the first to blend limited animation with the comics form for the purpose of longer narratives. The story, which first began appearing online in 2002, follows Jamie Black, a disillusioned dotcommer lured into the gritty world of private investigation. The series includes two full-length stories, "Remembering a Door" and "Pieces of Each Other," and a short story (illustrated by John Barber), "One Shot." Cahill is also the writer of Marvel's four-issue *Sable and Fortune* miniseries, a spy/detective adventure, illustrated by John Burns and Laurenn McCubbin.

DRAWING FROM LIFE & PHOTO REFERENCE

In the early stages of creating *Outside the Box*, Cahill was wary of using photo or life reference, thinking of it as "cheating." He has since changed his mind on this point and now uses much more reference. He finds fashion magazines particularly useful, along with Internet research through search engines, online reference sites, and stock photo collections. When using photo reference, though, he's careful not to reproduce the photographer's composition. "What I tend to do now is make reference drawings in my sketchbook based on other peoples' photography so that I can learn how to draw a certain person or thing *without* referencing it from the original photo in the future. Those shots I clearly label with a '[ref.]' in the sketchbook so I know never to make them public. I'm pretty prickly about that."

Cahill occasionally "casts" real-life actors in the roles of his characters, though again, he's cautious to avoid a perfectly faithful rendition. "Rather, I draw my 'actor' multiple times until I understand somewhat intuitively how to draw facial or bodily characteristics I'm looking for. Then I apply those to my character. So you may see me draw someone vaguely resembling Jennifer Garner, but it won't actually be a perfect copy of her." Cahill prints out his reference shots on an inexpensive, high-resolution, black-and-white laser printer, which he says is good for contrast, and tapes them to his drawing board.

TRADITIONAL TOOLS VERSUS DIGITAL DESIGN

While Cahill often uses digital tools for layouts and graphic design, his drawing and sketching process remains completely traditional, saving the digital drawing tablet for touch-ups and special effects. "Putting something on a blank sheet has to happen on the drafting table. Character creation typically involves a lot of start-and-stop, trial-and-error, loose sketches, and mistakes. At this point, a computer is still no good for those things—at least for me. No matter how advanced tablet technology gets, it probably won't ever be as fast or easy as pencil on paper. I like digital tools for creating finished, refined things, not for doodling." ▸

Above top: Jamie and Elizabeth, the lead characters in "Remembering a Door."

Above: Phillip, Adrian, and Big Man, the villains of "Remembering a Door."

Far left:
In Cahill's words Phillip is "Eurotrash gone evil," with his greasy, receding hairline, pencil mustache, and skeletal features.

Above middle:
Says Cahill, "Adrian was intended to look like a bartender in a good Irish pub—working class, but suave, and good-looking in a slightly busted-up way."

Above right:
Big Man is supposed to look "as much like an ogre as a human being can."

Left:
Faith Carlyle, the kidnapping victim in "Remembering a Door," is one of the first finished drawings Cahill did for *Outside the Box*. "You can see I'm still trying to emulate a cartoony look, but it's not really happening."

LIMITED ANIMATION

Cahill uses limited animation created with Macromedia Flash software in *Outside the Box* (*OTB*) primarily to set the pacing. The characters aren't animated, just the panels they appear in. Fades, sliding panels, and other transitional effects give the stories a cinematic flair, but the visual structure stays firmly rooted in the comics form. "It's possible that my initial inclination to make *OTB* more cartoony was due to an unconscious association with the simple look of cel-based [frame by frame] animation: I knew it was going to be Flash-based before I started creating the characters. But if this was the case, even my subconscious quickly learned that the Flash-based animation style was the medium, not the message."

THE IMAGINARY CHARACTER

In "Remembering a Door," the life of Jamie Black, ambitionless office worker, flips upside down when eleven-year-old Elizabeth turns up on his doorstep, claiming to be able to do magic and urging him to follow up on a mysterious phone call.

What drives Elizabeth's design isn't immediately apparent in the story: Elizabeth is a projection of Jamie's psyche, visible only to him. "She represents the child in him, the part of him that believes that anything is possible, that hasn't been killed or curtailed by the realities and compromises of adult life," Cahill says.

A challenge of creating an imaginary character is the need to balance a dual identity. Elizabeth personifies Jamie's repressed desires, yet remains her own character. When Cahill thought about Jamie's leap from an "adult" job to a more fantastic existence, "it seemed natural that his guide would be a child—someone for whom the concept of being a PI and having this exciting, dynamic life seems not only completely possible, but also completely normal."

Elizabeth's visual design followed directly from her role in the story. "She had to be cute and be able to wear a mischievous look convincingly. Thus, the pug nose, big eyes, wide smile, round cheeks. The long, unstyled hair is a definite sign of childhood. Also, her mannerisms are childlike: big, grand gestures, fidgeting, sitting in a chair any way except the way you're supposed to; that look kids are so good at directing to adults that says 'What are you, an idiot?'"

The final detail was Elizabeth's name, an often-overlooked aspect of character design. Cahill liked "Elizabeth" because "it's an old and proper-sounding name, and it has associations with British royalty, which to my mind fits a character who serves as a manifestation of something ancient and eternal about human nature." ■

Left: Says Cahill, "This shot nails down the most important of Jamie's features: floppy hair, slightly upturned nose, green eyes. His mouth is set quite low on his face, giving him less chin and making him look a little bit dorky, but also morosely cool."

Below left & right: Cahill uses physical features, posture, and mannerisms to convey the personality of his characters.

Background: In *Pieces of Each Other*, Cahill updates Jamie's design to reflect his new life as a more experienced PI. "He slicks his hair back and looks buff."

Opposite page: Jamie and Elizabeth's final designs changed little from Cahill's first sketches.

CASE STUDY:

METAPHROG

Left:
Left page: doodles from John (except Clean in red, by Sandra). Right page: sketches from Sandra based on doodles by John (except two inked doodles on newsprint, by John).

Franco-Scottish duo Metaphrog—Sandra Marrs and John Chalmers—began releasing comics and graphic novels in 1996 and have since gained worldwide acclaim for their series of disarmingly shocking and daringly deep *Louis* graphic novels that blur the line between children's literature and avant-garde comics. Generally, Marrs draws and paints the artwork, and Chalmers writes the scripts and creates the lettering.

They now reside in Glasgow, Scotland, and have been nominated for prestigious Ignatz and Eisner Awards in the United States. Metaphrog also published *Louis: Red Letter Day* as a webcomic on www.serializer.net between 2003 and 2004. *Louis: Dreams Never Die* was animated in 2004 (www.metaphrog.com and www.louisandfc.com).

Metaphrog consider the Louis books to be "scary-cute graphic novels for all ages." Louis, an unassuming little worker who lives with his pet bird FC (Formulaic Companion) in Hamlet, a colorful place in which all the houses are alike and fenced off, spends his days doing his duty (filling bottles with air and pumping vegetables), corresponding with an aunt he has never seen (a creation of his wicked neighbors Clean and Jerk) and dreaming of freedom. The stories follow Louis's misadventures and draw grown-ups and children alike into a scary-cute world where the citizens' lives are stifled and their actions more or less controlled by entertainment centers and obscure regulations. Four books are available so far, and Metaphrog is currently working on a fifth book.

"Some characters," Marrs says, "are inspired by real life; that is the case with Clean and Jerk, for example, who were partly based on our friends' small children (one of them had a squarish head, which Clean ended up having too). Jerk was to some extent inspired by Johnny Rotten (even if he doesn't look like him at all), while the postman character was inspired by our former postman (the moustache being the main inherited feature). Real-life characters can be adapted from nature to suit the fantasy-world simplified style of the books. For example, in *Louis: Lying to Clive*, the secondary characters of the worker bees and drones were based on real bees, and schematic drawings derived from bees were the basis for the character designs."

Sometimes, Marrs continues, shapes can trigger a character. For example, the head of The Fly Catcher in Chief in *Louis: Dreams Never Die*, "was discovered on our bathroom wall, where the old plaster was creating a shadowy textured shape." This was modified to look like a cross ▸

between Hitler (for the hair and moustache) and George W. Bush (for the eyes close together). At other times, the characters come from Chalmers, who doodles on papers or magazines, and the pair decide on the best examples.

With the design of Louis, Metaphrog wanted a "universal appeal." Marrs says Louis started out as a little mole-like character (because he cannot really see what is going on around him), with dungarees to show he is a worker. "He was supposed to be quite cute, and to be instantly likeable. Of course, the character evolved over time, becoming more childlike," says Marrs. Although Louis was not inspired by anything or anybody in particular, a source of inspiration was toddlers and small children, whose attributes Louis has increasingly been adopting. The works of creators like Hergé, Moebius, and Bill Watterson have also influenced the designs.

"Sometimes an interesting notion, a peculiar word or combination of words, can also suggest ideas for a character; using a fat dictionary to find words randomly is a process akin to serendipity," Chalmers says. The precise attributes of any character are then adjusted in accordance with the story's requirements. Some characters are deliberately satirical; others are more fully developed or rounded. ▸

Above top:
The development of the Louis character in sketches, from 1999 to 2006.

Above:
The evolution of Louis from *Red Letter Day* (2000) to *Dreams Never Die* (2004).

This page:
Study for secondary characters from *Louis: Lying to Clive* (2001), showing how the worker and drone characters were based on schematic drawings of worker bees and drone bees.

Some characters, Marrs says, are designed specifically to suit a personality when, in the script, Chalmers comes up with characters to inhabit the story, and sometimes it's the other way around. "But the best is when the designs come naturally, and when we can match a design with a personality we wanted to use."

Usually a character is sketched out in advance. Marrs never draws a character for the first time on the final page because the drawings for the Louis books are more drafted than immediate, and they are going to be painted and then inked. "There is no margin for error," she says, "it's all got to be quite precise. But in the layout stage, I can experiment and try more immediate drawings and look for shapes as they come out, and this is when a character design might change from its initial shape in the original sketch. It's important to keep a certain spontaneity."

The coloring process is much more spontaneous, Marrs says. The color schemes for character designs are decided on the final page (although sometimes also during the sketching process), in terms of personality of the character. The Fly Catcher in Chief, for instance, whose skin was left uncolored to give him a ghoulish aspect and also because he is leading a Ku Klux Klan-type troop, was designed in relation to the other colors on the page, the mood of the scene, and the scenes that precede it.

"Often characters must carry certain attributes, or perform necessary actions, which may be open to interpretation in order for the plot to function dynamically," Chalmers says. "Both actions and appearances can amplify character traits in a graphic novel or comic."

The question of "when to stop" designing, Marrs points out, applies to all stages of the creative process. "It's very much like walking in the dark. You simply don't know what will come next. I guess the answer is to stop when you are satisfied. Conversely, you should never truly stop, as a character will always evolve in some way, however minutely, over a long period of time, perhaps even years. You have a solid character if he or she manages to make all the personality traits they are supposed to have come across to the reader, and also if it looks graphically interesting enough, and has a real presence. In our case with the *Louis* books, the character ▸

Left & below:
The military gear was designed to match that of the Fly Catcher in Chief.

Left & below:
Process for designing the Fly Catchers in *Louis: Dreams Never Die* (2004). From the script, the characters were placed in the layout as arbitrary shapes, which brought about the idea of the conical-hooded heads.

Above top: Pages 10 and 11 from *Louis: Dreams Never Die.*

Above: Pages 24 and 25 from *Louis: Dreams Never Die.*

Left:
Clean and Jerk scheming with the postman on page 35 of *Louis: Dreams Never Die* (2004). Compare with the earlier image on page 65.

design has to express as much as possible with as few lines as possible. While the main attributes of a character will stay unchanged, details might evolve over time, such as Louis's posture becoming increasingly childlike, or camp in later books, or Jerk's eyebrows being removed altogether to simplify the design." It isn't always easy, Marrs notes, to know when you have finished the character, but "usually if you don't quite have it, you are left with a nagging feeling, and that's when you know there is more work to be done. Sometimes a character will come out in one attempt with no changes to be made at all; sometimes it requires a bit more searching."

In terms of writing, Chalmers sees the evolution and development of characters as integral to the story-telling itself, and seeing characters come alive on the page can be inspiring. "There is certainly a link between drawing and writing even before the final version sees the page," he says. "In general, we try and allow room for the reader to inhabit or interpret the characters and their actions, leaving space for both empathy and ambiguity." ■

TOTIVS
Sles wyck
Kappeln
SINUS
Oldenborg
Wagria

SECTION VI

THE EXPANDED CAST

Most often, the pages of a graphic novel are populated with a host of characters filling large and small roles, from the larger-than-life hero down to the anonymous passers-by on the street. Ultimately, all of these characters must function together as part of a single narrative logic. The degree of planning demanded by individual characters may vary, but every character who affects the course of the story requires attention. In this section, we will discuss ensemble storytelling, and the methods for managing many characters at once. The four case studies in this section present creators who have successfully incorporated large casts into cohesive stories, without compromising the depth of their character design. ■

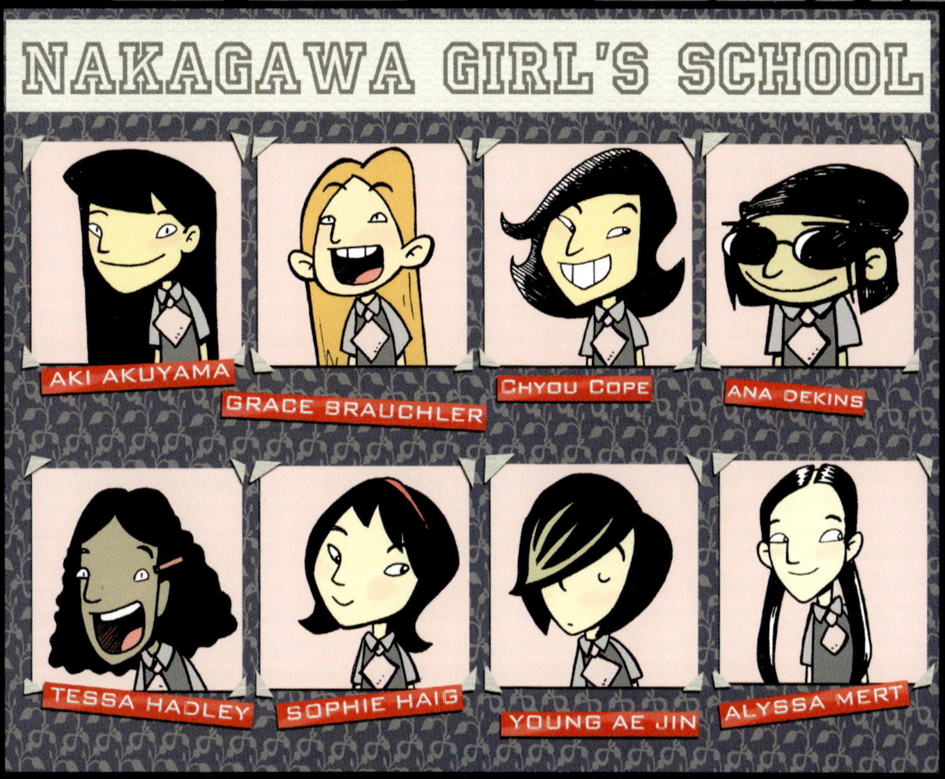

Above & right: Aki Akuyama and her classmates, from *Aki Alliance* by Ryan Estrada. These class photos function like a table of contents for the story, as Aki must "conquer" each girl in her class by winning her friendship. (For more information about Estrada, see pages 170–173.)

GROUP IDENTITY & STORYTELLING

ENSEMBLE CASTS

Not every story has a central character. Some stories feature an ensemble cast, wherein several characters play equal roles in bringing the story to its conclusion. Multiple points of view are often represented, and no character's perceptions dominate the narrative. In such stories, the primary characters must all be unified in some way—in purpose or in theme—so that they are all tied to the core of the story as well as to each other.

Not all large casts are ensembles; ensembles are defined not by the number of characters involved, but by a sense of group identification. If the reader identifies with a single character above all others, then the story is not an ensemble, no matter how many secondary characters with prominent subplots are involved. The true ensemble story asks readers to identify with multiple characters, sometimes simultaneously, with each point of view receiving equal or near-equal value. This diffusion of perspective can be achieved in two ways. First, an author maintains objective distance from all characters, relating events without direct access to any character's thoughts or emotions, as Scott Morse does in his sci-fi epic, *Soulwind* (Oni Press, 1997–2001). Second, the author allows the reader direct access to multiple characters' psyches, allowing common events to be reframed by each perspective, as Alan Moore and Dave Gibbons do in *Watchmen* (DC Comics; 1986–1987). *Watchmen* presents an especially intricate and orchestrated use of the ensemble cast. The primary cast is united in a common goal (the hunt for The Comedian's killer), but this goal is secondary to the exploration of the cast itself, examining their shared histories, the evolution of their relationships, and most importantly, the ethics behind their unique approaches to vigilante justice.

Group identity can take various forms: a family, a circle of friends, or a superhero or sports team. The characters need not all share common goals; Eric Shanower's *Age of Bronze*, for instance, follows entire armies of characters whose aims are in direct and indirect conflict (see pages 48–53). Neither the Achaeans nor the Trojans are given preferential treatment in terms of narrative focus.

Characters need not even be in close proximity; they may be part of a multigenerational epic, or they may each be ensconced in their own more or less independent stories that may (or in rare cases may not) be brought together by the story's conclusion. In *Soulwind* the stories of Nick, Sophie, Weaver, Cernunnos, and others are divided across time and galaxies, but all contribute to the climactic event in their own ways. In stories like this, discovering the hidden connections between the characters and their stories is a major part of the payoff.

A well-constructed ensemble story gives a clear sense of each character's function or purpose in the story and a sense of group identity. After all, it's not that an ensemble cast has no lead character—it's that it has multiple characters who lead the story in tandem. One character's personal crisis and climax do not define the story's resolution; rather, the story is resolved in aggregate, with each character emerging as pivotal to the greater change the story brings about.

REPERTORY CASTS

The ensemble isn't the only narrative structure that makes use of group identity. A similar form is the repertory cast, wherein a series of linked stories draw from a common pool of characters. Busiek, Anderson, and Ross's *Astro City* (1995) (see pages 120–125) is a prime example of this form. Samaritan or Winged Victory might be the star of one story and serve as the backdrop in the next, such that it is the city itself that emerges as the one constant that ties all the stories together. ■

Opposite page: Alex Robinson's *Box Office Poison* (Top Shelf Productions, 2001) features a large ensemble cast. Pictured here are just a few of the book's many characters.

BOX OFFICE
POISON

CASE STUDY:

JASON LITTLE

Jason Little was awarded a Xeric grant in 1998 for his self-published *Jack's Luck Runs Out*, a story of crime and gambling in Las Vegas, featuring characters inspired by classic playing-card designs. Little's more recent work, the *Bee Comix* series, offers high-energy mysteries, which Little describes as "bubblegum noir." *Shutterbug Follies*, the first Bee story, was initially published in installments online, before being collected by Doubleday in 2002. Bee's second adventure, *The Motel Art Improvement Service*, is scheduled for print publication by Little, Brown & Company, in 2007. (More of Little's work can be found at Little's website, Beekeeper Cartoon Amusements; http://www.beecomix.com/.)

In *Shutterbug Follies*, Bee is employed as a photo-finishing technician, a job she enjoys particularly for the view it allows her into the secret lives of her customers. Her natural inquisitiveness leads her inevitably into adventure and mystery when a new customer brings in a roll of particularly brutal photographs.

Little is very aware of the influences contributing to his design. "My Bee characters are mostly informed by Hergé's *Tintin* characters. The degree of simplification, the absence of tone and solid blacks are all of a piece with Hergé's style. Though there is a hefty dose of Daniel Clowes' [*Ghost World*] cute girl sensibility in there as well. I tried to bury that in Hergé since ▸

Left:
Unlike most comic-book heroines, Bee has a realistic physique, with broad hips and a generous bottom. She's attractive, but not in keeping with the mainstream ideal. "Bee's shape was a very deliberate decision. While there are a few nice female characters with big butts in alternative comics, relatively speaking there are few role models for young women in the media in general that are anything other than skinny. It's okay to have a big butt, or to be fat. In fact, it's nice."

Right:
In her latest story, Bee has set out to bike across the United States, but her travels are rudely interrupted when she is harassed by a car full of frat boys on a road trip of their own. The resulting destruction of her bicycle leaves her stranded at the Pine Inn.

everyone and his brother is influenced by Clowes these days. Also, in the bulk of *Shutterbug Follies* the characters have an art nouveau–style heavy outline, which came from Winsor McCay [*Little Nemo in Slumberland*], but which, particularly combined with the influence of Hergé's flat color, makes my stuff look heavily influenced by Chris Ware [*Jimmy Corrigan: The Smartest Kid on Earth*], who is also being imitated by hoards of cartoonists these days. So I'm trying to shake off the art nouveau outline in favor of a more varied line these days. I'm also trying to make my inking a little less cold lately (cold meaning super-clean, almost dead lines like Hergé and Ware) and warm it up with a little texture and dry brush (inspired mostly by children's books, like those by H.A. Rey and Robert McCloskey)." ■

Above:
Cyrus, lanky and mysterious, is an employee of the Pine Inn and a secretive painter. He "improves" the hotel's existing artwork by adding his own subversive imagery. In exchange for his efforts, he steals small doses of guests' medications.

Left:
The stylistic design of the title character from *Jack's Luck Runs Out* immediately conjures the spirit of Las Vegas casino life, where you live or die by the luck of the draw.

Above:
While Huey admires Bee's photography, Bee's attention is all on Huey. Bee's interest is made evident through body language—not a word is needed. Huey's obliviousness is equally evident.

Above:
Alice, "a dour, studious Korean lesbian," and Hector, a screw-up, have plans to sell a huge bag of home-made ecstasy to the villain, Private Rick Johnson.

CASE STUDY:

DYLAN MECONIS

Above:
Character profiles from the online graphic novel *Bite Me!*.

Dylan Meconis first made a name for herself with the online graphic novel, *Bite Me!*, a vampire comedy she describes as "Anne Rice by way of Looney Tunes." She is now self-publishing *Family Man*, a historical drama following the early life of one of the characters from *Bite Me!*, while working on *Self Portrait as Somebody Else*, "a strange autobiographical piece about my childhood and Greek mythology." *Bite Me!* and *Family Man* can be found at http://projectkooky.com/dylan/.

Dylan Meconis is clearly devoted to the concept of *character*. "I really enjoy the character design process, but not just for the purpose of visual design play. I started drawing because I had characters in my head, and I wanted to make them come alive any way I could. Drawing them gave them a whole new level of reality. The rest is great fun, but the joy is derived from bringing a person out of the paper."

In *Bite Me!*, each character initially seems to be a caricature of familiar vampire clichés, though ultimately it is the characters' complete inability to live up to those caricatures that makes them endearing and memorable.

In *Family Man*, Meconis blends nuance and minute movements with notes of amplification and exaggeration. Early in the story, she captures the intimacy of a family at home, defining her characters by interaction as much as by individual identity. These initial exchanges make clear that this is to be a story defined more by the personalities of its inhabitants than by sequence of events.

RESEARCH & AUTHENTICITY

While *Bite Me!* parodied existing period clichés, *Family Man* is more concerned with presenting a reasonably accurate picture of people living in the eighteenth century, necessitating a fair amount of research into the period. She has focused on such topics as the history of family life in the lands that would become Germany; the history of the university as a social institution; ▸

Above:
In *Family Man*, Meconis blends subtle nuance and minute movements with notes of amplification and exaggeration to create characters who are as striking for their familiarity as for their richness.

and religious and secular philosophy, a particularly important point, as the philosophies of each character provide much of the story's conflict.

In the area of visual research, she has studied period wardrobe, although this research presented some challenges. "It's quite easy to find out how the high and mighty befrocked themselves, because who *wouldn't* be interested in a woman with a sailing ship balanced on her hair, but it's much trickier to get a sense of real clothing for the middle and lower classes."

More difficult than maintaining visual authenticity is how to address the nonvisual aspects of period character design. Capturing the dialogue, the personal values and concerns, the complex social interactions, and other such nuances of character can be taxing. Sometimes, Meconis says, it's better to capture the spirit than the letter of the time period in question.

"Nobody writing in the twenty-first century could ever really recreate an eighteenth-century mind," argues Meconis. "I try to avoid certain phrases and behaviors that are obviously modern, and add some quaint inflections (without layering on romance-novel faux-historic jibber). And I give characters simplified versions of interests and behaviors that I've found actual evidence for. But the only way it works is to admit that these people would be very unusual for their time. So I've just embraced that by making Luther and his family (and the other upcoming characters) intentionally atypical, bordering on scandalous. This makes it relatable for a modern audience, and adds a zest of conflict." ▸

Characters

For every yang there is a yin, and for every fruity French vampire, there is a sarcastic Bavarian werewolf.

Most people come to Paris for the museums and the cuisine; Luther comes to make sure Lucien hasn't jumped off a bridge yet.

Plus, why spend an evening at the Opera when you can just take in the free street theater that is the Children of the Night?

Besides, *none* of them have fleas.

Occupation: *Skeptic*
Disposition: *Amused*

Luther

PROCESS & METHOD

Meconis does not belabor the visual development of a character; she uses no model sheets, turnarounds, or other such tools, and only sketches a character three to five times before dropping them into the story. When she feels a character bears a strong resemblance to an actor, she will use photos or film stills as a reference, though only in very early sketches. Her primary reference is her mental image of the characters, combined with existing drawings within the story itself.

Despite keeping her early process brief, she is concerned with the small details of character design, and has a particular fondness for the symbolic value of design elements. "Shapes, features, tones, and colors need to be significant to the character's personality or background. If two characters share visual elements, they'll share the related character elements, too."

Her attention to color symbolism is surprising given that her comics make very limited use of color—*Bite Me!* is simply black and white, while *Family Man* adds only green tones. But, as she points out, "Just because Hollywood filmed in black and white for the first half of the twentieth century doesn't mean the costume designers dressed stars according to their on-camera value. An actress will behave differently in a red dress than a blue one, if it responds to her character somehow. And likewise, for me, it's very important for getting a grip on the character. Additionally, you're always going to end up producing promotional or cover art that uses full color, so the audience is going to internalize that a little when reading the material. In a practical sense, knowing character colors also helps when assigning black-and-white (or green-tinted) values on the page." ▸

Left:
A character profile from online graphic novel *Bite Me!*.

DESIGNING & DEVELOPING LUTHER & FAMILY

While creating *Bite Me!*, Meconis decided to create a separate story using Luther, a German werewolf made to contrast with the French vampire characters, “who all had dark, severe designs with lots of sharp points and steep curves. So I made him shortish, stocky, rumpled, casually dressed, and cast him entirely in warm grays, with shapes that were organic rather than dramatic.” She added “a big trumpet of a nose to give him a wolfish snout that would contrast with the slender vampire noses.” For *Family Man*, she removed some of the “cartooniness” and made him about 20 years younger, before he becomes a werewolf. “Now, instead of being an animal symbol, the nose ties in with some of his problems about being identifiably half-Jewish,” says Meconis. “Nobody outside of the family has such an exaggerated feature in their design, so it’s a very easy way of having an immediately distinctive protagonist while still acknowledging how odd the feature is.”

As a young man, Luther’s body language is introverted, a little tired, and defensive. “In *Bite Me!*, Luther is still a bit exasperated, but he has elements of sly wolfishness mixed in—long nails, a toothy smirk, wisps of hair, and occasional pieces of transformation that alter his hair and eyes to be darker and wilder. In *Family Man*, he’s not yet acquired those elements, so he’s less physically self-assured, and his design has fewer lupine tip-offs.”

Adding to the design challenge is the early revelation that Luther has a twin brother, Johann. “Johann is a much more gregarious, self-assured character than Luther. To show this difference but to keep them similar, I took Luther’s design and tweaked it to be taller and jauntier, with a more feminine jaw, longer sideburns, and smokier eyes.”

Also connected, Meconis says, are the designs of the parents, whom she had to “retroactively design” to show where their children’s features came from, while still explaining the parents’ characters. ■

Left: Luther and his twin brother Johann are distinguished by visual tags, such as Johann’s sideburns and stubble, as well as by differences in body language and speech mannerisms.

Above left: For *Family Man*, Meconis had to redesign her existing character, Luther, as a much younger man. She accounted for both the physical and emotional effects of ageing.

CASE STUDY:

BUSIEK, ANDERSON & ROSS

Though many have argued against their inclusion in graphic novels, superheroes are wonderfully variable and viable metaphors that still have great potential in graphic storytelling. Just ask Kurt Busiek, Brent Anderson, and Alex Ross, who are unabashedly serious about the art of superhero design—a demanding (and in-demand) genre because of the core audience's near-encyclopedic knowledge of character continuity and the continual costume revamps and secret-origin relaunches.

Kurt Busiek's *Astro City* is a comic-book series written by Busiek and co-created by illustrator/designer Brent Anderson and cover artist/designer Alex Ross. First published by Image Comics in August 1995, the series is now published by Homage Comics (part of the Wildstorm imprint of DC Comics). In *Astro City*, superheroes have existed for more than a century, yet the ordinary citizens throughout each era of the city's history are as important in the anthologized stories as the high-flying heroes and villains.

Writing *Astro City*, Busiek says, differs from much of his other superhero comics work in that the series tells "how-does-it-feel" internal narratives rather than "what-happens-next" adventures. Instead of asking what if superheroes were real, the stories ask: What if we were there. What if there were a place like that?

The characters in *Astro City*—a series of short stories taking place in a shared setting, building up a portrait of a fictional place—form a "repertory group," Busiek says, rather than an ensemble cast. Each of the heroes and villains is rooted in archetype. "Archetype doesn't mean using Superman but with a different name, though. Samaritan [*Astro City's* central hero] and Superman share underlying archetypes: both fall into the role of the savior character, the person who has lost a world and seeks to save another, like Moses leading the Israelites to the promised land. Whether you're dealing with a manly superhero with a foppish secret identity, a trickster character, a scholar, whatever—the archetype is the pattern underneath. Characters aren't themselves archetypes, but any character has one or more archetypes underlying them," says Busiek.

The creative process varies from character to character, but all three creators are integral members—Busiek sometimes contributes basic sketches, while Ross and Anderson often contribute story and character ideas. There is often a great deal of back-and-forth by phone and e-mail among the three. Here are some details about the design of two characters: Samaritan and the armored hero N-Forcer.

SAMARITAN

Despite the fact that Samaritan is the figurehead superhero in *Astro City*, in its 10-year lifespan he's been the lead character in only a few stories. Busiek started with the concept of the "flying hero ... the experience of flight ... a superhero having flying dreams because he doesn't have time to enjoy it during the day because he's so busy. He's almost a monastic superhero with a religious calling."

A character's design often begins with deciding on a name. "The design evolves on the simplicity of what the name suggests," says Alex Ross. Busiek chose Samaritan, based on Jesus' parable of The Good Samaritan, from a list of possible names suggested by Ross. ▸

Above:
Sketches of various characters for *Astro City*, including Winged Victory, by Alex Ross.

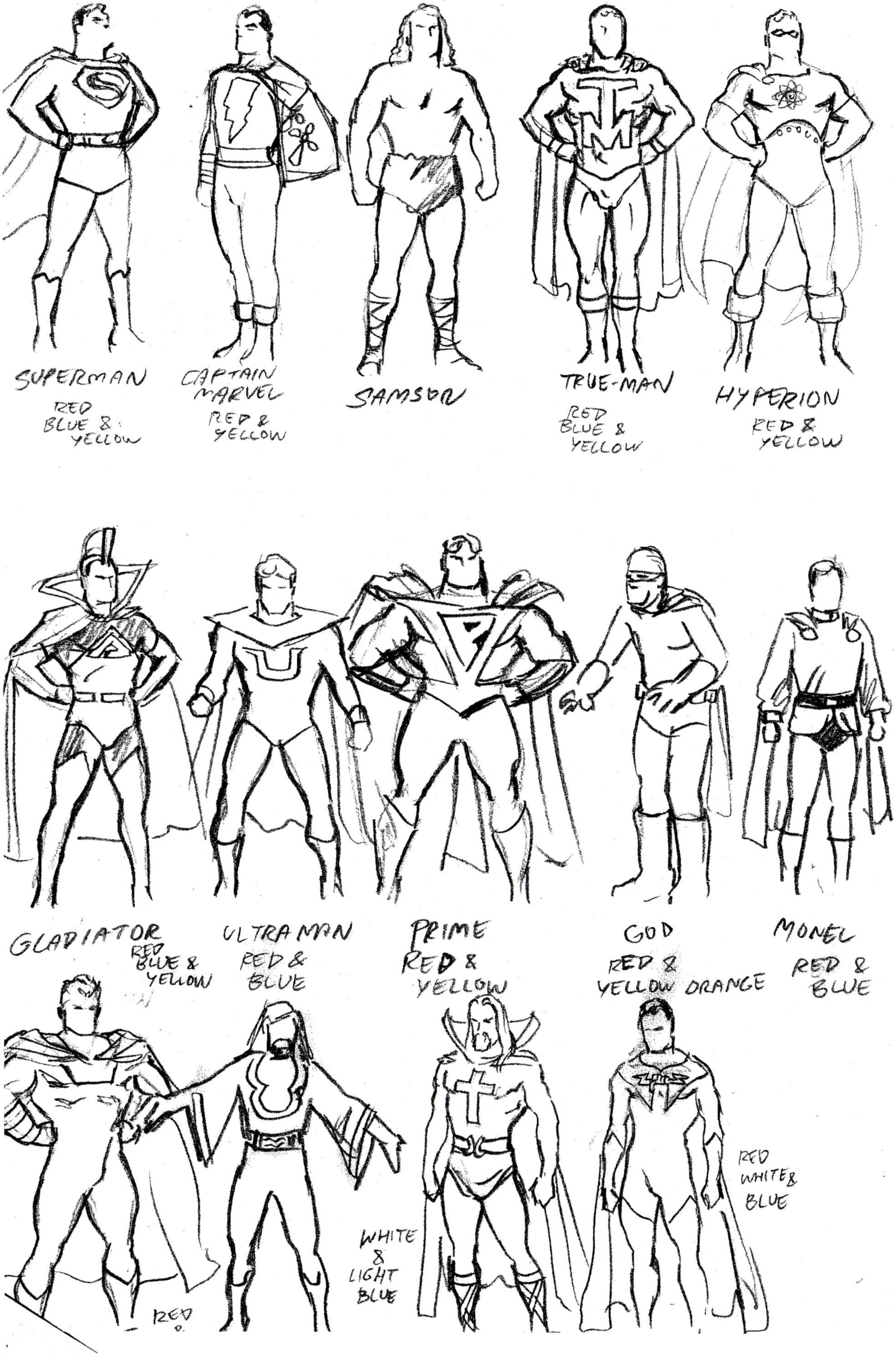

Left:
Ross studied many incarnations of the Superman model to reach Samaritan's final design.

For Samaritan, the first character designed for *Astro City* (about 1994), Ross wanted a design that could have existed in the 1930s; nothing exceedingly modern, but not overly dated. To accomplish this, Ross engaged in what he calls an "archeological study," comparing the original illustrations of classic characters such as Flash Gordon and Buck Rogers, then moving on to later versions. His finished design should correspond to his biggest influence, usually a hybrid of the original character and subsequent interpretations by other artists.

Ross's key inspiration for Samaritan was to ask himself what Jesus might look like as a superhero. "You don't want that to be overt; you want it to be very, very subtle," he says. "You try to find what the core influences are on a character, to study if it's coming from another form of art, or from other cultures. If you can find inspiration from outside of the comics world, it can widen the reader's perception."

Ross studied Renaissance, classical paintings of Christ and borrowed an element consistent across a vast majority of paintings: a red tunic with blue sash. He then took the challenge of making the Superman archetype subtly different, incorporating minor costume variations and reversing Superman's signature colors. He drew a series of 14 sketch shots of superhero archetypes. Samaritan's ceremonial, almost Romanesque cape going over one shoulder—a simplified, abstracted toga evoking the Biblical era—is reminiscent of the classic heroes Captain Marvel or Hyperion, Ross says.

For Samaritan's bodysuit, Ross was influenced by the original Human Torch, the classic Marvel Comics character. A very basic red bodysuit with very little detailing to it; a one-piece with a cuff overlap on wrists and ankles; it gives a streamlined appearance without it looking like one large stocking; it has a looseness to the material; more heft than spandex, ▶

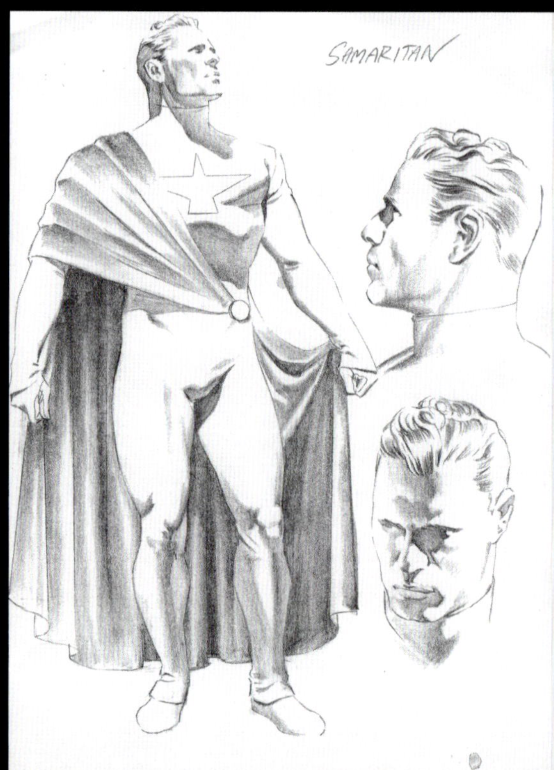

This page: Various Samaritan sketches by Alex Ross, culminating in a full-color illustration.

Opposite page: Samaritan, in his full-color glory, strikes a heroic pose.

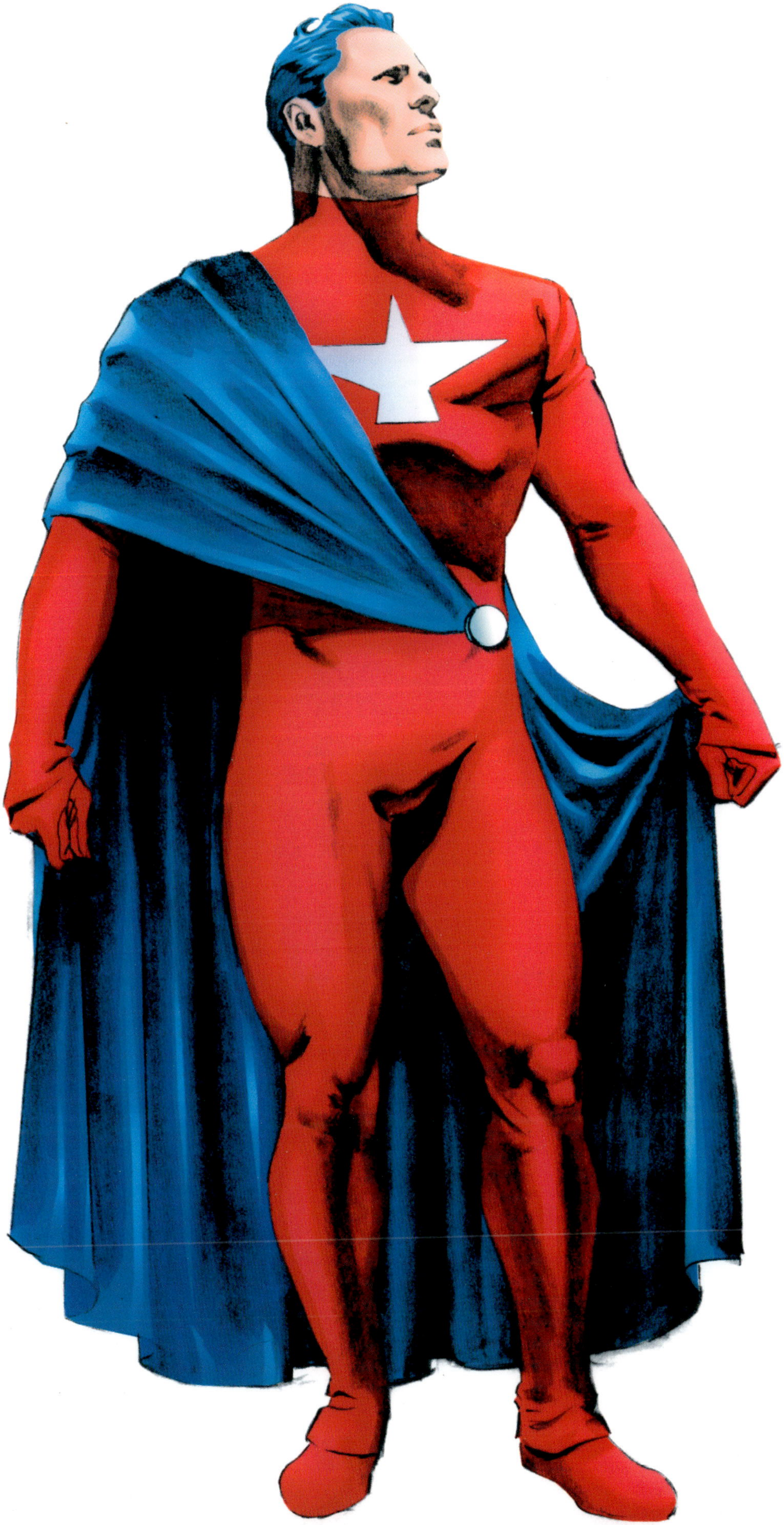

with a high collar; it is ever so slightly different from Superman archetypes, corresponding to Jerry Siegel and Joe Shuster's original version.

Ross used a friend as a model. Samaritan's facial features are distinctly, though not exaggeratedly, Semitic, "a subtle variation on what you'd think of as the idealized version, with a small curve to the nose and slightly fuller lips. It's just a shade off what could be considered an 'ideal' Caucasian face."

Brent Anderson, says Ross, is a perfect draftsman for this. "He saw every one of those details and used them to full effect. The hairstyle is simplified and short, with nothing to hint at Jesus—just Buster Crabbe's hairstyle from the original Flash Gordon serials. We used short, short sides of the hair, with a mass of curls somewhat matted down on top of the head." Ross intended for the character to have brown hair, but Busiek suggested blue hair as a nod to a character in Robert Mayer's *Superfolks* novel (1977).

For Ross, the touchstone of the design is the chest emblem. It is meant to be something a reader can identify instantly. Borrowing from graphic design and Alex Raymond's Flash Gordon, Ross chose an arrangement of triangles: three triangles pointing together to form a white dove, the Holy Spirit, the Trinity. "Combining the triangles in one way looked like a simplified bird shape but also like a star," Ross says. "This to me ended up being the simplest form of the graphic. Most think it's an abbreviated star symbol; but it's the image of a dove. Gold. White stands out to communicate one idea ... coming together in a harmonious, timeless emblem." ▸

Below left:
Kurt Busiek's initial sketch and notes for N-Forcer.

Below:
Alex Ross' "streamlined design," based on Anderson's rendition of the character.

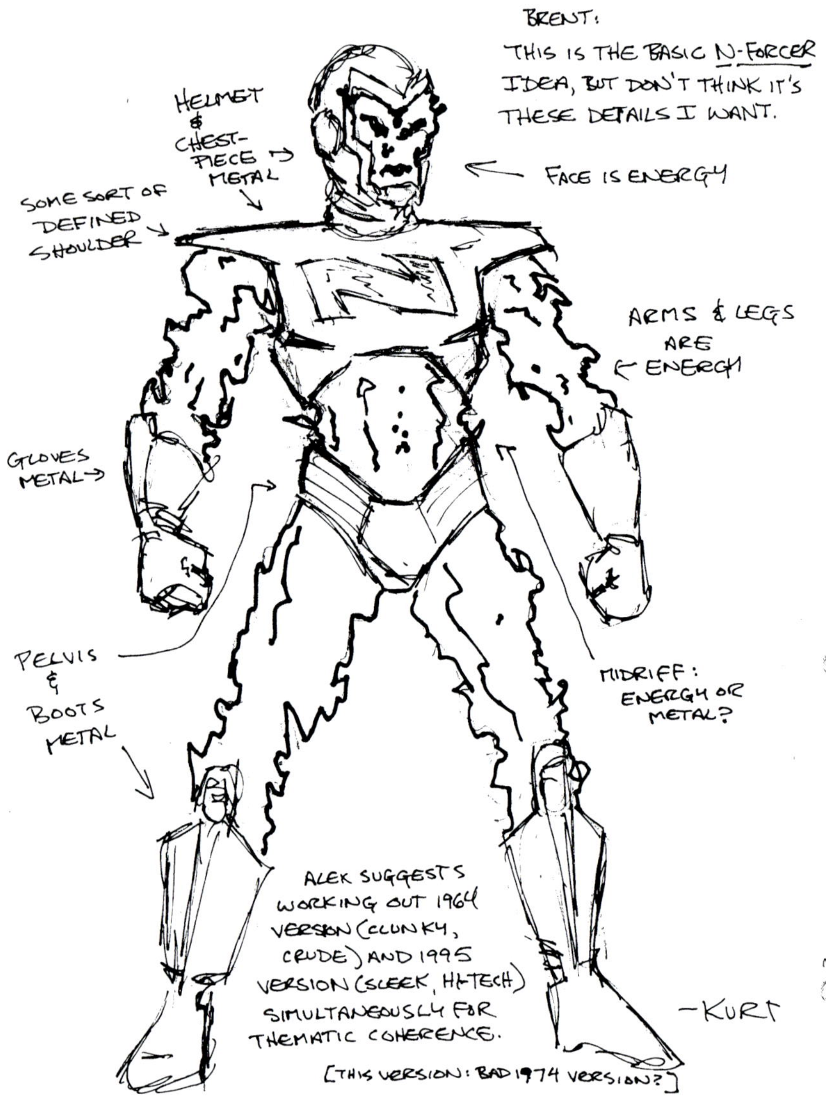

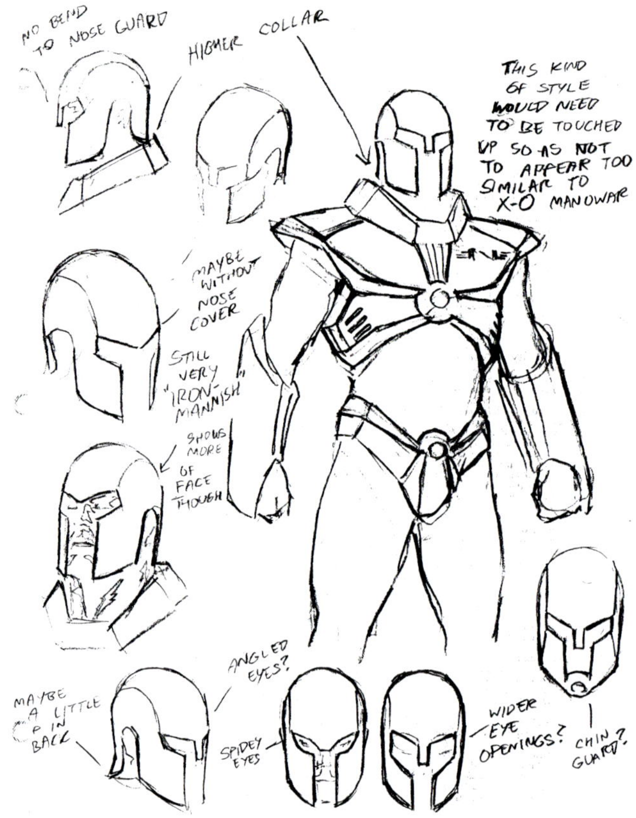

Most artists don't overthink such things, Ross says, but for him each design is a great process of trial and error. "Finding a variation on such a well-known model ... I had to discover it through study, through the application of different ideas."

Painting his characters in gouache, Ross says, is mostly the same process as working in pen-and-ink. However, "Because you have no limit to what you can render, in terms of life, shadow, and depth, anything can go wrong." This leads him to put more research and study into the designs. He draws fairly tight thumbnail sketches as guides for the final illustration. He puts together an extensive reference library of photos of live models, toys, etc., to get a close sense of lighting, detail, and color impacts. "My greatest concern," Ross says, "is that what I pump out artistically pulls from a very limited source: the substance of my memory."

N-FORCER

Anderson and Ross collaborated on Busiek's basic design of N-Forcer, a character who, Ross admits, is "not a particularly focused character... he's a combination of armor and energy," who shares an underlying archetype with Marvel's Iron Man. According to Busiek, N-Forcer has not been fleshed out in the comics yet, but he knows a lot about him that hasn't been revealed. "He's a corporate-backed hero, a trademark of his company, but there's a lot going on inside that shell."

Interestingly, Ross was a little at odds with Anderson's design concept. He felt there was "too much sophisticated structure and geometry with the shape of Brent's design. I would have turned the body into an illuminated structure. I was pushing more for the helmet to have a simplified ancient Spartan look ... already basic in design but pushing that a little more." In the end, he simply streamlined some of Anderson's lines for the "modern" version of the character.

Says Anderson, "I try to capture the feel of the character when I'm designing, and in doing so, inspiration can come from just about anywhere." He strives to convey a powerful feeling to the reader through his drawing, and to elicit an equally powerful emotional response. He draws from models and life when he can, but mostly resorts to photo reference from his extensive "swipe file" or "reference morgue," or, more likely these days, images taken from an Internet image search.

"An intriguing visual design can inspire an interesting character trait," says Anderson. "On the other hand, if I start with a well-thought-out character, many more visual ideas present themselves for consideration than the other way round. But then, I'm a visual person. I often think in a viscerally visual rather than a thematic way when creating a character design. I never draw a 'cool picture' and then try to create a character around it." ■

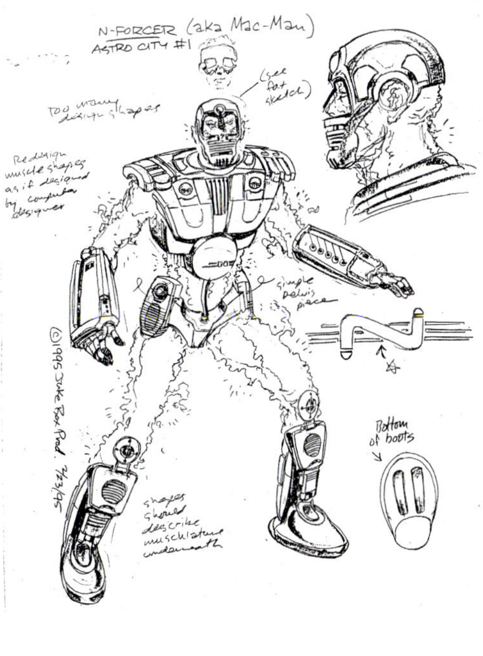

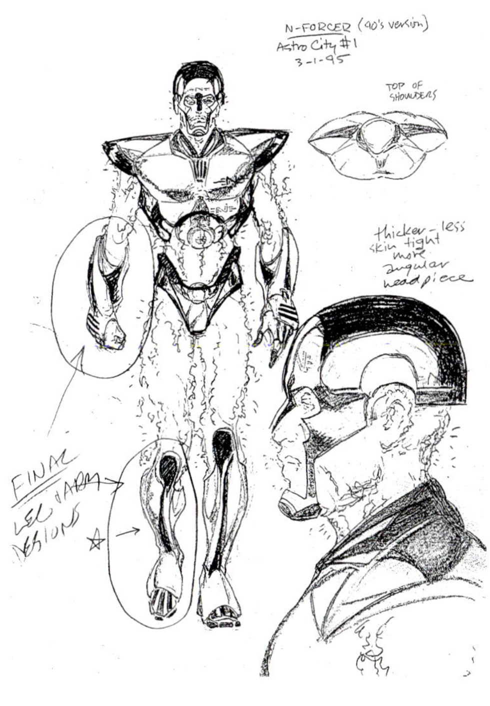

This page:
Four decades of N-Forcer design: 1950s, 1970s, 1980s, and 1990s.

CASE STUDY:

STAN SAKAI

Born in Kyoto, Japan, Stan Sakai (www.usagiyojimbo.com) grew up in Hawaii and now lives in California. He received a fine arts degree from the University of Hawaii and furthered his studies at Art Center College of Design in Pasadena, California. His most popular character, Usagi Yojimbo, was inspired by Japanese history and fiction, and based loosely on the life of Miyamoto Musashi, a samurai who lived in Japan at the turn of the seventeenth century. Usagi's stories, which feature many dozens of recurring and new characters, have evolved from simple "funny animal" parodies to a gripping, multilayered graphic masterpiece. Sakai, who is also the letterer of the *Spider-Man* Sunday newspaper strips and Sergio Aragonés and Mark Evanier's *Groo the Wanderer*, continues to influence graphic novelists worldwide and notes as his own major influences Steve Ditko, Sergio Aragonés, Milo Manara, Moebius, Jack Kirby, Bill Stout, Walt Kelly, Carl Barks, and Akira Kurosawa.

For Sakai, expressiveness and functionality are more important than originality and novelty. He has created wildly novel characters, but he feels that often they do not fit in the *Usagi Yojimbo* universe.

His creation of a new character happens in two ways. He might have a story written out with a new character, and has to come up with a design to match their personality or actions. Or he may create an appealing character design while sketching and then write a story around it. Sakai's most popular villain, Jei, the demonic spearman, started life as a quick drawing in one of his sketchbooks. Months later he wrote a story around that sketch.

Sakai says the more incidental the character, the more generic he or she is. He doesn't like the background people to be too prominent, and spends much more time developing the visuals for a new major character, because he wants to make the character memorable or sympathetic. For the most part, the species of a character is not an issue. Many times, he just chooses the kind of animal that looks good or fits well in the story, though in the past he has used a particular animal species because there are qualities of that animal he wanted to transfer to a character.

For example, Usagi's mentor, Katsuichi, is a lion. Sakai wanted to convey the nobility and power of the animal. The red coloring of Katsuichi's mane was taken from a kabuki play about the relationship between a lion and his cub. ▸

Left:
Evolution of the title character Usagi Yojimbo, from 1982 (one of the earliest sketches), through a classic pose from 1985, to 1994 (close to his present design, which continues to change).

Above:
Usagi Yojimbo (which means "rabbit bodyguard"), first appeared in comics in 1984 and today appears in a monthly series and trade-paperback collections published by Dark Horse Comics.

Above:
Jei, the demonic spearman and Usagi's perennial nemesis. Jei is a bridging character between the realistic and magical elements of the series—a human warrior and an otherworldly force.

Above:
Usagi with a village of visually diverse characters.

Left:
Usagi's mentor, Katsuichi Sensei.

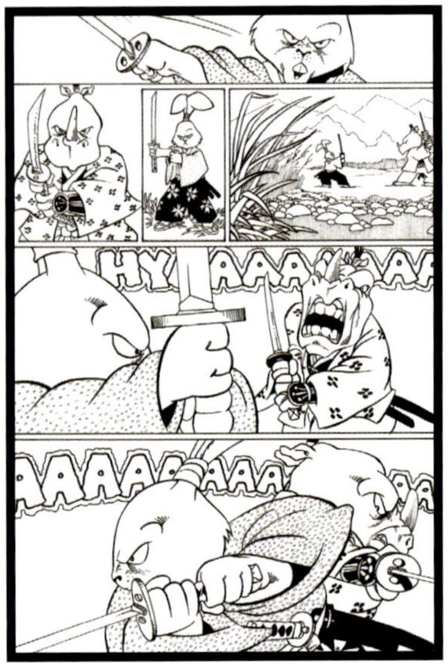

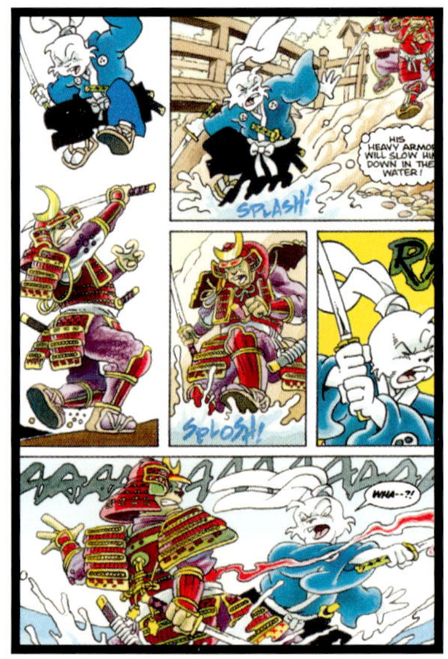

Top row:
Evolution of Gen, the rhino bounty hunter and Usagi's friend, from the first story to the present.

Middle row, center left & left:
The bat-like Neko Ninja attack from above, and Usagi clashes with an armored warrior.

Middle row, far left:
Mariko, Usagi's star-crossed love and the mother of Usagi's son, Jotaro.

Bottom row:
Images of Usagi's son, Jotaro, one of the most pivotal characters to emerge in recent years. Jotaro is a bridging character who unites the playful and earnest sides of Sakai's epic.

Gen the rhino bounty hunter's personality was inspired by Toshiro Mifune's roles in the movies *Yojimbo* and *Sanjuro*. Sakai made him a rhino because he liked the "massiveness" of that animal next to a rabbit. "They play off each other very well—visually, as well as with their personalities," he says.

Sakai's designs for his many central characters are now more or less set; at the same time, however, they continue to change, which Sakai attributes to his own maturity as an artist. "Sometimes the changes are deliberate, but often they are totally unconscious on my part. If you look at the earlier versions of Usagi, his proportions are very different compared to the present design. Back then, he was about three or four heads tall; now he is closer to five heads. He also obtained a little bump for his nose around Book Five. I had not planned these changes. It was not until they were pointed out to me that I became aware of them. I don't think this is uncommon in any series that has had a single artist for a sustained run. If you look at the earlier adventures of Sergio Aragonés' *Groo the Wanderer*, you'll see that his designs are markedly different than those of 20 years later."

Though *Usagi Yojimbo* is made primarily for a readership of one—the author—it is still pretty much an all-ages book. However, violence was a part of the samurai culture. That is something Sakai feels he can't, and doesn't want to, ignore, though he uses "floating skull" icons to tone down the reality of death. The early seventeenth century, he says, was a turbulent time in Japanese history. "The time of wars had just ended, a new military dictatorship was being established, the outside world was encroaching upon Japanese life, the merchant class was gaining more influence, and the samurai class was in decline." ■

This page: Sakai invented Space Usagi—a descendant of the original Usagi—in 1991 as a fun excuse to draw dinosaurs and futuristic monsters, and as an opportunity to place his characters in a wildly different context, expanding the Usagi mythos without betraying the spirit of the main story line.

SECTION VII

KNOWING YOUR AUDIENCE

For far too long, if you were creating comics, especially in the United States, it was generally a safe assumption that your target audience was almost exclusively teenage boys. Thankfully, that time has passed, and graphic novels today can be enjoyed by anyone from school children to senior citizens. More and more books that address audiences of diverse cultures, genders, and nationalities are being published. Likewise, each book published stands a very real chance of being exposed to a broader audience than would have been possible in previous decades. In this section we'll discuss issues of audience-targeted character design, such as writing for children, and address issues of globalization and cultural sensitivity. Case studies will focus on creators producing comics for an all-ages audience. ■

Above:
Once the best of friends, Miyumi San and Maribelle Mellonbelly are now bitter rivals in Dave Roman's *Astronaut Elementary* (collected edition; self-published in 2006). Roman combines cute and energetic characters with quirky dialogue that's especially fun to read aloud.

AGE APPEAL

For years, the rallying cry for adult comics enthusiasts in the United States has been "comics aren't just for kids anymore." In truth, comics have never been just for kids, barring a brief period following the formation of the Comics Code Authority in 1954, and prior to the underground comics movement of the 1960s. For a time, this perception, combined with the steadily rising average age of actual readers, resulted in some strangely conflictive comics with limited appeal for either adults or children. At the same time, since the late 1970s, there has been a small but strong undercurrent of "all-ages" material, and sporadic children's comics did appear (along with the international mainstays of *Tintin* and *Asterix*), but it was only with the stocking of graphic novels in libraries, bookstores, and classrooms that a large number of younger readers began to discover and devour the comics form, especially manga. And major publishers including Scholastic, HarperCollins, and First Second Books have recently launched successful imprints or titles for children, preteens, and teenagers.

It is important to know the audience you're creating for, to have a sense of their frame of reference and interests, and to communicate as clearly as possible without "talking down" to or alienating them with material they've grown out of, or are not yet ready for. Age-appropriateness is incredibly difficult to measure accurately. It can help to consult parents, teachers, and librarians, as well as kids, when designing characters for young readers.

In addition to providing good stories, graphic novels can also be effective literacy tools for reluctant and struggling readers. By integrating text and visuals, "Graphic novels model the reading process for you to some degree," says Sheila Keenan, executive editor of Scholastic's Graphix imprint. Readers construct pictures in their minds, and graphic novels assist in that "visualization" process without overtaking it, as television and movies are often said to do, as a graphic novel requires active reading rather than just passive watching. When a child moves beyond "read-alouds" and picture books but still grapples with the demands of text-only books, certain targeted graphic novels such as Jimmy Gownley's *Amelia Rules* (IBooks) and Jennifer and Matthew Holm's *Babymouse* (Random House), or other hybrids of chapter book and comics such as Dav Pilkey's *Captain Underpants* (Scholastic), can help boost verbal and visual literacy. ▸

Left:
Ultimate Spider-Man, by Brian Michael Bendis and Mark Bagley. Spider-Man: TM & (c) 2006 Marvel Characters, Inc. Used with permission.

Above:
A page from *Shark Hunters*, by Jef Czekaj. (See page 74 for more about Czekaj's work.)

Manga is by far the most popular category of graphic novel for teenagers. Interestingly, Japanese and manga-inspired character designs are sometimes criticized as being one-dimensional and indistinguishable ("all big eyes and elfish proportions"), but manga actually encompasses a wider range of character styles and "levels of reality" than most American and European comics do. Various theories account for the allure of manga within and outside Japan, but it might be this dynamic range that is the most immediate, visceral draw.

Marvel's Ultimate line of books is also a teen favorite, recognizing that young readers often prefer to read about characters who are their own age or slightly older. *Ultimate Spider-Man*, aimed at younger teens, features a teenaged Peter Parker struggling to live up to very adult responsibilities, while *The Ultimates*, aimed at a young adult audience, features characters in their twenties and thirties.

Perhaps the last "untapped" market for graphic novels is the reader over 40 years old. Emotionally rich, visually elegant stories, often featuring older characters and made by experienced creators—such as Art Spiegelman's *In the Shadow of No Towers* (Pantheon; 2004), Marjane Satrapi's *Persepolis*, Miriam Katin's *We Are On Our Own* (see page 76), and Seth's *Clyde Fans* (Drawn and Quarterly; 2004)—offer renewed appeal for readers who might have "left comics behind" decades before. ■

Left:
Mark Millar and Bryan Hitch's *The Ultimates*: TM & © 2006 Marvel Characters, Inc. Used with permission.

GENDER & CULTURE

While the long-standing perception that comics were for children was largely off base, a more accurate and unfortunate perception—that comics are for teenage boys and infantile, heterosexual, white men only—is now being openly challenged by a new generation of graphic novelists.

Books like Neil Gaiman's *Sandman* (Vertigo; 1993–1997) and Jhonen Vasquez's *Johnny the Homicidal Maniac* (SLG Publishing; 1997) have drawn sizable female audiences by tapping into the thriving goth subculture. High-fantasy fare such as Wendy and Richard Pini's *Elfquest* (see pages 136–141), Jeff Smith's *Bone* (Cartoon Books; 1996–2004), and Linda Medley's *Castle Waiting* (Olio Press; 2002–2003) draws men and women by featuring heroic figures of both sexes. Terry Moore's *Strangers in Paradise* (Abstract Studio, collected editions, from 1994) proved that by focusing on character development and meaningful relationships, romance comics can be complex and compelling, in contrast to the superficial, often condescending dating and fashion comics occasionally published to lure female readers.

Characters of alternative sexuality have been increasingly represented as well. DC Comics' announcement of a gay Batwoman was controversial, but independent comics prominently featuring openly gay or bisexual characters, such as *Strangers in Paradise* and Los Bros Hernandez's *Love and Rockets* (Fantagraphics Books, collected editions from 1985), have been pleasing audiences of all sexual orientations for years. By including well-developed characters of diverse sexual orientations without pandering or stereotyping, these books have transcended the need to appeal to any single demographic.

Depictions of ethnic and cultural diversity are also on the rise, especially as larger publishers and online publishing advance international distribution of graphic novels. Ethnic and cultural diversity has proven a considerable draw for graphic novel readers, as demonstrated by the success of books like Marjane Satrapi's *Persepolis* (Pantheon; 2004) and Derek Kirk Kim's *Same Difference* (Top Shelf Productions; 2004), not to mention the massive global success of manga. ▸

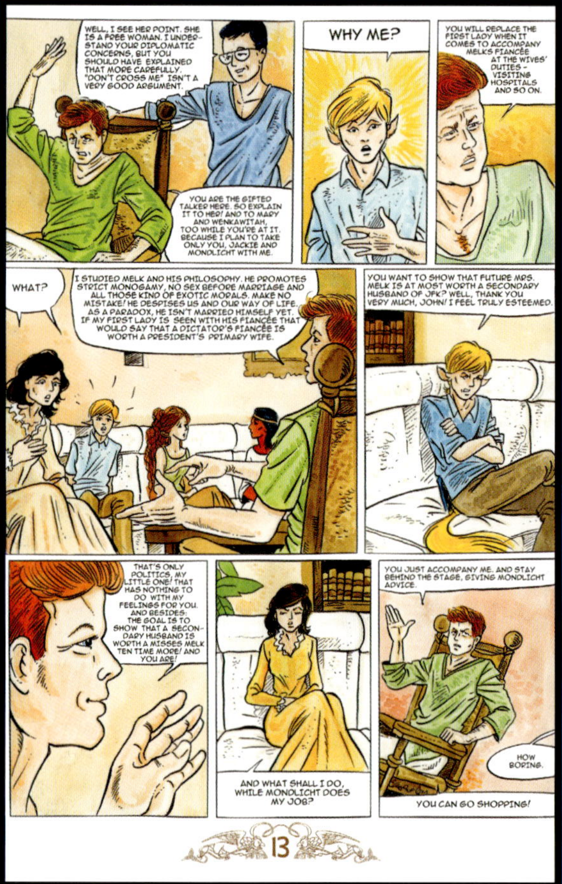

Left: European Diana R. Sassé has created a unique cultural mix in *Antique White House: The Kennedy Tales* by imagining the figure of John F. Kennedy as the pansexual hero of a decidedly alternative American history.

Left: Bryant Paul Johnson explores the hypocrisy of early American race and gender relations in *Cell Division*, a story from his series *Teaching Baby Paranoia* (www.moderntales.com).

A basic truth for any narrative art form is that people need identification figures—characters they can relate to, in whom they can see some aspect of themselves. A key element in the designs of such characters is *authenticity*. Whether or not the authors belong to the ethnic or gender group explored in the story, they will put off a large portion of their potential audience unless they create from genuine experience and observe rather than prejudge.

When designing characters for the modern graphic novel audience, your potential readership is more diverse than ever before. Make no assumptions about who graphic novel readers are—they can be anyone. But if you hope to reach that diverse audience, then you need to design for diversity, creating interesting and relatable characters that capture all aspects of humanity. One of the great appeals of reading is exploring lives very different from our own. Designing diverse characters isn't just about appealing to a target demographic—it's about providing a richer, more varied experience for *all* readers. ■

Left:
Culture needn't be foreign to be worth exploration. In *Blankets*, Craig Thompson explores the life of an artist growing up in a restrictive Christian community.

CASE STUDY:

WENDY & RICHARD PINI

Far left: Picknose the Troll.

Left: *Elfquest's* central male character Cutter in a typical samurai pose.

Wendy Pini (www.elfquest.com) grew up reading illustrated fantasy literature, fairy tales, and myths. Howard Pyle, Arthur Rackham, Maxfield Parrish, Gustav Doré, and Aubrey Beardsley all played a large part in shaping her vision of how other worlds—indeed, other dimensions—might look. The father of Art Deco, Erté, was a strong influence in the area of design, with his grace of line and elegant posture of the human form. She also garnered a powerful sense of shape and silhouette from the painter Eyvind Earle, a painter known for his background landscapes for Walt Disney's *Sleeping Beauty*.

Even as a child, Pini could see that Walt Disney used influences from some or all of these great illustrators. And so she realized the connection between illustration and animation. Disney cartoons were responsible for her initial love of the art of animation, and she tried writing and drawing comics based on cartoons she'd seen, or doing little "flip books." Then in the 1960s she discovered early *anime* films such as Toei's *Alakazam the Great* and *The Littlest Warrior*. Japanese animation, and the rare manga she could get her hands on, solidified her storytelling sensibilities.

By the time Pini discovered Marvel Comics in her teens, her drawing style was "pretty well set." She enjoyed interpreting Stan Lee and Jack Kirby's superheroes her own way, with a delicate, art nouveau touch. Yet, especially from Jack Kirby and Doug Wildey, she learned a great deal about how to solidify and masculinize the characters she was starting to develop on her own. Practising the art of comic-book storytelling in various fanzines, Pini learned the stylized shortcuts that, she says, "make all the difference between pure illustration and panel-to-panel graphics."

"The *Elfquest* cast of characters has been with me, in one form or another, since I was a kid. In high school I interpreted them as little insect beings with wings—'Hoppity Goes to Town' meets 'The Flower Fairies,'" Pini says. "But in the mid-1970s, when Richard [husband and partner in WaRP Graphics] and I set about getting the *Elfquest* saga out to the public, a kind of warrior spirit rose in me that wanted expression through scrappy little pointy-eared barbarians with swords. The idea of the small, cute, and seemingly vulnerable up against huge odds is very manga, very *anime*. *Elfquest* was one of the first American comic series to show obvious Japanese influences."

WaRP Graphics continues to create and publish the series through a licensing agreement with DC Comics. ▶

FACING LIFE

Pini believes that all comics artists, however stylized, interpret the human experience and, therefore, draw on what they've lived and observed. For an audience to relate to a character, she says, that character must be infused with a soul. That soul can only come from the artist's feelings and perceptions.

For instance, she might be having breakfast at a coffee shop and notice the way the waitress casts her eyes down, as if her mind were on some unspoken trouble. Says Pini, "I may not ask what's wrong, but my heart will stir. Instinctively, I record that moment in my arsenal of expressions and, later, it might become a shot of Leetah [a main female character] deep in thought."

"On the other hand," she continues, "I might latch on to a personal memory that angers me and apply that energy to Cutter's expression and stance as he's about to righteously fight."

For Pini, the character's personality shapes his or her appearance. Creating a face, she says, is something like designing a mask. And since she has knowledge of animated cartooning, she begins by choosing geometric shapes that embody certain psychological traits. Circles are harmless (witness Mickey Mouse); ovals convey feminine appeal; squares suggest reliability; triangles, aggression; and so forth. Savah and Lord Voll are, Pini says, both strong, authoritative characters, so she based their features on a diamond. ▸

Above left:
Leetah in thought.

Above:
Savah, the Mother of Memory.

This page:
The arrogant Rayek.

Above:
Cutter &
Yul Brynner.

Rayek is hotheaded and arrogant, so his face is an upside-down triangle. The wide dome of his head emphasizes his intimidating eye expressions. "Bill Everett took this design element to the extreme with the Sub-Mariner's triangular noggin in the 1940s," says Pini. (The Sub-Mariner is a classic aquatic superhero character, still popular in Marvel Comics.)

Cutter's face is based on a square. "That said, I must confess that his design is a broad caricature of the late actor Yul Brynner," Pini says. "Physically, Brynner personified the strutting rooster character. This he did naturally, unself-consciously, which made him the ideal model for the minihunk Wolfrider chief. If you analyze Brynner's face and physique (which I never get tired of), it's clear he's built on squares. Hence the heroic, larger-than-life parts he took, always playing, as he put it, 'a bastard with a heart of gold.' Cutter has occasionally been cranky enough to merit that description."

CHARACTER EVOLUTION

Pini approaches all her character designs three-dimensionally, and she likes to know how they'll look from all angles before she starts working with them. "Even so, with minor or background characters, I fudge a lot," Pini says. When she finishes an issue, she goes back over the art, in sequence, to make sure she hasn't made any huge costume or facial mistakes. Fortunately, she says, Adobe Photoshop is very forgiving.

According to Pini, if you have a character who plays a fairly major role throughout and you don't settle on his/her features right away, you can run into continuity problems—especially if you work on pages out of order, as she does.

From the beginning it was Wendy and Richard Pini's intention to "grow these characters up." For Cutter, because he's mortal and slowly aging, that's meant numerous subtle changes over the years. For Leetah, being immortal, the changes have been more in stance and expression (and costumes—she's a natural clothes horse!) than physical. ▸

Says Pini, "Leetah's design originated from everything I knew and felt about haughty, fairy princesses, blended with my gorgeous, sexy, belly-dancing coach Marlene Celia. Over the years, Leetah has aged only in the sense that her life experiences are reflected in her eyes, which are wider and show much less self-involvement than at first. Her wisdom and compassion are so deep at this point that she could be Savah's logical successor.

"As for Cutter, he's truly following the Hero's Cycle, going from untried boy-king, to young visionary, to King of Sorrows to fully adult father/king. Because he's an elf, he's not aging in terms of wrinkles or muscle loss, but he has facial hair in the form of 'mutton chops,' which signifies maturity in a male Wolfrider. As with Leetah, his most significant change is in the expression of his eyes. He's been through a lot in his 500-plus years. Gone is the naïve, innocent youth who had to learn to roll with every punch. In his place is a self-assured leader who, just lately, has been relaxed enough to sport a wry sense of humor."

According to Pini, *Elfquest* has a huge, racially mixed cast. She is currently working on a four-part miniseries for DC Comics that contains yet another elfin group, the aquatic WaveDancers. "This is an entirely different artistic experience for me because I didn't originally design the appearance of these characters. To work with them, I've had to 'make them mine,' so to speak. The basic formula of breaking them down into geometric shapes helps me solidify their personalities and meld them seamlessly with our familiar, original cast."

Pini says the androgyny of her elfin designs reflects two things: the Japanese manga influence and her own personal sense of how to project "otherness" into a humanoid but not human character. Manga's popularity with a largely young, female audience that's receptive to "pretty" artwork and well-written, soap-opera-type stories is precisely the unheard-of audience that *Elfquest* attracted almost 30 years ago. "Not that I set out deliberately to do so. I just drew what pleased me and, naturally, it pleased other women," she says. However, because Pini also had influences from Jack Kirby and other mainstream comics stars of the time, her work had "a solidity that attracted the guys—that, and the fact that *Elfquest* contained large doses of PG-rated sex and violence as well as soap opera."

Pini says it was necessary from the beginning that the elves were human enough for readers to identify with, but alien enough that the enmity between elves and primitive humans made sense in the story line. "Androgyny, even in this enlightened age, is unsettling. Extreme beauty coupled with a slightly threatening, feral aspect, is both scary and titillating. It's an eternal question mark. What are we dealing with here? Something cute and childlike or something you definitely don't want to meet in a dark alley? That's what I mean by 'otherness.' Yes, the elves can be lovable. So can a timber wolf, or a white tiger. We also know, all too well, what else such creatures are capable of."

"I never want my readers to be entirely comfortable," Pini concludes. "Shuna, the human girl whom the elves have adopted, expresses this idea for me. She loves them, regards them as family, and yet she knows she'll never truly be one of them. The tension, the joy and despair of her yearning, is my delicate sword dance with *Elfquest's* audience. I know what they want, but if I give it all to them, the spell is broken. That's the law of Faerie." ■

Above:
Leetah's design progression.

Left:
Leetah's design progression.

Below:
Cutter's design progression.

CASE STUDY:

BRYAN TALBOT

Along with Raymond Briggs (*Ethel & Ernest; When the Wind Blows*), Bryan Talbot (www.bryan-talbot.com) is often credited as Britain's first graphic novelist. Talbot cut his creative teeth while working in the underground comics of the late 1960s, where he created the character Chester P. Hackenbush, still an icon of the British counterculture, for a book called *Brain Storm*. He began publishing *The Adventures of Luther Arkwright*—a science-fiction epic—in 1978, and the series had various publishers until 1989. During this period, Talbot worked on the outstanding British comics anthology, *2000 AD*, among other works. In 1995, Talbot published *The Tale of One Bad Rat* through Dark Horse Comics, melding the bright hues of Beatrix Potter and the English countryside with much darker shades to reflect child abuse and loss of innocence. He returned to his former lead character in 1999 with *Heart of Empire: The Legacy of Luther Arkwright* (Dark Horse Comics). After brief runs on Neil Gaiman's *Sandman* and Bill Willingham's *Fables* (both from DC Comics/Vertigo), Talbot is now finishing *Alice in Sunderland*, a documentary graphic novel about storytelling, myth, history, and the roots of *Alice in Wonderland*.

According to Talbot, stories and scenes can be constructed and worked on, but character design tends to be the most intuitive area of storytelling. The characters have to "sound real" to him (in their own context), and usually they come, almost fully formed, once he knows their role or function.

Occasionally he will base a character on someone he knows—Sam in *The Tale of One Bad Rat*, for example, was based on a friend—and infrequently he will incorporate some elements from a movie or TV character. The best example of this is Harry Fairfax in *Heart of Empire*, some of whose mannerisms Talbot based on those of Wilfred Bramble's old Steptoe character in the British 1960s TV series *Steptoe and Son*.

Talbot doesn't make character sheets for his own books (though he drew them once commercially for a comic company). He tends to prepare a few sketches to develop the character's appearance. For a graphic novel, he spends a great deal of time on the structure of the whole before he draws a single page. This is the point at which, he says, the characters really come into focus. ▸

Far left: The first three issues of *Brain Storm Comix* formed the now iconic *Chester P. Hackenbush Trilogy.*

Left: Title character from *The Adventures of Luther Arkwright.*

ON LUTHER ARKWRIGHT

The Adventures of Luther Arkwright, though basically science fiction in essence, is a cross-genre story that also includes elements of horror, espionage, and historical fiction. For this reason, Talbot says he avoided creating a *Star Wars/Buck Rogers* atmosphere. He loosely based the inking style on the engravings of William Hogarth, the eighteenth-century illustrator and painter who, according to Talbot, was the father of both British art and the British comic strip, to give the book "a sort of historical patina," though he varied the style for different sections to give each an individual feel.
The storytelling was deliberately experimental, drawing in a lot of influences from then-contemporary cinema, including Nic Roeg (*The Man Who Fell To Earth*, 1976), Sam Peckinpah (*Straw Dogs*, 1971), Francis Ford Coppola (*The Godfather*, 1972 and *The Godfather Part II*, 1974), and Sergio Leone (*A Fist Full of Dollars*, 1964).

With Luther Arkwright being, in the story, the next stage of human evolution, Talbot wanted him to look semidivine, even angelic—with "the aura of demigods." The white hair was an attempt, Talbot says, to make the character appear "slightly alien, to have some sort of purity." The center parting, he confidently decided at the time, was to denote equilibrium, but, looking back, he thinks it was lifted from David Bowie in the film *The Man Who Fell to Earth*—a big influence on the look of Arkwright. "At a time when all comic heroes were muscle-bound and macho, I wanted Arkwright to be slender and androgynous. I suppose that my choices were given the 'all clear' by gut reaction, but only after I'd considered them thoroughly," Talbot says. ■

Left & above left: Pages from *The Adventures of Luther Arkwright.*

ON THE TALE OF ONE BAD RAT & ALICE IN SUNDERLAND

Talbot thought long and hard about both books before beginning. The choice of style for both was very deliberate. According to Talbot, *Bad Rat's* job was to be easily accessible to readers with no acquired knowledge of comic grammar, and to be clear and straightforward. For that reason, he used a clear-line technique and based all the pages around the nine-panel grid—keeping the focus always on the main character. He based the look of Helen, the book's central character, on a girl he'd seen begging at London's Tottenham Court Road tube station. "*Bad Rat* is the only book where I 'cast' the whole story and used photo references for all the main characters. This meant that I had to find someone for the role of Helen who looked like my character sketches. I was very lucky to find Kate Housden, a 16-year-old drama student at the time and a great little actress," he says.

Says Talbot of his latest book, "*Alice in Sunderland* is a very different kettle of fish and is not a story as such—it's a documentary within which a multitude of short stories are told." Although he does describe the life of Alice Liddell (the "real" Alice, who inspired the lead character of *Alice in Wonderland*), it's told from a distance, narrated by a third party, so she doesn't have a speaking part, and her look is totally based on photos of Alice Liddell. ■

This page & opposite: Helen and her father from *The Tale of One Bad Rat.*

ON CONSISTENCY & BEHAVIOR

To Talbot, it's important that the character is recognizable from most angles and from a distance. Getting a character that's produced purely by imagination (as opposed to one based on a real person) that looks consistent and has its own distinct mannerisms, is a real skill, he says.

When at work on a comics or graphic-novel story, Talbot usually pencils the whole thing and then goes back to do the inks. This gives him enough time to get used to the characters so that he can make any changes at the inking stage. "This is also good for getting the continuity right," he says. "If I introduce an element into a scene later on, then I can place it into earlier scenes, if appropriate, retrospectively."

Alice in Sunderland, again, is very different, Talbot says. "The whole idea behind the book is that things are changing all the time and the characters are fluid in appearance. Different styles come and go. The two main characters' faces, though always recognizable, change drastically throughout the book."

Talbot believes that body language and facial expression are important storytelling tools, and each pose should emphasize what you're trying to put across in the story. Says Talbot, "As for pantomime, it should be possible to follow the story or perceive the situation just going from the visuals. I usually always try and have a character's mouth open when they are talking, in a way that expresses what they are saying, and very often I reinforce this with their hand or head gestures or body position. I have a mirror attached to the drawing board for this purpose—to pose for the characters. One comic I saw had a really long scene of a heated conversation, and in every single panel the characters' mouths were firmly clamped shut!" ■

CASE STUDY:

ANDY RUNTON

Andy Runton (www.andyrunton.com) is the author of three all-ages graphic novels, all published by Top Shelf Productions: *Owly: The Way Home & The Bittersweet Summer* (2004); *Owly: Just a Little Blue* (2005); and *Owly: Flying Lessons* (2006). The *Owly* stories are all wordless, with dialogue expressed in the form of simple iconic images. In 2005, Runton's work on *Owly* earned him the Ignatz Award for Promising New Talent.

Before turning to comics, Runton completed a degree in industrial design, culminating in a thesis about applying principles of character design to the process of industrial design, to create what he called "Products with Personality."

To date, Runton has poured all his comics-making efforts into his *Owly* stories, saying that these characters are precisely what he'd been seeking for years. Runton's books and characters represent the kind of comics he himself always wanted to read. "When I couldn't find what I was looking for out there, I decided to make it myself."

Runton's chief character is the eponymous Owly, a small, flightless owl who lives in the woods, raises plants, and does his best to help out the small animals around his home. Each book features Owly's first encounter with a new creature and his efforts to befriend it, from saving a worm from a flood, and building a home for bluebirds, to taking flying lessons from a flying squirrel. The only actual text in the *Owly* books is in Owly's reference volumes about small birds and animals—which provide nature facts for the reader. ▸

THE AESTHETIC OF FRIENDLINESS

Owly is unapologetically cute and nonthreatening. His childlike proportions—a soft, round body low to the ground, and huge, egg-shaped eyes—give him a look of honesty and vulnerability. Owly plays both friend and parent to Wormy and others. He is innocent and independent, eager to grow and learn, yet reliable and responsible—the perfect projection of a child's self-image.

And yet, Runton is resistant to labeling his stories "children's books." He prefers simply "friendly," since he feels they hold as much appeal for adult readers as for younger audiences. In fact, his readership is just about evenly split between children and adults. The key to this crossing of age boundaries is Runton's obvious sincerity in his approach to character design—he makes little attempt to appeal to market trends, or to tap into "what the kids like today." He creates a character he loves and presents him simply, for a result that's fun and energetic, but without the frenetic quality typical of much contemporary children's material. The result is a character as soothing as he is entertaining, and with an ageless appeal. ▶

Opposite page:
The cover of the first *Owly* book, which gathered two of Runton's stories.

This page:
Owly and Wormy. Though tiny and easily injured, Wormy is enthusiastic and eager to help; he is willing to put himself in harm's way for the sake of others, even though he relies on Owly for his own protection against the whims of nature.

THE INSPIRATION & ORIGIN OF OWLY

Runton's lifelong love of children's entertainment and cartoons has not faded with adulthood. "I always loved cartoon characters, whether they were animated, in comics, or even if they were corporate mascots. I especially loved The Muppets, the Disney characters, especially *Pete's Dragon*, *Dumbo*, and *The Rescuers*, anything in School House Rock, Paddington Bear, all kinds of children's books, and the list goes on..."

As an industrial-design student, Runton's coursework often required him to work through the night—a standard rite of passage for students in his field. The changes in his sleep habits concerned his mom, who took to calling him her "little night owl." As a way of easing her mind, Runton started leaving notes for his mother, letting her know when he had gone to bed—and signed all the notes with drawings of a round little owl. "Owly evolved over years of tiny drawings" before Runton decided to try crafting stories about the character.

Some of Runton's friends advised him to add a more distinctive accessory—clothes or a funny hat. Instead, Runton gave him a friend, Wormy, who often rides on Owly's head. "Wormy is his accessory," says Runton. ▸

Top left:
In *Just a Little Blue* Owly and Wormy attempt to build a house for a pair of bluebirds, but the bluebirds are suspicious of Owly's intentions.

Top right:
In *The Bittersweet Summer*, Owly and Wormy befriend a pair of hummingbirds. But hummingbirds are migratory, a challenge to friendship that Owly has difficulty overcoming.

Above left & left:
These tiny doodles are some of the earliest drawings of Owly, and reveal much of the character's evolution. In particular note the rounder body and more prominent feet of later drawings.

Since Owly lives in the forest, Runton draws a great deal of inspiration from the natural world. "I do look at a lot of animals ... looking for nuances, studying features. I also look at a lot of interpretations of animals to see what I can use. What's been exaggerated? What works and what doesn't?" When Andy and his mom built a home for bluebirds, only to have their efforts rejected by the birds they had hoped to help, he turned that experience into the book, *Just a Little Blue*. According to Runton, autobiographical comics are "unique because they are so personal. Trying to build a house for bluebirds isn't something that everybody does."

METHOD & PROCESS

When creating characters for his graphic novels, Runton doesn't draw model sheets, turnarounds, or other formal design sketches, even though those processes were a big part of his industrial-design studies. He explains the different process in terms of the very different end products. "When you're designing a logo, one drawing is the final end result. A lot of conceptualizing goes into that. Comics are more organic. You have to go on instinct, because you have a lot of pages to create."

This is not to say that he never sketches characters before putting them into books. When considering a new critter to add to Owly's circle of friends, he will often sketch the character while signing books at conventions. The process is unstructured but allows him to work out the basic look of a new character. The character isn't finished until it's been drawn many times in the context of a story. For this reason, Runton pencils the entire book before he inks a single page so that each character will maintain consistency.

"The characters and their designs tend to evolve as I write and draw my stories. I'm usually dealing with a pretty large page count, so by the time I pencil everything out I have a better feel for what they're all about. Once I start inking, it's pretty much finalized. But that's not to say things don't still evolve. Despite my familiarity with Owly, he's still evolving." ■

Right:
A color illustration of one of Owly's bluebird friends.

CASE STUDY:

MARK CRILLEY

Below left: Cover from *Akiko.*

Below middle: Early sketches of Miki (left) and Reika from *Miki Falls.* Both blend manga designs with Crilley's unique visual sensibility.

While teaching English in Japan in 1992, cartoonist and writer Mark Crilley (www.markcrilley.com) invented his best-known character, Akiko, and fashioned her first all-ages adventure, a 33-page comic-book story titled "Akiko on the Planet Smoo." Returning to his native Michigan in 1995, he found an eager publisher for the tale in Sirius Entertainment, who published the story as a one-shot comic book in December 1995, with a new series, *Akiko*, to be launched the following spring. In those first years of creating comics, he managed to produce new issues of *Akiko* at a rate of 10 or more per year and found a small but dedicated readership among comics fans. He also toured the United States with Jeff Smith, Stan Sakai, Linda Medley, Charles Vess, and Jill Thompson for the Trilogy II Tour in 1998. That same year, Random House Children's Books invited him to write and illustrate a series of novelized adaptations of *Akiko* for young readers. The first in the series, *Akiko on the Planet Smoo*, was published in March 2000. Random House will publish 10 Akiko books in all. In 2004, Random House published Crilley's first new creation since *Akiko*, titled *Billy Clikk: Creatch Battler*. Crilley now lives in Michigan with his wife, Miki, and their son, Matthew. His latest project is a series of four graphic novels set in Japan, under the title *Miki Falls*, to be published by HarperCollins Children's beginning in 2007. Crilley's character designs rise above simple classification, expertly melding inter-galactic imagery with earth-bound emotion, and his artistic approach is continually evolving with each new story and each new vision.

Crilley says *Miki Falls* is in essence a "what-if" story that asks the question: What if Cupid isn't a myth? What if romantic love really is controlled—not by some guy with a bow and arrow—but by a vast number of quasi-celestial beings that live among us? In the story (which takes place entirely in Japan), an unsuspecting high-school girl, Miki, meets one of these beings and slowly unravels his secrets. And, as the title implies, her interest in him soon goes far beyond merely wanting to find out who he really is.

Crilley initially jumped into *Miki Falls* "thinking it would be a 'Crilley-style-manga' project; my attitude was just about that shallow." But as he went along, he found that this project allowed him to "truly reinvent myself as a comic-book storyteller" and he has discovered a drastically different way of laying out pages, dispensing with panels whenever possible, and conveying visual information in ways he "never came close to doing in the *Akiko* series." ▸

Opposite page, top & bottom: The design of Spuckler, Akiko's roguish yet loyal companion, has clearly evolved since the beginning of the series ...

This page: ... but perhaps not as much as the design of villainous Lloza Throck.

Probably the first thing readers will notice about *Miki Falls* is that the characters are drawn with manga-like faces. But rather than do a line-for-line copy "bent on fooling people into accepting this as authentic Japanese manga," Crilley is filtering the manga approach to drawing faces through his own sensibilities. He picks and chooses the aspects of manga that he likes—giving Miki a very small nose and mouth, for example—and stays away from manga elements he doesn't much care for, such as outrageously large eyes, or faces that briefly morph into icon-like cartoons to express particular emotions.

The primary manga technique Crilley is using is the tendency to allow an entire figure to break out of all the panels of the page and occupy its own "panel-less" space. He had hardly ever done this in *Akiko*, but in *Miki Falls* is doing it frequently: much more often, he says, than most manga artists do. Pages filled exclusively with rectangular panels are quite rare in *Miki Falls*, and there are a great many pages that have no panels at all.

A technique Crilley discovered while working on the project is something he calls "text snaking." The idea is, whenever possible, to place narration boxes and word balloons in an instantly perceivable line that snakes its way from the top of the page to the bottom. "Comics creators have been doing this on splash pages [full-page pieces of art usually found on the first page of a story and including credits] for ages, but I'm attempting to do it on the multi-panel pages as well," he says. "The idea is to make the reading order of the word balloons and text boxes so clear that the reader—even the uninitiated comic reader, I'm hoping—never has the slightest doubt which thing to read next. I'm striving to keep the reader in the story at all times and never allow even the possibility of someone wrestling with the nuts and bolts of 'which panel comes next?'"

In the early days of character creation, Crilley has a general sense of the sort of person he's going for, which includes some idea of the physical presence. Says Crilley, "I'm not the type to sit down and create some highly detailed 'bible' on the character with background history and so forth, so I'd never have been able to say, 'Spuckler moves his arms like this, but not like this,' back when I was first inventing him. At least 90 percent of what the character eventually becomes is a natural outgrowth of the story. I discover the posture and typical gestures only after I've started putting him or her into situations. It's all pretty intuitive rather than following some grand master plan." ■

Left:
Rough sketches of scenes from *Miki Falls*.

Opposite page:
The lead character from *Miki Falls*, doing just what the title says.

MODERN METHODS

Digital technologies are an undeniable reality in today's graphic-novel landscape for even the most staunchly technophobic, ink-on-the-fingers cartoonists. Scanners and drawing tablets, image-editing and 3-D rendering software, and of course the World Wide Web are becoming (or have long since become) essential creative and distribution tools for thousands of graphic novelists. In most cases, somewhere in the process from conception to completion, from idea to published page, a computer is involved. We are merely skimming the surface of what is possible and already in practice in an enormously complex aspect of character design for graphic novels—offering a few elegant examples to help guide your way through an ever-evolving electronic realm. ■

Left:
Canadian cartoonist Jim Zubkavich is one of the earliest and most influential among the growing number of creators who are publishing self-contained, long-form graphic narratives on the Web. His deft use of monitor-friendly, monochromatic colors and horizontal layouts elevates *The Makeshift Miracle* to near the level of modern art. A complete, 180-page graphic novel, it was serialized online at www.makeshiftmiracle.com from September 2001 to March 2003. It chronicles "the surreal coming-of-age adventures of Colby Reynolds, a teenager who is disillusioned with life and his future."

DIGITAL DESIGN

While many artists have begun turning to digital tools for touch-ups and coloring, a growing minority use electronic tools for every step of character design and art. Some creators utilize drawing tablets, such as those made by Wacom, to reproduce their natural drawing style on the computer. Other creators, such as Joe Zabel and demian.5, prefer to explore design possibilities unique to the digital drawing board. As demian.5 points out, "Drawing digitally has its own optical characteristics and peculiarities, just as analogue techniques, like pencil-scribbles or watercolors, do."

VECTOR GRAPHICS

Vector-graphics programs, such as Adobe Illustrator or Macromedia Flash, differ from bitmap programs such as Adobe Photoshop in that they treat image files as a series of mathematical statements rather than as a conglomerate of individual points. On the practical side, this results in smaller file sizes and scalable images that can be exported to any resolution, regardless of original size.

Creatively, vector-based design allows artists to work with each element of a drawing as a discrete object to be manipulated, reproduced, or repositioned independently of other objects in the image. The result is something akin to poseable models. For instance, all of demian.5's characters are constructed such that "Legs, arms, neck, and tail (if existing) are made with one single path each. The real form of the limb will be laid on this path later, as a brush. This way the characters have something like a skeleton, which makes it easy to show them later in different movements." The poseability of vector images makes programs such as Macromedia Flash a common choice for creators incorporating animation into their comics as well.

Additionally, many creators use vector-graphics software to add lettering to the finished page, since the consistent, sharp lines of vector art produces highly legible lettering—just one of the many additional techniques made possible by vector-based design.

3-D DESIGN

Joe Zabel illustrated his *Trespassers Mysteries* in traditional line art for years before he was seduced by the realism of the 3-D modeling software Poser. Moving to digital design has radically transformed Zabel's approach to the visual design process. "I no longer think in terms of line art; I think instead in terms of colors, textures, and shapes in depth. It also opens the door to incorporating your source material (i.e., photographs) directly into the work; it gives you the tools to manipulate source material and radically transform it to suit your artistic goals."

According to Zabel, working within Poser does have its limitations. "You need to work with the models and the skin textures that are commercially available. If you're skilled enough at 3-D art you can build your own models, but I haven't developed that skill."

CUTTING-EDGE TECHNIQUES

Internet distribution has opened up yet more possibilities to the digital designer. Brendan Cahill, demian.5, and B. Shur have all incorporated limited animation into their comics, broadening their characters with a sense of movement. (See pages 100–103 for more on Brendan Cahill and pages 160–163 for more on B. Shur.) Other creators experimenting with movement, sound, and interactivity include Daniel Merlin Goodbrey (e-merl.com), Cayetano Garza (www.magicinkwell.com), and John Barber (www.johnbarbercomics.com), to name a few. B. Shur has incorporated all three into portions of his *I Am a Rocket Builder* series, demonstrating a wide range of new techniques for the adventurous designer to explore. ■

Above:
Kay, the title character of Joe Zabel's online GN, *The Ice Queen* (2006, www.joezabel.com, originally published by Modern Tales).

Left & opposite page left:
An early painting of Joe Zabel's amateur detectives, Raymond Fish and Delphinia Morgan, along with a 3-D image of Delphinia from Zabel's *The Ice Queen*.

Below:
Some creators, such as Gil Agudín, use 3-D modeling as a design aid, but not as final artwork. Agudín enjoys 3-D models because he can play with different head shapes and with different expressions—he's able to see the character from every angle possible before drawing a single line.

Bottom of page:
In addition to vector graphics, Demian.5's innovative online novel, *When I Am King* (1999–2001, www.demian5.com), makes use of 3-D models and animation.

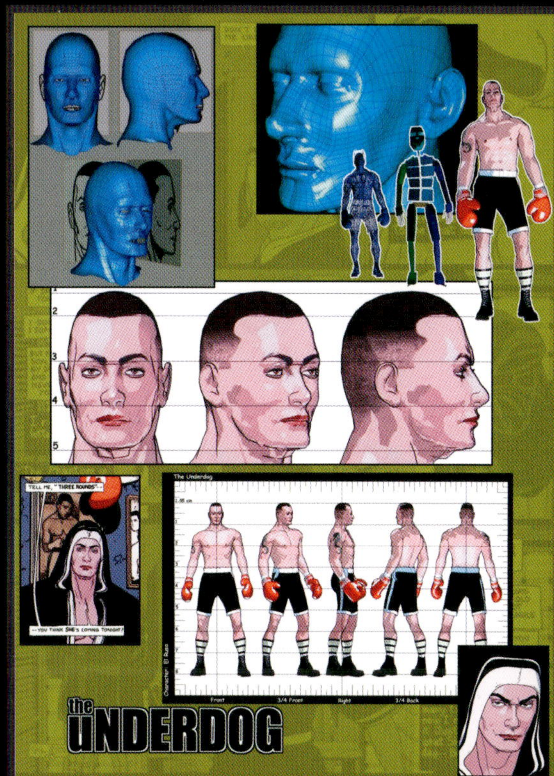

RESEARCH IN THE DIGITAL AGE

While there may not be a consensus among graphic novelists as to the best use and value of 3-D modeling, digital sketching, animation, or other modern design technologies, nearly everyone has embraced at least one modern technology as part of their design process: the Internet as a research tool. Whether a creator is seeking to fact-check small details, find quality photo reference, or simply explore visual resources for inspiration, the Internet has brought all the essential tools right into the artist's home office.

The Internet provides an unlimited, yet easily searchable, quantity of information and images. In addition to the general search and research portals such as Google or Wikipedia, some of the wealth of resources available to graphic novelists include stock photography (Getty Images, Corbis, FotoSearch, etc.), fashion photography (Hint, Elle, Vogue, GQ, etc.), celebrity images (IMDB.com), and public-domain images covering everything from historical reference (The Library of Congress), to works of art (The National Gallery, The Louvre), to military images (Defense Visual Information Center, Department of Defense), or even agricultural reference (USDA Agriculture Research Service).

What's more, the resources available online can provide more than just targeted research; they can also be a great source for inspiration and idea generation. While traditional research tends to be decidedly linear—identify a topic of research, find resources, read them, then move on to the next specific topic—Internet research is structured around the concept of browsing, bouncing from site to site, taking in a stock of random information. While it's certainly not uncommon to peruse the library shelves aimlessly, hoping for something to jump out at you (librarians call this "serendipitous browsing"), Internet research is ideal for this sort of mental stocking. And as Brendan Cahill explains, this sort of unstructured research can have surprising benefits.

BRENDAN CAHILL ON RANDOMIZED RESEARCH

A Google search is both faster and *more random* than traditional library research. It's the randomness that I really find useful. If I'm trying to come up with a character who has a retro-Futurism look, I can input very general search terms and come up with stuff I wouldn't expect. Searching for "modernism" might get you pictures of buildings, sculpture, and a toaster. I may not have thought to look at toasters when trying to come up with the character's hat, but suddenly, the form of the toaster is exactly right. It's great for aggregating unexpected details. Also, the hyperlinked nature of the World Wide Web means that research journeys can take much less expected (and much longer) paths. Try looking up anything of interest on Wikipedia and then see if you can stop jumping to related (or semirelated, or essentially *unrelated*) topics before an hour or two has passed. The ideas come a lot faster and from unexpected directions, which can, in turn, take character design to new places. ■

Above:
As well as simplifying the production of reference photos, digital photography opens up possibilities for making photocomics like this strip from Joey Comeau and Emily Horne's *A Softer World.*

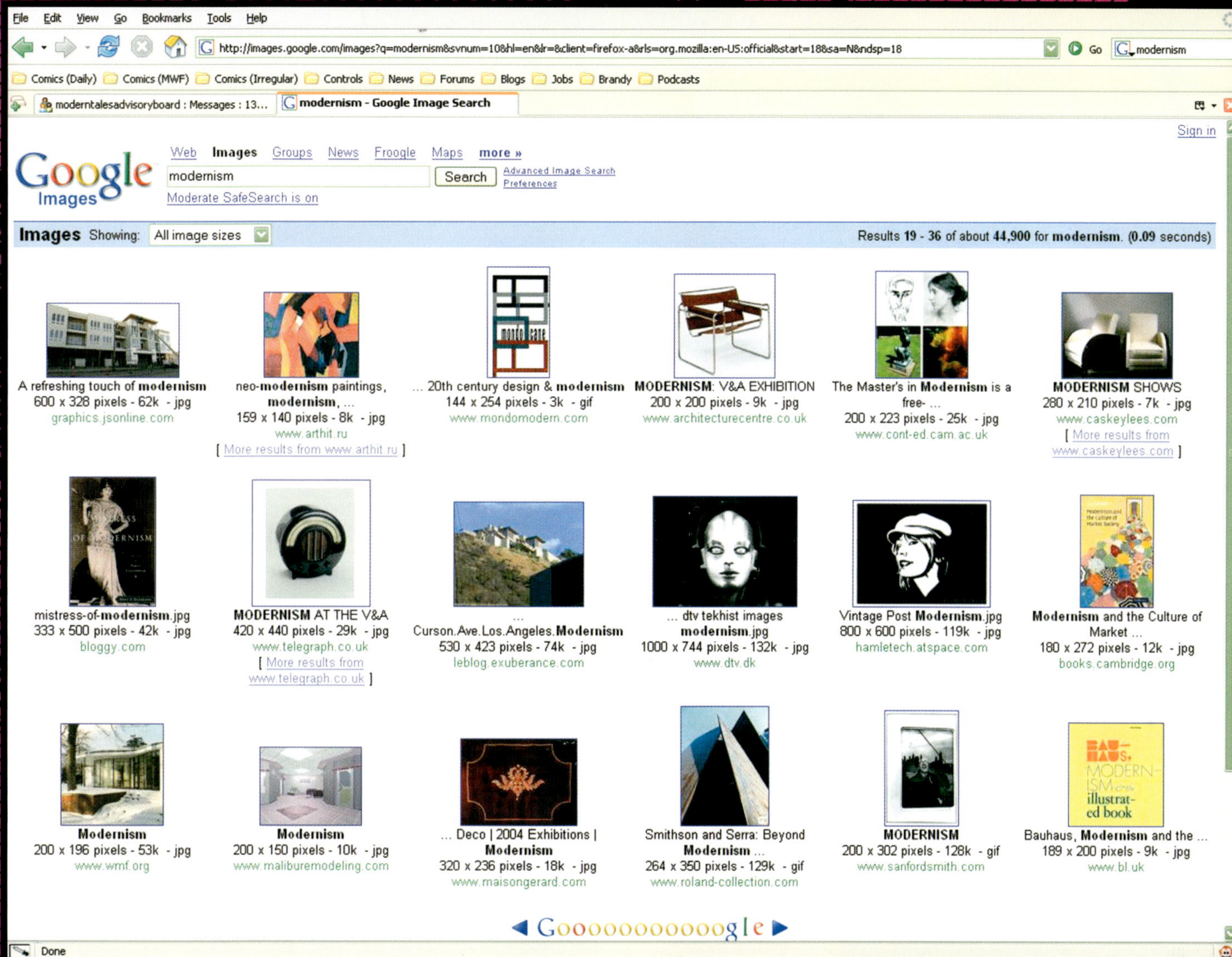

DIGITAL PHOTOGRAPHY

While the Internet has made it easier for graphic novelists to find existing reference photos, the advent of digital photography has made it much easier for creators to produce their own reference shots. Affordable digital cameras have made it possible for creators to shoot reference photos and instantly download them to their computer for immediate use or to archive them for later. There's no need for a private darkroom, expensive and laborious developing, or keeping voluminous reference files. Cheaper, faster, and more flexible, digital photography has greatly simplified the process of creating reference photos. ■

Above: Searching for the term "modernism" on Google Images returns a wide variety of results.

CASE STUDY:

B. SHUR

Below left: In the title story of *I Am a Rocket Builder*, Emma has just moved to a tiny shack in the countryside to build her rocket without interruption.

Below: The inventor is plagued by self-doubt and self-absorption.

B. Shur's online comic *I Am a Rocket Builder* (iamarocketbuilder.com) is actually a collection of four self-contained, but interconnected stories that will form a single narrative when complete. Each of the four ("The Pocket Witch," "The Politics of Flight," "The Reference Section," and the title story) is set in a different location with its own set of characters. Rory, king of the birds, is the one character who has appeared in all four stories. New pages are added to the stories on an alternating basis, so that they are all developing simultaneously, even though they don't take place at the same time.

Like many Web-native creators, Shur's work is consistently in vibrant full color. On some pages, he takes even greater advantage of the digital medium, working in bits of animation, sound, or even reader-interactive elements.

PROCESS & METHOD

Shur's process is fairly loose; he works without a script and designs new characters right on the page of artwork. Like most creators, he begins with a sense of who a character is rather than what he or she looks like, but he allows identity to develop as he works with each character. "Before I draw a character, I have a pretty good idea of what's going on inside his brain. Then, I'll draw most of the page with no script, just an idea of the action and the mood and maybe an image that'll be stuck in my head. The dialogue comes last, and that's where I find out that I have no idea what these people (or birds) are thinking. That's the really awkward part. I'll write the dialogue for a page at least three or four times, and it always comes out differently than I expected. It's then the characters start to find their personalities."

The nonlinear structure of *I Am a Rocket Builder* poses an extra challenge, since Shur's attention is divided among four casts. "I think I have a long way to go in defining the cast of *Rocket Builder*. Because of the way I've set it up, I haven't spent a lot of time on anyone yet. I'm looking forward to getting to know everyone better, especially the humans."

Shur works entirely in Macromedia Flash, from drawing frames to designing new characters. This method allows great flexibility for trial and error, since mistakes or missteps are easily removed. Successful drawings that don't suit the current pages can be stored for later use, and everything on the page remains editable throughout the process. "When I get close I start tweaking. Using the lasso, I'll grab big chunks and features and move and rescale them. For example, when a head needs to be wider or the eyes need to be smaller. When I'm happy with the basic shape, it gets smoothed out with the brush tool, zoomed in to about 300 percent. Then I'll do more tweaking and more smoothing. I'll play with the colors for about as long as the whole rest of the process until I tell myself to leave it alone. Sometimes I'll draw a whole page before deciding that something doesn't work, so I'll go back to each drawing and change a color or shrink an eye." ▸

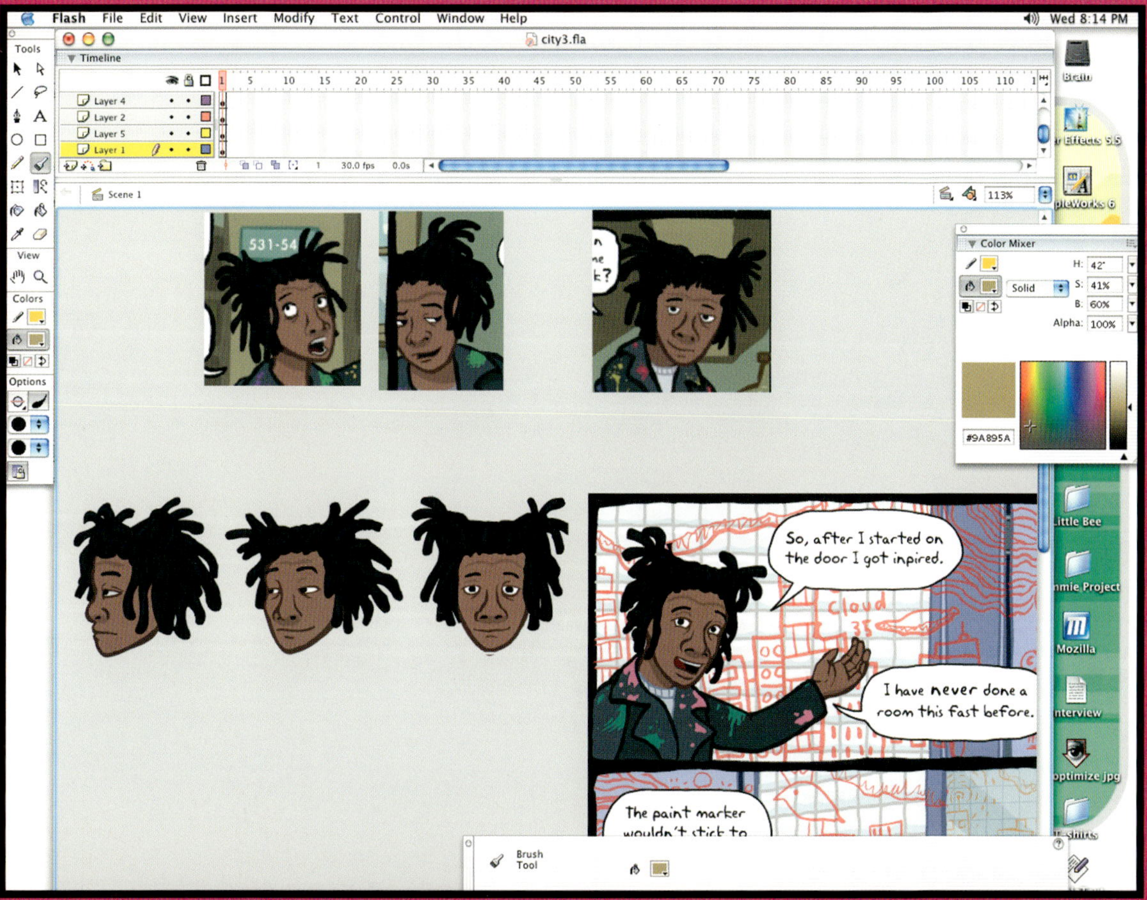

IDIOSYNCRASIES OF DIGITAL DESIGN

As a young artist, Shur has been drawing with computer tools since the moment he first learned to draw, when he used Mac Paint "to draw little pixel monsters dot by dot." Today, he even finds working manually to be more of a challenge. "The control and freedom of working digitally are great. When I try to draw on paper, I find myself reaching for the 'apple-z, undo' function, and it gets frustrating."

As valuable as these tools are, Shur finds that the lack of a tactile product can have a profound effect on his attitude toward his work. "Sometimes, since everything is so easy to change, there's a weird feeling that nothing has any weight. It's easy to get very picky when all your mistakes disappear into space. I've drawn at least a dozen fully finished strips that I just don't use. Some of them I think are better drawn or more funny than stuff that I post, but for some reason they don't fit. It's so easy to throw things away, it messes with any idea of value." ▸

Above left: Working in Flash allows Shur to keep turnarounds and previous instances of Samo, the graffiti artist, visible on screen while drawing him into a new panel.

Left: After a blow to the head, deposed King Rory receives a visitation from his late father.

INSPIRATION & INFLUENCE

Shur attributes much of the mood of his character design to an early love for *The Muppets*, and to the active screen-printing culture he encountered while attending college in Providence, Rhode Island. "There was an art collective called Fort Thunder, and some guys from there made a space and these posters that just looked like your childhood exploded. When I get thoughtful about the way I draw, I really wish I could make such ballsy color decisions. I try it in my own meek way."

Shur's character inspiration can come as much from observation as imagination. While some characters are talking birds or inventive witches, others are based on figures from real life, researched through books and Google image searches.

For additional modeling, Shur uses a mirror to observe his own hands and poses, though he plans to acquire a copy of Poser software to provide additional 3-D modeling reference. He recently acquired a pet cat as well, which will help in drawing Bones, the one-eyed cat.

Of course, even the characters inspired by reality are treated with a cartoonish flair. "I've never been great at real observational drawing, so the characters end up being more icons than drawings. I guess that's not so unusual for webcomics, but for me there's a sense that I'm getting away with something. It's probably just art-school guilt." ▸

Below:
Cat anatomy gives Shur more trouble than human, so he has shown mainly just Bones' head.

Above & right:
An early sketch and the final design of Rick, the drunk and depressed librarian.

Below left:
All the birds are based on the same original model, which can be tweaked into any new characters.

THE UNDIFFERENTIATED CROWD OF BIRDS

In the "Politics of Flight" story line, the majority of the characters are part of a flock of small, greenish birds undergoing a political revolution. Though initially indistinguishable, save for King Rory and his advisor, after the king is deposed and the political movement begins, more and more individual characters come to the fore. "There's this sort of undifferentiated crowd of birds, and every time I get to pull one out, it feels like we're accessing another clue about the weird tree-living society we're spying on."

Says Shur, "I have a lot of fun making new birds. When I draw a new bird, I'm working with a lot of limits. They have a set color scheme, a certain basic arrangement of parts, and a certain scale. I started thinking of them like the Smurfs … defined by one prop or trait and be almost interchangeable. When I played around with new birds, though, I found it was a lot of fun pushing the boundaries of those rules."

When creating a new bird, Shur starts with a copy of Rory himself, which he can then tweak into a new character. Creating many copies of a character in progress allows Shur to test different variations on the new design. While a human character can take several days to design, a new bird always takes Shur under an hour. ▸

THE POSSIBILITIES OF INTERACTIVE DESIGN

In "The Pocket Witch," Shur experiments with interactive design elements, from squirming worms that chase the mouse cursor, to a squid-like creature that waves its arms and sprouts new eyes every time the reader clicks on its head. In one sequence, the reader is able to alter Rory's form, as the witch has placed him into a "transmogrifier" that changes the bird king's color and shape when the reader presses the device's buttons. This technique allows Shur to experiment with design ideas that wouldn't work in a static context. "The eyeballs and worms in the early interactive strips don't have a lot of interest just as designs. If you freeze those strips, they'd be boring. The motion and interaction are parts of the design."

The limitation on Shur's interactive design is that these elements only exist within individual panels or pages. The reader has a sense of game-like involvement, but no matter what the reader does, the comic reaches the same narrative end. But Shur has larger ambitions for reader participation. "It would be nice to extend the audience involvement to a broader level than can be contained in one page ... I have a dream that I'll learn to use cookies and all sorts of fancy coding so that decisions a reader makes in one strip (like the transmogrifier bit in the Witch's house) will affect the way that things appear in future strips." ■

Above:
The pocket witch returns home. On a later page, the witch is interactive; a variety of critters peek out of her many pockets with some prompting by the reader.

CASE STUDY:

SCOTT CHRISTIAN SAVA

Scott Christian Sava wears many hats in the comics and animation industries. Founder of Blue Dream Studios (www.bluedreamstudios.com), former partner with Mike Kunkel in The Astonish Factory (original publisher of Sava's *The Lab*), and artist of *Spider-Man: Quality of Life* (a Marvel comic book rendered in 3-D), Sava is most energized by his creator-owned, all-ages, epic-fantasy project, *The Dreamland Chronicles* (now serialized online at www.thedreamlandchronicles.com).

Sava's original idea for *The Dreamland Chronicles* sprang, in part, from Winsor McCay's *Little Nemo in Slumberland* and C.S. Lewis's *The Chronicles of Narnia*. It tells the story of Alexander Carter, a college student who returns to his childhood dream world, where he reunites with old friends Kiwi the Fairy, Paddington Rumblebottom the Third, and Nastajia the Elf Princess. ▸

Main image: 3-D environment designed and modeled by Stefano Tsai.

PRODUCTION PROCESS, STAGE I

The 24-issue story has more than 200 characters and more than 100 environments. Since he already had an animation studio with designers, modelers, riggers, and software engineers at his disposal, Sava decided to treat it as a 3-D animated feature film—writing a script, drawing the layouts in the manner of movie storyboards (pencil sketches of each page detailing how the story will be told), and designing some characters. "It's definitely not as cheap as 2-D. But it's really coming along. It's becoming its own thing, and I think that in itself is a good enough reason why," says Sava.

Sava started by plotting out the entire 24 issues. For each issue, he thumbnails the pages on paper, scans the sketches, and colors them in Photoshop. (He also created Excel spreadsheets to determine how many characters, environments and props would be needed.) He turns all of this material over to character designer Karen Krajenbrink, who gives him back turnarounds of the characters in that issue. The two spend "quite a bit of time together getting costumes, hair designs, body proportions, and just plain attitude down correctly." Krajenbrink's turnarounds are e-mailed to character modeler Ivan Perez Ayala in Spain. While Perez models the characters, Krajenbrink helps Sava with the initial environment designs. Next, Stefano Tsai of Taiwan and Antero Pedras of Portugal model the environments. Working in 3-D, Sava says, depends on the modeler's preferences. If a modeler wants to give creative input, a single sketch is all that is needed. Other modelers prefer to see every angle, color designs, notes, and swatches for materials.

Sava says it is most difficult for Krajenbrink to work with modelers who would load her pictures into a 3-D program and copy them line for line. "Since Karen's designs are very organic, the turnarounds weren't always correct, and this drove the modelers crazy. We eventually worked it all out, and everyone was happy." ▸

Sava has also enlisted an international band of modelers, riggers, and morph targeters (a digital artist who builds characters as a series of vertex positions; an alternative to the common "skeletal" design process of 3-D digital art) to assist in the production. Lead morph targeter Peter Wong, together with Frank Lenhard from Germany, Peter Starostin from Russia, Jenn Downs from the United States, Kobi Alony from Israel, Joel Carlson from Canada, and Marcello Bortolino from England. Animator Heather Shipman also helps to set up scenes, by taking Sava's layouts and setting the characters in the proper environment, putting all the props in the right place, posing the characters in the general position, and even adding proper facial expressions. ▸

This page & opposite: Alexander Carter is more or less your basic cartoon hero, Sava says.

PRODUCTION PROCESS, STAGE II

Once Sava receives all of the component parts, he loads up the environment in Autodesk's 3D Max software. He then sets up the lights to give it the proper mood. After that, he brings in the actors (most of whom have multiple layers of clothing so that they're not in the same clothes throughout the series). He hides the clothing they aren't wearing and poses them for the first frame. Once they're posed correctly, he positions their eyes to look where he wants them. Then he selects one of the premade facial expressions and uses the 3-D software to select that face for the head. Once everything is just right, he renders the scene.

Because the computers are still too slow for calculating lighting, shadows, and all sorts of other intricate things in real time, a render has to be set up so that the computer can calculate everything needed to make the final page look right. "If I didn't do this, it would look like video-game art. And since I'm trying for a more Pixar-type look, I want to let the computer do its job," he says. Within an hour, a frame is usually rendered (though some frames can take as long as 24 hours), and he then brings the frames into Photoshop to combine them for a single page. "Just 48 more times, and I have a book." ■

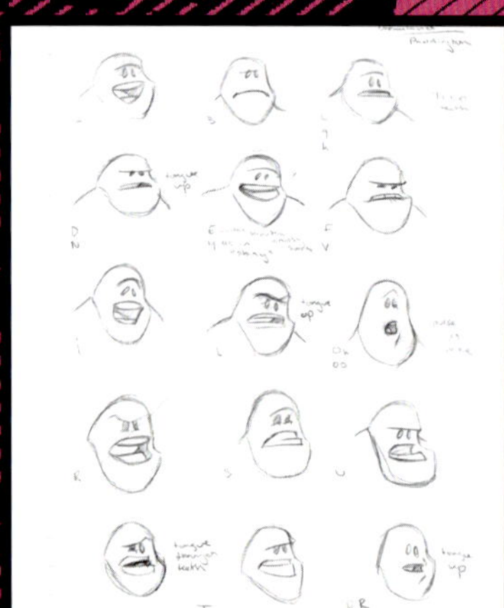

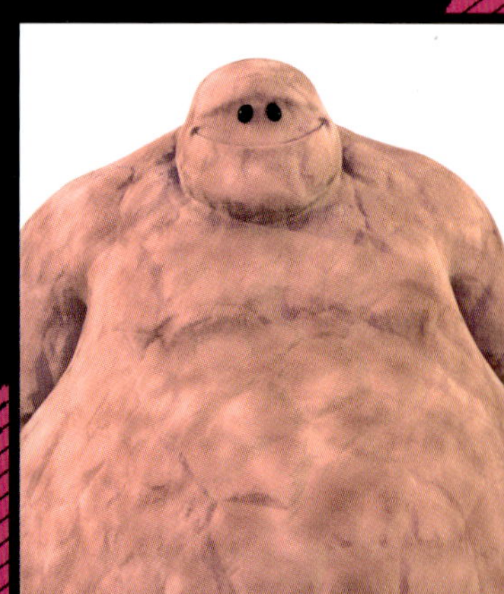

This page: Paddington, Sava says, is a mixture of The Thing from Marvel's *The Fantastic Four* and images of giants from fantasy books.

Left:
Kiwi the Fairy is a feisty, twenty-first-century Tinkerbell.

Below & below left:
The design process, including Sava's initial concept; Krajenbrink's gesture drawing, turnaround, and color study; and the finished 3-D character—for Nastajia, who Sava says is a bit of Disney princess mixed with a Japanese anime type of elf.

CASE STUDY:

RYAN ESTRADA

One of the most prolific Web-focused comics creators, Ryan Estrada has produced dozens of short works, utilizing a variety of methods, from hand-drawn illustrations to Flash-based navigational mechanisms. He is currently maintaining three separate ongoing series: *Aki Alliance*, published by Girlamatic.com; *Welton Colbert*, a satirical webcomics review published monthly by the webcomics news magazine Comixpedia; and *Frank: The Comic Strip*, the official comic strip of the LiveJournal community. Many of his shorter works are archived at www.ryanestrada.com.

Inspired by the 24-hour comics challenge created by Scott McCloud, Estrada has repeatedly set records for "consecutive comic making." His most recent achievement in this regard is *Ped-Xing*—a 175-page graphic novel, hand-drawn and inked in 175 contiguous hours.

Aki Alliance is perhaps Estrada's most artistically ambitious work to date, combining a large cast, a quest-like narrative, and an array of artistic methods. Most of the comic is created digitally, including backgrounds, colors, and such elements as the clear tape and shadows between the panels and the scrapbook "pages." The characters themselves are usually hand-drawn, except when they are abstracted to reflect character perceptions in contrast to the "actual" situations. The elements are compiled in Photoshop as a digital collage, to create the effect of the comic itself being a scrapbook maintained by the lead character, Aki, whose first appearance was in Estrada's previous book, *Ped-Xing*. According to Estrada, "The book itself is as much a character as anyone in it. Reading it is like getting into Aki's mind. So I designed the two as one and the same. Aki's uniform is a dark and light gray, with a pink tie for accent. Each page of the comic is filled with a pattern of the same two colors, with accents of the same pink in text blocks and backgrounds. I also use a lot of patterns in the designs, like the plaid on Aki's skirt, and the crosshatching in some of the hairstyles to add to the crafty feel of the book. I want everything to feel handmade so that the characters don't clash with the tape, glue, and faux cut paper that the pages are designed with." ▸

Above right:
Aki Akuyama as she appears on the cover of *Aki Alliance*. The story begins with Aki's entire school mad at her because of her penchant for joining various activities, dropping one and moving on to the next just as her teammates are beginning to rely on her. This leads to her quest to befriend every girl in her school, one at a time.

Right:
Aki as she first appeared in *Ped-Xing*. Aki is in constant motion—both physically and mentally—as she flits from one pastime to the next. Though she is able to master whatever she puts her mind to, she is incapable of keeping her mind on any one thing for very long.

ON CONSISTENT DESIGN & THE DIGITAL CANVAS

Working on a digital canvas helps me keep my characters more true to my original sketches. If I'm working on a conventional comics page, and I've doodled a character design I really like in the margin of some document from work, I'll then redraw the character in the right size and position on the page, but it may be difficult to recapture exactly what I liked about the original drawing. With *Aki Alliance*, though, I can just scan that drawing directly from the report I sketched it on, and paste it right onto the page. ■

Left:
The faux cut-paper characters are created digitally, using a Wacom tablet and Photoshop tools, including a selection of filters and texture fills. The visual presentation of these supporting characters, who appear as they are perceived by Aki rather than as they actually are, adds depth to Aki's own character development.

PROCESS WALKTHROUGH

The following step-by-step walkthrough by Ryan Estrada details his creation of a recent page of *Aki Alliance* using a mix of digital and traditional art tools. All of the characters in *Aki Alliance* are drawn on paper, but the backgrounds, props, text, and all other elements on the page are done digitally in Adobe Photoshop with a Wacom tablet. "The characters are not necessarily drawn the way they'll appear on the page, but rather doodled out on whatever scrap of paper I have handy, and compiled at a later stage." ▸

Right: A selection of the original art for the first half of Chapter 2.

1. I had a pretty good idea of how I wanted the page laid out, so the drawings are fairly close to where they'll be on the finished page. I decided afterward, though, that I needed one more character in the top row, so I added her on another sheet. The materials used at this stage are a pencil, Uniball Visions (both fine and ultra-fine), and whatever black marker I have to hand. ▸

2. I scan these pages into Photoshop as grayscale, then I darken the inks and drop out the pencil lines using Levels. I set this layer to "multiply," which allows me to color on a separate layer underneath. I have one layer for flat colors, and another at about 30 percent transparency to add the highlights and shadows by coloring over the flat areas in black, white, or yellow. ▸

3. After that's done, I take a blank page, with the standard backdrop pattern, cut out the characters from the other file, and drop them onto the page. This step is a lot like making a collage. I often don't know what the finished page is going to look like until this step. I sometimes cut out drawings that seem unnecessary at this point, or draw new poses because the page looks empty. ▸

4. I start drawing backgrounds on a new layer in between the characters and the page pattern. I do this by filling in selected shapes with solid color. After that I'll add details, usually with the line or shape tools, to keep a geometric shape for the images. Within the book (where Aki is keeping the book as a scrapbook), these backgrounds are supposed to be made with cut paper. ▸

5. I type the character's dialogue on top of this, and then use the "rounded-edge rectangle tool" to make word bubbles. I set a drop shadow on that layer so that the bubbles look like paper that Aki has glued to the page.

Voila! A finished page! ■

SECTION IX

PUTTING IT ALL TOGETHER

Design is problem solving, and the more you understand the problem you're facing, the more effective your solutions will be. That said, as important as it is to consider all the individual details that contribute to character design—the series of tiny or tremendous challenges you meet along the way—it's important always to be working toward the final, fully fledged character. After all, even if every facet is individually well-crafted, if they don't collectively mesh into a well-balanced design, the character will be unsatisfying. In this section we will discuss methods for critiquing your design, as well as strategies for revision, and conclude with a brief look at the future of graphic novels, and some useful supplementary resource materials. ■

Left: Hope Larson continues to explore themes of burgeoning adulthood in her second graphic novel, *Gray Horses.*

SYMMETRY & SYNTHESIS

According to *Webster's Dictionary*, symmetry is "beauty of form arising from balanced proportions … in size, shape, and relative position of parts on opposite sides of a dividing line … or about a center or axis …" Symmetry is a factor of both organic anatomy and inorganic construction. Symmetry enhances a sense of visual order, recognition, and completion.

But don't forget the importance of asymmetry. Nature is a tug-of-war between order and chaos, and graphic novels—unless a story's world is meant to be perfectly mannered or permanently skewed—should follow suit. Distorting an expected symmetry, by exaggerating or underplaying it, is a central component of comics art. When juxtaposed against or integrated with symmetrical forms, disproportionate shapes and figures can be powerful visual metaphors for any type of story.

This integration of expected and unexpected visual elements to form a coherent whole is also called *synthesis*. As Kevin Hedgpeth and Stephen Missal write in *Exploring Character Design* (Thomson Delmar Learning, 2006), "The mixing of two differing visual sources into a single design relies on both prior visual expectations and the surprise of new visual results from the synthesis for its success."

Synthesized characters ("hybrids") are blends of disparate anatomies (including species and genders) and of the animate and inanimate. Myths and folktales are the province of such hybrids—centaurs, mermaids, angels, demons, hippogriffs, totemic spirits—and graphic novelists should consider the metaphoric power of such combinations. By modifying—altering, adding, deleting, or substituting—one or more of a character's expected anatomical features—placing a wolf's head on a man's body, for example—we offer immediately identifiable associations for the reader.

Synthesis can be even subtler and involve more conceptual visual elements, such as scale. By shifting scale, we can call attention to one part over another, or quickly compare and contrast otherwise similar figures. ▸

When all the characters are roughly the same scale, adding a giant character catches the reader off guard, soliciting more attention, as does introducing a miniature character. (However, it should be stressed, not all genres allow quite the same level of exaggeration.)

With his simplified, wide-open line work (often colored by Rico Renzi), artist Craig Rousseau strives to achieve on paper what's in his head as closely as possible. Many of his characters are modeled after classic hybrids from myth and contemporary fantasy, but it's important for Rousseau to create distinct figures and body shapes/types without veering too wildly from natural forms. He says, "If you're not careful as a cartoonist, you develop a shorthand—you stylize and stylize and stylize—it deviates too far from reality." ■

This page & opposite:
Craig Rousseau's character designs and commissioned sketches from *Tellos* (written by Todd Dezago and co-created by Mike Wieringo) and *The Perhapanauts* (Dark Horse Comics) are examples of functional symmetry and synthesis.

JUDGING & REFINING YOUR CHARACTER DESIGN

One of the most difficult decisions in the character-design process is picking the moment to call a character *finished.* Too little planning, and you find you've completely misjudged how a character fits into a story, requiring significant reworking of earlier pages. Too much planning, and you run the risk of never even beginning the story at all. What's more, front-loading too much detail into a character can inhibit the discovery process that comes from actively working with characters in the context of the story.

A certain amount of character revision is to be expected—both in terms of adjusting the future growth to fit what you've already written and in terms of going back and reworking existing pages to bring them in line with a new conception of the character. Of course, as Tom Gauld points out, revision raises its own risks. "You could go on forever, but at some point you just have to get on with the finished work. I suppose I get to a point where I feel the character is ready to do something, to be put in a scene. The difficult thing is that the character tends to evolve a little as you go through the story, and by the end you are usually drawing him much better than at the beginning, and you want to go back to the start and redraw. But that would lead to a never-ending cycle of redrawing the same story, so you've just got to fix anything that's really dreadful and move on." (See page 72.)

The trick is in knowing when you find a particular character moment unsatisfying because you're stressing over minor details, as opposed to when you've genuinely made a mistake that works against your story. Consistency and accuracy are important, but striving for perfection can be a trap.

The proper balance of planning and revision also varies from book to book. In *Clumsy*, for instance, Jeffrey Brown seems to have done little if any revision to his early drawings; the look of his characters changes noticeably over the course of the book, as Brown refines both his art style and his story. But revision in this instance seems unnecessary, as the changing style fits the honest, almost diary-like quality of the book.

Jason Little, on the other hand, is more concerned with maintaining consistent design throughout. "I generally only need to draw a body a couple of times to feel I've got it right for a character, but the heads take forever. I feel like I have to draw a character's face at least 20 times in each position (front, profile, three-quarter) as the story is being written before it starts to become consistent. Even then I usually end up redrawing faces at the beginning of a story once I'm done with it." (See pages 114 and 115.) ▶

Left:
Jason Little's very first drawing of Bee. Compare with later designs on pages 114 and 115.

Far left:
By the third installment in his *Girlfriends* trilogy, Jeffrey Brown's designs had naturally evolved into a smoother, more refined look. (See page 73.)

By contrast, Jenn Manley Lee revisits existing pages of *Dicebox* (see pages 94–99) often, to ensure that existing character work is consistent with her future plans for character development. This is especially true of characters who are relatively minor in the early pages of the story, but who will become increasingly important as the story progresses, such as Donny Grae and Rande Yong. Although these two travelers have only played a major role in one chapter so far, these scenes lay the groundwork for their future encounters with Molly and Griffen, so it's important to capture their personalities accurately. ■

THE ESSENCE OF A CHARACTER

It can be helpful to write short, pithy descriptions of your characters that cut to the essence of who they are. These descriptions can serve as references to keep you from straying too far from the characters' core identities. Of course, they can be modified as your understanding of a character grows.

For instance, Jenn Manley Lee currently uses the following descriptions for Rande and Grae:

Rande Yong
Navigator and Pilot who allows his ambition to be dictated by his partner in most things, Donny Grae.

Donny Grae
Corps operative unsure of what fight she's after, although she's rejected many and continues to seek more. ■

This page & opposite:
An adjustment to Grae's body language markedly changes the tone not only of Grae's character but also of the scene as a whole. Refining a character's early moments can be pivotal in achieving the desired character arc through the rest of the story.

JENN MANLEY LEE ON THE REVISION OF DONNY GRAE & RANDE YONG

Even though [Rande and Grae] have been with me just about as long as Molly and Griffen, I have the most difficulty nailing them, in look, body language, and speech pattern. And they are going to play a big role in *Dicebox*, probably as big as Griffen and Molly toward the end. I knew that from the start, and yet everything has been a bit more of a struggle with them, mostly I think because they are more removed from me than Molly and Griffen. Things did start to get better after I worked out their back and forward stories—what happens to them after *Dicebox*. They are the ones I've been concentrating most of my character design thoughts on recently. I made a huge breakthrough while doing their character vignettes for Dicebox.net, specifically my redo of Grae's a couple months back.

I'm very excited about the pencil redo so far ... the panel [shown here] has some significance [also see pages 94–99], and this time I think I nailed it. This was largely due to a change in semantics of how I think of Grae in particular—instead of her default body language being uncomfortable or uneasy, it should be restless and on guard; she should be very confident physically. It's Rande who's always a bit unsure. ■

CONCLUSION:

INTO THE FUTURE

If the flurry and flux of the past two decades are any indication, graphic novels—the creative movement, artistic form, and publishing format—will likely see monumental changes in the coming years. As generations, cultures, and technologies shift, so will concepts of storytelling and characterization. While no one can say just how these changes will manifest, we can at least point out three trends already in progress, of which a graphic novelist or character designer should be aware.

THE GEOGRAPHIC NOVEL

The comics centers of the world, where the majority of graphic-novel publishing takes place, have long been North America, Western Europe, Scandinavia, Italy, Japan, and South Korea—with pockets of activity in other places. But such pockets on the periphery are showing signs of becoming fully fledged industries with the potential to reinvent the medium. In India, China, South America, Eastern Europe, Israel, Australia, New Zealand—even African and Arab countries—imported and homegrown comics and graphic novels are steadily becoming more commonplace. Egyptian publisher AK Comics recently debuted four superhero comics series, including *Jalila, Protector of the City of All Faiths*, hoping to bring Middle Eastern stories in comics form to international readers.

THE PICTURE-BOOK CONTINUUM

The children's picture book is the close cousin of the graphic novel—but the two have, until recently, remained on opposite sides of a wall imposed by parents, publishers, booksellers, librarians, and teachers. Words-and-pictures storytelling for older children and teenagers—once frowned upon by librarians and educators—is now becoming an acceptable, even championed, reading form, so children should now discover a seamless continuum of books at ▸

Left: Germany's Markus "Mawil" Witzel—whose graphic novel *Beach Safari* was published by Top Shelf Productions in 2003–enjoys making comics despite the lack of what he calls "a big comics culture" in his native country. This art comes from the semi-autobiographical story "Carpe Diem," which is included in Mawil's collection, *Action Sorgenkind* (Reprodukt, 2007).

Below:
The title character from Jennifer and Matthew Holm's *Babymouse*.

Bottom right:
Simple-in-appearance yet complex-in-nature digital character from an online work by Swiss artist demian.5.

each stage of their lives: picture books and illustrated storybooks, to "middle-grade" comics chapter books, and then later to young-adult and adult-oriented graphic novels.

A great example of a "beginner book" for children learning to read comics is brother-and-sister team Jennifer and Matthew Holm's *Babymouse* graphic novel series (first published by Random House in 2005). Of the series, artist Matthew Holm says, "What really strikes kids is [comics] seem very attainable. It's something that you can aspire to do yourself."

ONWARD & ONLINE

Graphic novels are still largely the print-based province of the solo creator or small team. However, digital technologies including Web publishing and blogging software, handheld devices, and peer-to-peer networks have given creators an array of new artistic, distribution, and collaboration options. It is unlikely that digital will completely replace print as the standard format, but even if you intend to produce and publish your work traditionally, knowing something about pixels and vectors, rasters, wikis, avatars, and hyperlinks can only improve your chances of success in an increasingly electronic marketplace.

IN CONCLUSION

Character design is an essential facet of comics storytelling, no matter the format or genre or style. Without believable, sustainable, identifiable characters, a story is no more than an exercise in plotting. In all but the most frivolous and farcical of comics (not necessarily a bad thing), without a determined and discerning artist at the helm, even the most outwardly appealing character will rarely engage a reader for more than a few pages, unless there's a sense that the character's outer life—the "look" as it were—is merely a reflection of a richer inner life. For ultimately, in a sort of comics Zen, we graphic novelists do not draw simply to represent what can be seen—we draw to illuminate what remains always in the dark. ■

ONLINE RESOURCES

TYPEFACES

BLAMBOT
www.blambot.com

COMICRAFT
www.comicraft.com

FONTIFIER
www.fontifier.com

ONLINE COMICS COLLECTIVES AND ANTHOLOGIES

01COMICS.COM
www.01comics.com

ACT-I-VATE
http://community.livejournal.com/act_i_vate

BLANK LABEL COMICS
www.blanklabelcomics.com

THE CHEMISTRY SET
www.chemsetcomics.com

DUMBRELLA
www.dumbrella.com

GIRLAMATIC
www.girlamatic.com

GRAPHIC SMASH
www.graphicsmash.com

KEENSPOT
www.keenspot.com

KOMIKWERKS
www.komikwerks.com

MODERN TALES
www.moderntales.com

NEW BODEGA
www.newbodega.blogspot.com

ROCKETPIRATES
www.rocketpirates.com

SERIALIZER.NET
www.serializer.net

WIREPOP
www.wirepop.com

CHARACTER DESIGN

CHARACTER DESIGN BLOG
characterdesign.blogspot.com

PICTOPLASMA
www.pictoplasma.com

POSER RESOURCES

PLANIT3D
www.planit3d.com

POSERWORLD
www.poserworld.com

RENDEROSITY
www.renderosity.com

COMICS ORGANIZATIONS

CARTOON ART MUSEUM
www.cartoonart.org

THE CENTER FOR CARTOON STUDIES
www.cartoonstudies.org

THE COMIC BOOK LEGAL DEFENSE FUND
www.cbldf.org

FRIENDS OF LULU
www.popcultureshock.com/lulu

NATIONAL ASSOCIATION OF COMICS ART EDUCATORS
www.teachingcomics.org

THE NATIONAL CARTOON MUSEUM
(formerly The International Museum of Cartoon Art)
www.cartoon.org

WORDS AND PICTURES MUSEUM
www.wordsandpictures.org

INSPIRATION AND REFERENCE

CORBIS
(stock images)
www.corbis.com

DEFENSE VISUAL INFORMATION CENTER
(Department of Defense)
www.dodmedia.osd.mil

ELLE
(fashion)
www.elle.com

FOTOSEARCH
(stock images)
www.fotosearch.com

GETTY IMAGES
(stock images)
www.gettyimages.com

GQ
(fashion)
www.gq.com

HINT
(fashion)
www.hintmag.com

IMDB (CELEBRITY IMAGES)
www.imdb.com

THE LIBRARY OF CONGRESS AMERICAN MEMORY COLLECTION
(historical reference)
http://memory.loc.gov/ammem/index.html

THE LOUVRE
(art images)
www.louvre.fr

THE NATIONAL GALLERY
(art images)
www.nationalgallery.org.uk

THE NEW YORK PUBLIC LIBRARY DIGITAL GALLERY
(rare images)
http://digitalgallery.nypl.org/nypldigital/index.cfm

STYLE.COM
(fashion)
www.style.com

USDA AGRICULTURE RESEARCH SERVICE IMAGE GALLERY
(agricultural images)
www.ars.usda.gov/is/graphics/photos

WIKIPEDIA
(general reference)
www.wikipedia.org

WEBCOMIC DIRECTORIES

COMIXPEDIA'S WEBCOMIC ENCYCLOPEDIA
www.comixpedia.org

FULL STORY: AN INDEX OF COMPLETED WEBCOMICS
www.twentysevenletters.com/fullstory

ONLINECOMICS.NET
www.onlinecomics.net

THE WEBCOMIC LIST
www.thewebcomiclist.com

SELF-PUBLISHING RESOURCES

BOOKSURGE
(print on demand)
www.booksurge.com

COMIC GENESIS
(free Web hosting for webcomics)
www.comicgenesis.com

COMIXPRESS
(print on demand)
www.comixpress.com

LULU.COM
(print on demand)
www.lulu.com

WEBCOMICS NATION
(Web hosting and business tools for webcomics)
www.webcomicsnation.com

SUGGESTED READING

COMICS THEORY AND TECHNIQUE

COMICS AND SEQUENTIAL ART
Will Eisner
(North Light Books, 1994)

DIGITAL PREPRESS FOR COMIC BOOKS
Kevin Tinsley
(Stickman Graphics, 1999)

EARLY WRITINGS ON VISUAL LANGUAGE
Neil Cohn
(Emaki Productions, 2003)

GRAPHIC STORYTELLING AND VISUAL NARRATIVE
Will Eisner
(North Light Books, 2001)

MAKING COMICS: STORYTELLING SECRETS OF COMICS, MANGA AND GRAPHIC NOVELS
Scott McCloud
(HarperCollins, 2006)

REINVENTING COMICS: HOW IMAGINATION AND TECHNOLOGY ARE REVOLUTIONIZING AN ART FORM
Scott McCloud
(HarperCollins, 2000)

UNDERSTANDING COMICS: THE INVISIBLE ART
Scott McCloud
(HarperCollins, 1994)

VISUAL STORYTELLING: THE ART AND TECHNIQUE
Tony Caputo
(Watson-Guptill Publications, 2002)

WEBCOMICS: TOOLS AND TECHNIQUES FOR DIGITAL CARTOONING
Steven Withrow and John Barber
(Barron's Educational Series, 2005)

HISTORIES AND WRITINGS ON COMICS

THE ART OF THE COMIC BOOK: AN AESTHETIC HISTORY
R. C. Harvey
(University Press of Mississippi, 1996)

DREAMLAND JAPAN: WRITINGS ON MODERN MANGA
Frederick L. Schodt
(Stone Bridge Press, 1996)

FASTER THAN A SPEEDING BULLET: THE RISE OF THE GRAPHIC NOVEL
Stephen Weiner
(NBM Publishing, 2003)

GRAPHIC NOVELS: EVERYTHING YOU NEED TO KNOW
Paul Gravett
(Collins Design, 2005)

GRAPHIC NOVELS: A BIBLIOGRAPHIC GUIDE TO BOOK-LENGTH COMICS
D. Aviva Rothschild
(Libraries Unlimited, 1995)

A HISTORY OF WEBCOMICS
T. Campbell
(Antarctic Press, 2006)

MANGA! MANGA!: THE WORLD OF JAPANESE COMICS
Frederick L. Schodt
(Kodansha America, 1988)

MANGA: MASTERS OF THE ART
Timothy R. Lehmann
(Collins Design, 2005)

MANGA: SIXTY YEARS OF JAPANESE COMICS
Paul Gravett
(Collins Design, 2004)

TOON ART: THE GRAPHIC ART OF DIGITAL CARTOONING
Steven Withrow
(Watson-Guptill, 2003)

ILLUSTRATION AND DESIGN

3D CREATURE WORKSHOP
Bill Fleming (Charles River Media, 1998)

THE ANIMATOR'S SURVIVAL KIT
Richard Williams
(Faber & Faber, 2001)

THE ANIMATOR'S WORKBOOK
Tony White (Watson-Guptill, 1988)

DIGITAL CHARACTER DESIGN & PAINTING: THE PHOTOSHOP CS EDITION
Don Seegmiller (Charles River Media, 2004)

EXPLORING CHARACTER DESIGN
Kevin Hedgpeth and Stephen Missal (Thomson Delmar Learning, 2006)

EXPLORING DRAWING FOR ANIMATION
Kevin Hedgpeth and Stephen Missal (Thomson Delmar Learning, 2004)

FLASH CHARACTER ANIMATION: APPLIED STUDIO TECHNIQUES
Lee Purcell
(Sams Publishing, 2002)

THE HISTORY OF ANIMATION: ENCHANTED DRAWINGS
Charles Solomon
(Alfred A. Knopf, 1989)

THE ILLUSION OF LIFE: DISNEY ANIMATION
Frank Thomas and Ollie Johnston
(Hyperion, 1995)

PEOPLE AND POSES: COMIC ARTIST'S PHOTO REFERENCE
Buddy Scalera
(Impact Books, 2006)

WRITING TECHNIQUE

STORY: SUBSTANCE, STRUCTURE, STYLE AND THE PRINCIPLES OF SCREENWRITING
Robert McKee
(Regan Books, 1997)

SCREENPLAY: THE FOUNDATIONS OF SCREENWRITING
Syd Field (Delta, 2005)

JOURNALISM AND CRITICISM

ARTBOMB.NET
www.artbomb.net

THE BEAT
(Publishers Weekly)
http://pwbeat.publishersweekly.com/blog/

BORDERWALKER
www.borderwalker.com

COMIC BOOK GALAXY
www.comicbookgalaxy.com

COMIC BOOK RESOURCES
www.comicbookresources.com

COMICON PULSE
www.comicon.com/pulse

THE COMICS INTERPRETER
http://tci.homestead.com

THE COMICS JOURNAL
www.tcj.com

THE COMICS REPORTER
www.comicsreporter.com

COMICS WORTH READING
http://comicsworthreading.com

COMIXPEDIA
www.comixpedia.com

DIGITAL WEBBING
www.digitalwebbing.com

FLEEN
www.fleen.com

THE GRAPHIC NOVEL REVIEW
www.graphicnovelreview.com

ICOMICS
www.icomics.com

INDY MAGAZINE
www.indyworld.com/indy

NEWSARAMA
www.newsarama.com

POPIMAGE
www.popimage.com

SEQUENTIAL TART
www.sequentialtart.com

THE VISUAL LINGUIST
www.emaki.net/blog

THE WEBCOMICS EXAMINER
www.webcomicsreview.com

WIZARD ENTERTAINMENT
www.wizarduniverse.com

GLOSSARY

ACTION LINE
An imaginary line that indicates the flow of action through a figure's body. Action lines are common in gesture drawing.

ANIME
Japanese animation.

ANTHROPOMORPHISM
The practice of conferring human characteristics on nonhuman ideas, creatures, or objects. Such characteristics may be physical (wearing clothes, walking on two legs, etc.) or nonphysical (sentience, ambition, emotion, etc.). Examples include humanlike animals, such as Snoopy in Charles Schulz's *Peanuts*, or The Grim Reaper as the humanlike incarnation of death.

ARCHETYPE
Classic character models that often underlie contemporary characters. Examples include the tragic hero, the trickster, the brute, etc. (See pages 22 and 23 for more detail.)

BANDE DESSINÉE (BD)
French language comics from France and Belgium. Literally, "drawn strip."

CARTOON
A broad term encompassing the entire spectrum of semiabstract illustration styles, from minimalism to realism. Scott McCloud defines cartooning as "amplification through simplification."

CLEAR LINE (LIGNE CLAIRE)
A drawing style popularized by the Belgian creator Hergé. Common characteristics of clear-line illustration include bold and consistent line weight, prominent outlines, lack of shading, and strong colors.

COMICS
A storytelling form in which words and pictures are often used interdependently. Defined by Scott McCloud as "juxtaposed pictorial and other images in deliberate sequence, intended to convey information and/or to produce an aesthetic response in the viewer."

CONSTRUCTION LINE
Lines of variable weight (visual density) and character (emotional quality) that compose a figure and help to position anatomical elements correctly in space relative to one another. Construction lines are common in gesture drawing.

CONTOUR
A structural outline that indicates form or volume.

CONTOUR DRAWING
A form of line drawing that emphasizes tone over line.

ENSEMBLE CAST
A cast of lead characters of roughly equal importance within a story. Stories based around ensembles do not have an identifiable central protagonist, focusing instead on a group dynamic or central theme.

FLASH
Macromedia's software package for creating and viewing low-bandwidth animation.

FUMETTI
Comics that use photographs of live models or staged sets instead of illustrations. Also called photocomics.

GESTURE DRAWING
Simple drawings of an object that convey only the object's most essential details.

GRAPHIC NOVEL
A form of unified comics narrative. Also, alternately, a publishing format, an aesthetic movement, or a book-length work of comics fiction. (See pages 12 and 13 for more detail.)

HATCHING
The use of parallel lines to create shading effects in visual artworks. A related technique, crosshatching, involves the use of crossed lines.

HYPERREALISM
A style of painting that attempts to recreate subjects in photographic detail. An outgrowth of photorealism.

ICON
A simple, but broadly recognizable image that bears a resemblance to the person or object it signifies.

ILLUSTRATOR
Adobe's software package for creating vector-based illustrations.

MANGA
Japanese comics. May also refer to non-Japanese comics using styles and conventions derived from Japanese comics.

MINICOMICS
Short and often handmade comics, common among independent creators.

MINIMALISM
A very spare art style defined by the aesthetic of "less is more," in which only the most essential details are represented.

MODEL SHEET
A functional reference for composition, character likeness, posing, and accuracy and consistency of detail. The most common types of model sheets are: character sheet, concept sheets, turnarounds, action sheets, expression studies, value studies, and color studies. (See pages 38 and 39, for more detailed definitions.)

MODULAR DRAWING
The construction of a figure from simple shapes and forms.

MOTION LINE
A visual shorthand used to indicate direction of movement.

PHOTOCOMICS
See *fumetti.*

POSER
e frontier's software package for creating 3-D illustrations.

REPERTORY CAST
A cast of characters who each take the lead role at different times. This is more common for ongoing series or anthology series than for self-contained stories. Many team superhero books can be considered to have repertory casts.

SEQUENTIAL DRAWING
A series of gesture drawings placed in chronological order to demonstrate a complete action. (Also called stop-action drawing.)

STIPPLING
The use of small, closely spaced dots to create shading effects in visual artworks.

SUBTEXT
The implied meaning beneath the surface of what is openly expressed.

SYMBOL
A visual metaphor used for comparison, wherein a literal object, trait, or event serves to convey non-visual, usually abstract, information.

SYMMETRY
The balance of form across a dividing line or axis.

SYNTHESIS
The integration of expected and unexpected visual elements to form a coherent whole.

TAG
A visual cue used to differentiate one character from others in the story, so as to make the character easily identifiable to the reader.

TURNAROUNDS
A particular type of model sheet providing reference for composition from various angles and viewpoints. (See *model sheet.*)

VECTOR GRAPHICS
Highly scalable image files that are composed of a series of mathematical statements, rather than a conglomerate of individual points.

VERISIMILITUDE
The appearance of truth or the quality of seeming to be true.

WEBCOMIC
A comic published on the Internet. Usually used exclusively for comics using the Internet as the primary means of distribution, though sometimes used to refer to any comic utilizing web publication, including those primarily published in print.

ACKNOWLEDGMENTS & PICTURE CREDITS

Steven thanks all the graphic novelists and publishers who were so generous in contributing words and images to this book—especially Bryan Talbot for his insightful foreword; everyone at RotoVision; Alexander for his superb coauthorship; and most of all, Lesley and Marin Jeanne.

Alexander thanks Steven for sharing this opportunity, as well as all the creators and editors who generously contributed their time and material. Thank you to my family for a lifetime of encouragement; to Brandy, for her enduring patience and support; and to James, for introducing me to the world of comics in the first place.

FRONT COVER:
© Brendan Cahill.

IMPRINT/TITLE PAGE:
© Mark Crilley; © Eddie Campbell (*From Hell* written by Alan Moore).

CONTENTS SPREAD:
ASTRO CITY TM & © 2006 Juke Box Productions. All rights reserved.

FOREWORD:
© Bryan Talbot.

GRAPHIC NOVEL CHARACTERS:
© Matt Kindt.

BACK COVER:
© Spike.

SECTION I:
THE GRAPHIC NOVEL
Page 10 © Arvid Nelson and Juan Ferreyra; Page 11 © Jeff Nicholson; Pages 12 and 13 © Max Estes, © Ted Slampyak, © Bryan Talbot; Pages 14 and 15 © Art by Tom Scioli with colors by Bill Crabtree, © Will Eisner Estate, © Osamu Tezuka (English translation now published by Dark Horse Comics), © Gene Yang, used by permission of First Second Books, © Lewis Trondheim, used by permission of First Second Books, © Emmanuel Guibert and Joann Sfar, used by permission of First Second Books; Pages 16 and 17 © Craig Thompson; Pages 18 and 19 © Arvid Nelson and Juan Ferreyra.

SECTION II:
THE CHARACTER
Page 20 © Craig Thompson; Page 21 © 2006 Stan Sakai; Pages 22 and 23 © Jim Zubkavich, © Eddie Campbell, © 2006 Stan Sakai, © Nate Piekos; Pages 24 and 25 © Metaphrog, © Diane Sasse; Pages 26 and 27 © Metaphrog, © R. Kikuo Johnson; Pages 28 and 29 © Craig Thompson, © Jason Little; Pages 30 and 31 © Spike.

SECTION III:
ELEMENTS OF DESIGN
Page 32 © Eddie Campbell (*From Hell* written by Alan Moore); Page 33 © Eric Shanower; Pages 34–37 © Jef Czekaj, Bone ® is 2006 Jeff Smith, ASTRO CITY TM & © 2006 Juke Box Productions. All rights reserved, © Miriam Katin, © Colleen Coover (script by Root Nibot), © Don MacDonald; Pages 38 and 39 © Matt Kindt; Pages 40 and 41 © Nate Piekos, © Ted Slampyak, © Dylan Meconis; Pages 42 and 43 © kristin studio inc., © Gil Agudín, © Dave Roman, © Bill Duncan, © Eric Shanower, © Hope Larson; Pages 44 and 45 © Mike Mignola, © Paul Chadwick, © Jenn Manley Lee; Pages 46 and 47 © Nate Piekos; Pages 48–53 © Eric Shanower; Pages 54–57 © P. Craig Russell (characters from "The Devoted Friend" by Oscar Wilde), © Don MacDonald, © Todd Dezago, Craig Rousseau, © David Petersen, © demian.5; Pages 58–63 © Eddie Campbell (*From Hell* written by Alan Moore).

SECTION IV:
DESIGN STYLE
Page 64 © Tom Gauld (www.cabanonpress.com); Page 65 © Metaphrog; Pages 66 and 67 © Jef Czekaj, © Brett Weldele, © David Petersen, © Joey Comeau and Emily Horne; Pages 68 and 69 © Jeff Mariotte and Jeremy Huan, © T.J. and Jason May; Pages 70 and 71© Neil Cohn, © David Petersen, © Steve Lafler, © Jason Little; Pages 72 and 73 © Tom Gauld (www.cabanonpress.com), © Jeffrey Brown; Pages 74 and 75 © Jef Czekaj, © Colleen Coover (script by Root Nibot); Pages 76 and 77 © Miriam Katin, © Don MacDonald; Pages 78 and 79 © Jeff Parker, © Colleen Doran; Pages 80–83 © Lea Hernandez; Pages 84 and 85 © Jeff Nicholson.

SECTION V:
APPEARANCE & REALITY
Page 86 © Brendan Cahill; Page 87 © Jenn Manley Lee; Pages 88 and 89 © R. Kikuo Johnson, © Jeff Mariotte and Jeremy Haun, © Craig Thompson; Pages 90 and 91 © Jenn Manley Lee, © R. Kikuo Johnson, © Scott McCloud; Pages 92 and 93 © Neal Von Flue; Pages 94–99 © Jenn Manley Lee; Pages 100–103 © Brendan Cahill; Pages 104–109 © Metaphrog.

SECTION VI: THE EXPANDED CAST

SECTION VII: KNOWING YOUR AUDIENCE

SECTION VIII: MODERN METHODS

SECTION IX: PUTTING IT ALL TOGETHER

INDEX

CONTRIBUTOR LIST

GIL AGUDIN
http://underdog.dreamcomics.com

BRENT ANDERSON
www.brentandersonart.com

ASTRO CITY
www.astrocity.us

BABYMOUSE
www.randomhouse.com/kids/babymouse/

JEFFREY BROWN
www.margomitchell.com/thc/jb.htm

BRENDAN CAHILL
www.brendancahill.com

PAUL CHADWICK
www.paulchadwick.net

NEIL COHN
www.emaki.net

COLLEEN COOVER
cooverart.com

MARK CRILLEY
www.markcrilley.com

JEF CZEKAJ
www.czekaj.com

DEMIAN.5
www.demian5.com

TODD DEZAGO
www.perhapanauts.com

COLLEEN DORAN
www.colleendoran.com

BILL DUNCAN
www.moderntales.com/comics/pst.php

WILL EISNER
www.willeisner.com

MAX ESTES
www.maxestes.com

RYAN ESTRADA
www.ryanestrada.com

TOM GAULD
www.cabanonpress.com

LEA HERNANDEZ
www.webcomicsnation.com/divalea

R. KIKUO JOHNSON
www.seabread.com

BRYANT JOHNSON
www.tragi-comix.com

MIRIAM KATIN
home.nyc.rr.com/miriamkatin

MATT KINDT
www.supersecretspy.com

STEVE LAFLER
www.stevelafler.net

HOPE LARSON
www.hopelarson.com

JENN MANLEY LEE
www.jennworks.com

JASON LITTLE
www.beecomix.com

DON MACDONALD
www.donmacdonald.com

JEFF MARIOTTE
www.jeffmariotte.com

T. J. AND JASON MAY
www.summ.net

SCOTT MCCLOUD
www.scottmccloud.com

DYLAN MECONIS
www.projectkooky.com/dylan

METAPHROG
www.metaphrog.com

MIKE MIGNOLA
www.hellboy.com

JEFF NICHOLSON
www.coloniapress.com

JEFF PARKER
http://parkerspace.com

DAVID PETERSEN
www.davidpetersen.net

NATE PIEKOS
www.realmofatland.com

WENDY PINI
www.elfquest.com

REX MUNDI
www.rexmundi.net

ALEX ROBINSON
http://members.aol.com/ComicBookAlex

DAVE ROMAN
www.yaytime.com

ALEX ROSS
www.alexrossart.com

ANDY RUNTON
www.andyrunton.com

P. CRAIG RUSSELL
http://pcraigrussell.net

STAN SAKAI
http://usagiyojimbo.com

DIANA SASSÉ
www.webcomicsnation.com/sasse/

SCOTT CHRISTIAN SAVA
www.bluedreamstudios.com

TOM SCIOLI
www.geocities.com/sciolit

ERIC SHANOWER
http://ericshanower.com

A SOFTER WORLD
www.asofterworld.com

B. SHUR
www.iamarocketbuilder.com

TED SLAMPYAK
www.jazzagecomics.com

JEFF SMITH
www.boneville.com

SPIKE
www.ironcircus.com

BRYAN TALBOT
www.bryan-talbot.com

OSAMU TEZUKA
www.tezuka.co.jp

CRAIG THOMPSON
www.dootdootgarden.com

NEAL VON FLUE
www.ape-law.com/hypercomics

BRETT WELDELE
www.brettweldele.com

JOE ZABEL
joezabel.com

JIM ZUBKAVICH
www.makeshiftmiracle.com